AF778854

UNCAPPING FAMILY WISDOM

Recognizing, Treating,

and Reconciling

Transgenerational

Dysfunction

UNCAPPING FAMILY WISDOM

Recognizing, Treating, and Reconciling Transgenerational Dysfunction

Sandra S. Pate
D. Phil., MSW

Phillip Monroe Publishing Company

©2012 by Sandra Pate

ISBN 978-0-6154554-4-0

Library of Congress Control Number: 2011903434

Editor's note: All the stories in this book are based on actual experiences. The names and details have been changed to protect the privacy of the people involved. In some cases, composites have been created.

All rights reserved. No part of this book may be reproduced in any form by any electronic or mechanical means (including photocopying, recording, or information storage and retrieval) without written permission.

Phillip Monroe Publishing Company

Phillip Monroe Publishing Company
P.O. Box 2585
Rogers, AR 72757-2585
479-925-3400
http://www.patecounseling.com

Printed in the United States of America

Design and layout by Martha Nichols/aMuse Productions®

With love to my family…

John, my husband and friend

Phillip, my son, and his family,

Shannon, Zach, Abby, Molly—Logan and Pug

Eric, my son, and his family,

Yami, Adriana, and Joshua

Table of Contents

List of Tables and Charts

Tables

Charts

Introduction

Many of you who read this book will be familiar with the problem described on these pages. From your own experience, you could add many details to any descriptions you might find in the writing. Please use your experience to add to the body of knowledge as you discuss this book with others and when you participate in continuing education meetings and workshops.

Uncapping Family Wisdom: A Program for Recognizing, Treating, and Reconciling Transgenerational Dysfunction is about a treatment program that can electrify latent human development potential in families, as barriers to progress are removed. In fact, this program, designed to assist people in trauma-organized family systems, has proven to be useful for therapists and staff who treat the people for whom the program was designed. Almost everyone who has been involved in working around this program has used its principles to look inside themselves and their own families to see how they are progressing. Realizing that different types of groups of adults and children will be coming together for treatment, for ease of flow, the words "parent" and "parents" are used to symbolize the adults in authority in the family, with special appreciation to all those who are taking on parental roles.

The Population

When we identify populations, we automatically take the risk of using labels that excuse responsibility, release shame, appropriate blame, and risk a static evaluation for these populations. The problem addressed in this book belongs to our culture and the English language we speak, not to the population that is the focus of this presentation. The population, in varying degrees, is showing the stress of being in the third or fourth generation of dysfunction which has traveled down through their linguistic heritage.

Phelps observes (Bailey 2007, p. 5) that words culturally bind our thoughts, our beliefs, and subsequently our emotions and behaviors. Since belief systems rely heavily on semantics, the use and meaning of language, one might also conclude that the use of semantics and grammar figure as the largest independent variables in understanding human condition and interactions. Boyd and Richerson (Bailey 2007, p. 5) observe that these insights highlight the tremendous impact grammar has on emotions, behaviors, and perceptions across cultures as well as between species.

The term *linguistic determinism* refers to the idea that, *to some extent*, the language we use determines the way in which we view and think about the world around us. Wisdom potential, somehow limited in any population, may be only lying dormant, waiting to be released (Campbell, 1997).

Whorf explains:

> ...the problem of thought and thinking in the native community is not purely and simply a psychological problem. It is largely cultural. It is moreover largely a matter of one especially cohesive aggregate of cultural phenomena that we call a language (Carroll, p. 65, as cited in Alford, 2010, May 28).
>
> ...Which was first: the language patterns or the cultural norms? In the main, they have grown up together, constantly influencing each other (Carroll, p. 156, as cited in Alford, 2010, May 28).
>
> ...a language is a system.... Large systematic outlines can change to something really new only very slowly, while many other cultural innovations are made with comparative quickness (Carroll, p. 156, as cited in Alford, 2010, May 28).

The purpose of *Uncapping Family Wisdom* is to hasten the process of change for populations not exposed to certain types of conceptual language which could expand the probability for future human development.

Learning How to Be a Family

Transgenerational dysfunction affects almost every population group to some degree, but a special excitement and dramatic change can occur when the *Uncapping Family Wisdom* methodology is applied to individuals and families who recognize that something is terribly wrong within their family system. I recall a day in family therapy with an adolescent, who was part of my caseload at a children's hospital. Her mother had been transported from a psychiatric unit at another hospital for the therapy session. At one point in our conversation, after a silence, the mother said, "We would like to be a family, we just don't know how." This is what *Uncapping Family Wisdom* is all about. No matter how severe the circumstances, all families deserve to be exposed to the highest conceptual understanding of how to be a family, interpersonally and intrapersonally.

Uncapping Family Wisdom offers a path to follow for difficult cases. Gaining information from different disciplines enables individuals and families to move past the stagnant condition so aptly described by the mother above. Like the mother above, many people seen in shelters for those who are battered or homeless, in psychiatric units, among the incarcerated, or even in private practice, are from families who have difficulties and who are missing conceptual information, a legacy which, through the family linguistic pattern, has continued through several generations. Because the parents themselves have not passed through some of the developmental stages and are not aware of how to provide an environment where normal development will occur in their family, the children have missed developmental markers.

How Large Is this Population?

An estimated 809,800 federal and state prisoners have minor children. Almost 1.7 million minor children have a parent in prison—an increase of more than 206,000 children since 1999

(Bureau of Justice Statistics, 2007). These children are most likely in a state of crisis, understanding that a father's or mother's imprisonment can be the final, lethal blow to an already weakened family structure. In 2007, members of households with children made up approximately 23 percent of persons using emergency shelter and transitional housing programs (U.S. Conference of Mayors 2007 Status Report on Hunger and Homelessness). Because more families with children than unpartnered people enter and leave homelessness during a year, families represent a relatively large share of the annual population. As a result, during a typical year, between 900,000 and 1.4 million children are homeless with their families (Institute for Urban Research, 2010). Children are the fastest growing segment of that population. Many of the problems found in these families did not begin in the present generation but have extended into the present from two, three (and sometimes more) generations ago.

The Theoretical Basis for the Program

Before any actual discussion begins on the steps of the treatment program, some background might prove helpful. Although the program is basically simple when brought down from its abstract beginnings, a long process of experimentation, testing and integration of theory from several disciplines has contributed to the final form of the *Uncapping Family Wisdom* program.

If you have worked in mental health very long, you realize that there are some families who have been fighting dysfunction now for many generations. Some ancient traumas put a family on the wrong track. Adjustments in later generations could have gone either way, but many times the problems became worse. Now, a growing social services crisis exists in the inability to provide the necessary assistance to the number of children and families who are in need of their services.

When the numbers of troubled families enlarge and communities become unstable, society itself begins to lose its cohesiveness. Families impact their community and community impacts the families with norms for appropriate behavior. Strong organized communities with established behavioral norms protect families from some outside stressors. Families who establish behavioral norms, which almost all families elect to follow, build strong communities which stay interconnected.

Questions that Must Be Asked

So, where do we begin? These are the questions that must be answered:

- How do we start to restore communities?
- How can we provide an environment where families can heal?
- How can we supply the information the families need to overcome transgenerational dysfunction?
- How can we empower the families to move into leadership positions where they can impact their communities with rich conceptual information and healthy norms?

Finding the answer to these questions is the objective of *Uncapping Family Wisdom.* A program is provided that deals with the root of problems with families and communities. The program can restore communities, provide an environment where families can heal, and help families overcome transgenerational dysfunction. Families can be empowered to move into leadership positions where they can impact their communities with rich conceptual information and healthy norms. John Nist (1974, pp. 75-81) and Basil Bernstein (as cited in Nist 1974, pp. 203-204), both sociolinguists, discussed the basic two lects,[1] acrolect and mesilect, and one basic dialect, basilect, found in the English Language. Nist was also able to discern the manner in which all three language groups reared their children. One group spoke a highly specialized lect, acrolect, which contained conceptual information that allowed their children to achieve normal development. Generation after generation the families who spoke this lect were successful in keeping this heritage of normal development intact.

The method appeared to be coded within their language. Depending on their linguistic code, families in all three groups reached different levels of achievement as far as human development was concerned. Conceptual information that gave needed developmental permissions was a natural byproduct of their language. The basilect speakers had the most difficulty with healthy generational legacies containing the needed conceptual information. The families often became traumatized and remained so, generation after generation.

Carroll (1964, pp. 1-54) found that concepts, forming a conceptual informational base, were important to human development. Concepts were described as

- existing mostly outside of one's awareness,
- encompassing mostly learned responses,
- affecting reasoning,
- enabling the degree of problem-solving skills,
- setting the emotional tone of language, and
- forming a critical test for the acceptance of premises.

General semanticists work to improve the habitual response of human beings to their environment and to one another by

- training persons to have a critical awareness of the use of words and how the communication helps or hurts relationships,
- demonstrating the importance of using language that truly reflects reality,
- showing families how they enter conflict in the systematic way they use interactive language in the family, and
- connecting language with problems that hinder optimal human development in the family and in the community.

Count Albert Korzybski was a semanticist who wrote in the 1930s. His native language was Polish, and he was familiar with eight different languages. In his observations of the English language, Korzybski explained that if a person was born into the English language, the person was exposed to speech that was dysfunctional in eight different ways. He believed that these twists of the English language distorted reality and caused conflict. Korzybski believed that

1 *Lects* refer to classes of Standard English, and *dialects* refer to classes of sub-standard English.

language influenced not only thinking but also all of human behavior. The effect, he felt, was part of our nervous systems. Thus, if language habits were immature or distorted, behavior was also less than mature. Indeed, most of human behavior, from Korzybski's point of view, was *unsane*.[2] He was as much concerned with psychology as with mere words.

Aside from the linguistic and semantic observations, developmental studies are readily available from seminal writers[3] in moral, cognitive, psychosocial and social categories. A component of *Uncapping Family Wisdom,* these studies are valuable as evaluative and educational tools for the families who exhibit generational dysfunction.

Finding Content for the *Uncapping Family Wisdom* Program

Taking into account all that was learned about the use of language and its effect on human development, *Uncapping Family Wisdom: A Program for Recognizing, Treating, and Reconciling Transgenerational Dysfunction* codifies the conceptual information used by the population that speaks the highest functioning lect in the English language. The program then transfers the information incrementally to families with lower levels of information. The highest functioning families have valuable conceptual information in the language of their family units. They have a pattern of thinking that reflects reality and a developmental legacy that can be shared with families in other language groups.

The levels of study found in the *Uncapping Family Wisdom* program represent the conceptual information found in the language code of the Standard English language, the acrolect. The conceptual information is the formational design that acrolect speakers use to rear their children. These persons are able to pass along internalized information that allows children to pass through major developmental stages. The dynamics appears to transfer through the language over to future generations. Ideally, in studying the levels in *Uncapping Family Wisdom,* the rich conceptual information is introduced and practiced in a secure community setting.[4] In addition, one developmental instrument and one semantic inventory, both self-evaluative, will be used on two of the levels to show the families exactly where they can put to use developmental conceptual information and semantic conceptual information.[5]

New behavior will spring from an understanding of how their family operated before and how it operates after the application of the new information. The participating families will know why the old information and behavior did not work and why the new information and behavior achieve the desired results. By learning and becoming competent, each family can experience the emotional stability that comes with putting the information into practice and having the

2 At that time when these labels were applied freely, Korzybski believed that insane vs. sane was a polarization of speech which did not reflect reality and was unfair to the persons who were labeled insane. He saw everyone behaving on a continuum between the extremes of sane and insane. He chose the word *unsane* for his work and used this word as a description of behavior appearing abnormal.

3 *Seminal writers* in this case refer to the original writers who introduce new ideas of development in their particular area of development on interest. Other writers may have later challenged or expanded the original theories.

4 This secure community setting is modeled after the natural way the information is shared in a community that speaks the acrolect.

5 Even though learning in community is the ideal, this method has been used in private practice settings for over twenty years with individuals and families.

acquisition of the information followed by desired behavior. The process is self-rewarding and reinforces the desired behavior.

The Process of the Program

In order to achieve optimal success, the process must be learned and practiced in a secure and supportive setting, the way in which social learning is naturally absorbed. Many of the families who bear the symptoms of a cycle of generational dysfunction have not experienced a sense of community or have lost their community.

Families who are without communities have a difficult time dealing with negative behavioral invasions into their family boundaries. In an ideal community setting, these negative behavioral invasions would normally be stopped by community boundaries. The families can become overpowered if the community boundaries are not there to stop inappropriate behavior. To offset this problem, the treatment program is administered in a secure community setting with the community acting as a large group, and the families participating as a small group within the larger group community.

When everyone is learning the same thing at the same time, working independently, and looking at the family from a sociological level, shame can be bypassed. The facilitator establishes safe boundaries for the community that ensure safety for the families as they acquire needed conceptual information from which appropriate behavior will come. Highly-structured exercises that ensure continued safety and shield the families from shame are presented within this supportive community environment. With protection and assistance, the families are able to learn and practice the individualized new skills needed for their own family system.

Changing Patterns

How can the patterns that prevent forward progress in families be changed? One thing we know: Because patterns travel through the language of the family, and language defines reality for these speakers, a framework is needed, so that linguistic legacies that affect development can be understood and overcome. Many families have inherited a speaking pattern which distorts reality for the family. The adults in these families, through their inherited language patterns, do not know how to instill in their offspring the basic conceptual information and affirmations considered necessary for optimal moral, cognitive, social, and psychological development. Unfortunately, in many cases, the language the children hear from significant others largely determines the potential for development in these children. The children hear and learn defective language patterns, ensuring further dysfunction in succeeding generations. According to Bentovim (1992), because of the emotional pain incurred in the interactions in dysfunctional families, these families become "trauma organized." The pattern of behavior that causes trauma is called "transgenerational dysfunction."

A Program for Treating Transgenerational Dysfunction

Transgenerational dysfunction refers to configurations of dysfunction which limit the potential for human development and are passed down through verbal and non-verbal linguistic patterns. Transgenerational dysfunction is a growing phenomenon found in virtually every social strata in varying degrees, but is especially perceptible in alternative school settings, court-ordered counseling situations, substance abuse and mental health treatment centers, homeless shelters, and prisons. Most experienced mental health professionals can readily identify severe transgenerational dysfunction.

To understand what you will find in this book and how you will be equipped, let's get an understanding of the meanings behind certain terms found in the title, *Uncapping Family Wisdom: A Program for Recognizing, Treating, and Reconciling Transgenerational Dysfunction.* The program has a positive premise that latent wisdom resides in the family system. Three steps are necessary to uncap the latent family wisdom:

1. Recognizing transgenerational dysfunction: A self-evaluation tool allows the parents to reveal the developmental level of their children and then the level of their own development. Another self-evaluative exercise focuses on the specific general semantics of conflict found in their family.
2. Treating transgenerational dysfunction: Conceptual information is transferred incrementally to family units in a community setting by the use of interactive educational presentations to the community, family self-assessments which assess and instruct, structured exercises which allow the family to apply what they learn immediately, and specific techniques for bypassing shame. As the family acquires information, they determine the desired change. The family learns in a safe community environment with healthy norms maintained by the therapist.
3. Reconciling transgenerational dysfunction: Filling in gaps in conceptual information occurs by providing educational steps in life skills in the structured exercises. In the midst of a protective nurturing community, the family members practice the educational steps and learn how the family fits into a community.

The simply-structured program is easy to follow. The difficult work of cross-disciplinary integration has been done for you and is now built into the program, simplifying the facilitation. Exposure to new information is a very important part of the program. The families use the assessments to better understand their strengths and define exactly where interventions need to occur. Then, through the carefully structured exercises, the families proceed in the integration of each concept and fill in gaps in their information base. Participation is self-rewarding due to the growing freedom from disquiet in thoughts and feelings as the family members receive important developmental permissions.

A Community Setting

Although parts of the program can be used in private practice, one important facet of the program described in *Uncapping Family Wisdom* is the administration of the program within a supportive, controlled community setting. The program assumes that many of the problems come from societal impacts and immediately invites the families to find out how their family has been impacted by society. This process takes the blame for the problems off the individuals for a time until they have more information with which to address problems they find in the family. Knowing that others are learning is also affirming. In time, the responsibility for family discord becomes a family goal with choices that will build the self-esteem of the family.

Pinsof (1995) described the safe, warm envelope for family therapy in a private setting as a "holding environment." In this program the community acts as the safe, warm, holding environment with the community as a large group and the family acting as a unit within that group. The facilitator sets the norms for the community. Understanding the pressures placed on the families, the facilitator acts to focus the community on norms that the community requires for safety and structure. With needed norms in place, the family can relax within the supportive environment of families, evaluate their own progress, and acquire missing conceptual information.

This type of intervention is necessary because many of the families with generational dysfunction often have no sense of community. The families usually have been handling problems that could have been stopped by community boundaries if an organized community existed. Sometimes, families also have stressors coming from their family of origin. The stressors coming from the lack of community boundaries cause additional strain. Then, if the families begin to show the strain, they are blamed and stigmatized. The *Uncapping Family Wisdom* program maintains that given the right conceptual information, within a consistent holding environment, the family can gain confidence in their successes and work toward healing their family. They also have the opportunity to learn how they are connected to society and can become a powerful force for change.

Since many families have probably not experienced a community with knowledge of civilized established norms for the members, they are especially vulnerable to shame. Shame lies in the core of one's personhood and is an overwhelming debilitating feeling that one may have done something wrong, improper, or immodest, perhaps even outside of one's awareness. While guilt has to do with something one has done that is perceived as wrong or stupid, shame lurks in the very essence of a person's perception of himself or herself. Shame can be very devastating in the process of self-scrutiny. The very language used by these families often includes shaming in direct and indirect communication, so addressing the potential for shame is critical to continuing treatment, attendance, and participation in the meetings. In *Uncapping Family Wisdom*, special forethought is given to techniques designed to bypass the element of shame in the program community setting.

Uncapping Family Wisdom offers a program which is flexible and easily specialized to various populations. In future chapters, you will read about three programs specialized to different populations. The linguistic and semantic information may be largely new to you, but the information is integrated in a style that is easy to learn. I think you will enjoy the assessments, based upon developmental observation and general semantics. The assessments are completed and evaluated by the families themselves, giving them more control of the interventions and allowing them to protect needed family boundaries. Careful directions are given to the community facilitator for the formation and process of the community environment. For the most part, all of these techniques bypass shame and prevent any resistance.

Significance to the Field of Therapy

Uncapping Family Wisdom: A Program for Recognizing, Treating, and Reconciling Transgenerational Dysfunction

This program introduces a method that moves families toward wholeness. The program illustrates an application of a living systems model, which intertwines sociological, psychological, semantic, and linguistic models. The method is noteworthy because it uses important information regarding linguistic competence to address the sources of problems that are impacting the entire culture. The comprehensive approach is in marked contrast to the practice of treating only the symptoms of the problems, which may change behavior but may not instill conceptual information that is basic to self-moderation and internalized control.

Uncapping Family Wisdom also highlights developmental issues in adults. It suggests a way to self-assess arrested development in adults, along with that of the children, and fills in the gaps of development. Clarke and Dawson (1998, pp. 218-242) offer specific affirmations for development stage progression and suggest that affirmations from preceding stages be offered in family linguistics, along with needed age-appropriate affirmations. They suggest a comprehensive model of linguistic intervention for parents who recognize they were raised in dysfunctional homes and realize they lack the necessary skills for parenting their own children. In this manner, the adults are empowered to avoid the missteps found in their family legacies. Clarke and Dawson (1998, p. 290) discuss developmental affirmations, some of which will be included in the program.

Clarke and Dawson argue that even as adults, we are continually recycling previous stages from day to day, so all the suggested affirmations are appropriate for adults. The treatment described in *Uncapping Family Wisdom* recognizes that adults are in need of developmental intervention. The program has found a way to show the family how transgenerational dysfunction is actively operating in their family and to give the family the tools to address what they see.

To sum up the process, the program diagnoses and provides missing conceptual information in a protected, structured environment so that the cycle of generational dysfunction can be reversed and optimal development restored. The program allows parents to evaluate the developmental gains of the family and provides a self-evaluative inventory that identifies semantic problems which cause conflict in the families. The program leads individuals and families toward restoration as functioning units and equips them to pass on healthy functioning as a new generational legacy in the community.

The overall intervention by the facilitators into the family dynamics in the community will consist of three parts:

1. the knowledge of the theory behind the project,
2. the content of the extracted conceptual information from the highest lect, and
3. the process of supplying an appropriate environment for change.

The Role of the Family in Society

Society affects the development of families, and families affect the development of society. Future families become symptom bearers of the growing degeneration of society, which, in turn, will reflect the developmental health of its families. The *Uncapping Family Wisdom* program provides a means to meet this challenge, while bypassing shame and allowing people to learn in an environment much like that in which high-functioning individuals absorb their conceptual information.

How the Book Is Organized

Uncapping Family Wisdom is ordered into three major sections:

Part I	Chapters 1-5 contain the background material needed for the application of the program.
Part II	Chapters 6-11 contain the application of the process and content of the program.
Part III	Chapter 12 contains the summary of the linguistic interventions, the developmental progress for each study, and the comparative study for four case study research investigations.

Part I—The Background Material Needed for the Program

Part I contains Chapters 1-5. Chapter 1 is the "origin story," the driving force behind a search for a treatment program for persons and families exhibiting symptoms of transgenerational dysfunction. The chapter contains information on what historians have called the "four turnings," which are divisions of history that occur about every 80 to 100 years and contain information about the events in the crisis time in which we live. Chapters 2, 3, and 4 provide basic background information that the therapist will need to know for facilitating the program. Each of these chapters contains overviews, glossaries, and bibliographies. In these chapters, readers are initiated into the content of the program. Chapter 5 covers the process of the program. Creating an environment for the program application provides safety and structure. A method for shame intervention is carefully described. This chapter presents a detailed explanation of the process for building an environment for conducting interventions into transgenerational dysfunction.

The background material found in Part I, Chapters 1-5, integrates and flows into the process and content of the treatment program which begins with Chapter 6 in Part II. The background information presented in Part I will be featured in the concrete objectives in the handouts as part of the actual treatment program found in Part II.

Part II—The Application of the Process and Content of the Program

Part II begins with an explanation of case study research which will prepare you to follow the four case studies which are included. The careful assimilation of the information learned in the first five chapters begins in Chapter 6 and continues through Chapter 11. These chapters constitute the actual recommendations, suggestions for timing, and handouts for the participants who will be going through the program. Each chapter offers detailed explanations for the facilitator of the program. The chapters are

Chapter 6 Characteristics of a Strong Family
Chapter 7 Communication in the Family System

Chapter 6 presents the beginning progress of four subjects studied in the case study research. This chapter demonstrates the actual use of the program with individuals and families. Chapter 7 provides the information for semantic intervention into the language patterns of families. Chapter 8 provides intervention into developmental arrests which may be affecting the families. Chapter 9 moves business management theory into the home environment. Chapter 10 addresses behavior modification which helps children internalize a locus of control and gain confidence in knowing how to take responsibility in order to enhance their chances of success in the future. In Chapter 11, the emphasis moves to the families, what they have learned, and how they can use what they have learned to influence their communities. The process and content of the program has been designed to protect the families from shame. In fact, at the end of the program in Chapter 11, an effort is made to "shame proof" the families. Here they are schooled in the nature of shame and how it might have impacted their family. Each of the families has an opportunity to highlight their progress and be affirmed by the community. The families are recognized as having the ability to impact their communities as positive building blocks of society.

Part III—Comparative Summary of Linguistic Interventions and Developmental Progress for Case Study Research

Chapter 12 is the summary of the individual linguistic observations, semantic evaluations, and developmental progress for the four subjects in the case study research are compared in Part III, completing the case study research. Two of the subjects have been followed over time and the long-term effects of their interventions over time will be reviewed.

Continuing Process

For some families who experience the program, the experience will be the beginning; for others it will be the answer; and for still others, it will prepare them for further intervention with a private therapist or support group. In residential treatment centers and group home settings, don't be surprised if the staff environment improves with the application of this program. Staff training is highly recommended.

My very best wishes to you as you open up understanding for your clients and have an opportunity to participate in their recovery.

Sandra S. Pate
D. Phil., MSW

References

Alford, D. C. (1980). Part I: Demise of the Whorf Hypothesis: *Phoenix: New directions in the study of man. Vol. IV*, 1-2. Retrieved from http://enformy.com/dma-dwh.htm.

Bailey, C. E. (2007b). Semantically Mediated Integration of Cognition in *Homo sapiens*: Evolution, Grammar, Uncertainty, and Cognitive Accuracy. *Cognitive Sciences 3*(1):85-142.

Bentovim, A. (1992). *Trauma-organized systems: Psychological and sexual abuse in families.* London, UK: Karnac Books.

Bureau of Justice Statistics. (2007). *Parents in prison and their minor children.* Retrieved from *http://www.bjs.ojp.usdoj.gov/content/pub/press/pptmcpr.cfm.*

Burt, M. (2001). What Will It Take to End Homelessness? *Urban Institute.* Retrieved March 5, 2010 from http://www.urban.org/url.cfm?ID=310305.

Campbell, J. (1997). *The Sapir-Whorf hypothesis*. Retrieved March 21, 2006 from http://www.venus.va.com.au/suggestion/sapir.html.

Carroll, J. (1964). *Language and thought.* London, UK: Prentice-Hall.

Clarke, J., and Dawson, C. (1998). *Growing up again* (2nd ed). New York: Hazelden Press, Inc.

Institute for Urban Research. (2010). Retrieved August 5, 2011, from http://www.esri.com/news/arcnews/spring10articles/mapping-urban.html.

Mumola, C. (2000). Incarcerated parents and their children. *Bureau of Justice Statistics.* Retrieved March 5, 2010, from http://www.bis.ojp.usdoj.gov/index.cfm?+pbdetail&iid=981.

Nist, J. (1974). *Handicapped English: The language of the socially disadvantaged.* New York: Charles C. Thomas Publisher.

Pinsof, W. (1995). *Integrative problem-centered therapy: a synthesis of family, individual and biological therapies.* New York: Basic Books.

U.S. Conference of Mayors. (2007). *Status report on hunger and homelessness*, p. 13. Retrieved March 5, 2010, from http://www.usmayors.org/HHSurvey2007/nhsurvey07.pdf.

Uncapping Family Wisdom

Part I

PART I

UNCAPPING FAMILY WISDOM: THE BACKGROUND MATERIAL NEEDED FOR THE PROGRAM

Chapters 1-5 contain the background material needed for the application of the program. The information regarding the origins of the program and predictions of historians help locate the focus of the program in time. The explanation of the program begins with an introduction of a common vocabulary.

Language and its lects demonstrate how different speakers view reality in their environments and how they survive in their cultures. The linguistic legacies of the speakers may affect human development potential and contribute to developmental arrests. Specific interventions can be created for trauma-organized families to address the problems concerning any tendencies toward developmental arrests.

In Chapter 1...

In this chapter, the origin and the development of the program called *Uncapping Family Wisdom* is explained. The program has been used in various settings. The program was drawn from several disciplines and addresses the problem of transgenerational dysfunction. The dysfunction interferes with the human development potential in family systems. The program reveals distortions of the language and conceptual language which are missing in the language of family systems exhibiting transgenerational dysfunction. The program interfaces with individuals and families, eliminating distortions and supplying conceptual language designed to uncap the inherent family wisdom. The reasons that the *Uncapping Family Wisdom* treatment program has been successful are

- The program is enjoyable because the families are ready for answers. When families are put in an affirmative, healthy environment and are given conceptual information, family wisdom can be released. The participants in *Uncapping Family Wisdom* groups grow to recognize that the ability to understand and live the characteristics described in the program lie latent within them and within their own families.
- Good research provides information which forms a foundation for proper internal investigations by the family.
- Trained, skilled facilitators bring their specialized knowledge and information about the specific needs of the population they serve and can adapt the flexible program to meet those needs. Using the program can enrich environments and benefit treatment center staffs who struggle with problems which come with chronic turnover.

Cross-disciplinary content made the development of such a program possible. A search for the cause of the cause of the cause of the cause of the cause, and the baseline underlying cause, is needed for bottom-line solutions.

The predictions from historians lead us to believe that the time is ripe for change and new paradigms. According to Strauss and Howe (1997), in times of crisis, the family and the community become increasingly important and society moves away from individualism to solve its problems. These authors report that by the 2020s, America could become a well-functioning society that has regained confidence in itself.

Uncapping Family Wisdom offers one method for addressing family difficulties which have continued in family systems for generations. Some family problems may have lasted through many cycles of change and are waiting for an opportunity to be resolved, providing a way for solid community building with healthier families as the building blocks.

CHAPTER 1

ORIGIN AND ORACLES

Early in my life, I learned something was wrong. At the time, I did not have the words to describe the situation. What I learned was that some children are born into families who have severe gaps in their informational base. The indications of these severe gaps in their informational base are want, need, toxic shame, and loss. A few are "down on their luck," while some of this population are the people for whom bells are rung and kettles are filled with coins at Christmastime. The individuals in these populations spend their lives looking for answers or just trying to survive. Others with different legacies, or with less severe gaps in their informational base, do not have to search to a comparable degree, because they were born into a family system that had the needed conceptual information and a menu of possibilities and choices.

How all this works in childhood psychotherapy is under investigation. Over the past decades, research into early attachment has stimulated general interest in the roles of relational processes and internalized representational systems. Lyons-Ruth (1995) observes that relational processes and internalized representational systems are seen as the basis for understanding continuities and discontinuities in psychopathology over time and across generations. Conceptual information is learned indirectly in the interplay between a parent and a child and determines how well one gets along with others and one's potential quality of family relationships. Conceptual information can even affect how much income one may accumulate during a lifetime. Conceptual information is a matter of learned responses, which are mostly out of a person's awareness. Persons who have different levels of conceptual information may have very different early childhood experiences with their children than those who have a larger degree of conceptual information.

Transgenerational Dysfunction

Transgenerational dysfunction is a growing phenomenon found in most environments and to some degree in virtually every social stratum today. Transgenerational dysfunction is especially visible in alternative school settings, court-ordered counseling situations, migrating populations, rehabilitation centers, homeless shelters, and prisons. Looking at only two areas, the prisons and the homeless, one can see how children are affected. Families with children constitute a substantial part of the urban homeless population. In prison populations, a substantial number are parents of children younger than 18 years of age. These families are in need of a systemized exposure to conceptual information, which will aid in the quest for optimal human development for all.

These and other families may not know how to instill in their offspring, through their language patterns, the basic conceptual information considered necessary for optimal moral, cognitive, social, and psychological development. The absence of this conceptual information leads to arrests in early childhood development and creates dysfunction within the family. Adults in many of these families appear to be passing down faulty language patterns, leading to further dysfunction in succeeding generations. The faulty language patterns distort reality for the speakers, deny developmental permissions, and limit prospects for the future.

As a child, I did not know these things. I only viewed the impact of the difficulty through an incident that happened to me on a special day long ago. This incident would eventually send me on a long search to understand what conceptual basis would be needed and would inspire me years later to write a treatment program for families trapped in a cycle of transgenerational dysfunction across all social strata.

Origin

My Friend

In the 1940s, Memphis did not have subdivisions. In my neighborhood, once fine old homes built at the turn of the century mingled with homes of different sizes built in succeeding years. I lived in a home next to a two-acre lot with a large old home that had been turned into a boarding house. The large old house could not be seen from the street; a tall iron fence surrounded the property. I had never met anyone from that house until one September day when I was four years old.

The day began as many others. I woke up to a man selling his produce calling, "Tomato Man! Tomato Man!" Later, after breakfast, Mother opened the front screen door for me to go out to play. Blinded by the morning light, I stopped before I reached the edge of the shade of the porch. The screen door closed on the aroma of sweet potatoes baking in the oven heat left from breakfast. Mother reminded, "Stay close, now." I knew that Mother would come out every ten or fifteen minutes to call my name. I would answer her promptly with "Yes, ma'am." If I called out "Yes," she would say, "Yes?" Then I would say "Yes, ma'am." But if I said, "What?" to her call, she would not answer at all. One never replied "What?" in answer to a grown-up.

All my routine stops would be places I had marked as locations with special meaning. My daily outside ritual began with a stroll over to the opposite side of the porch to kiss the post. To most people the post was a post, but to me the post was the love of my life, Gene Autry, my favorite cowboy, whom I knew from Saturday afternoon movies.

I then went down the steps to the maple tree and touched the leaves with their velvet bottoms and smooth tops. The tree had been planted when I was two. Turning toward the driveway, the next stop was the tree where a bat had come to cling with wings spread wide for several days. The neighbors had come at different times to see, and all had come back as a group when the animal control officer came to capture the bat.

I then turned and traveled down to the place in the driveway where my father's Studebaker would be parked after work. After that, I went on down the hill to the sidewalk, turning left to the spot by the street where Mr. Howard, who always brought candy for the children, parked his

Argo's Cleaners truck on Tuesdays and Fridays. My next stop was the place where the iceman stopped his truck and used his large scissor hooks to bring ice into our home.

At last, I reached the tall iron fence and turned left to follow the fence back to my home. As I turned toward home, I closed my eyes. Stretching my right arm back as far as I could, I grabbed a bar of the fence as I passed. Now, with my left hand held forward stretching in the air, I leaned forward, pulling hard, "digging" in my feet; until, at last, when I could hold on to the bar no longer, I released the bar and then grabbed the next bar to keep me from falling forward. I repeated these movements, advancing little by little, making a hard and challenging progress toward home. Finally, while holding onto the bar in my right hand, I stopped, blindly swinging around to grab a bar with my left hand, too. I held on to the bars with both hands, stood up straight, and relaxed. Still holding on to the bars of the fence, I leaned backwards with my arms outstretched and opened my eyes to the sky…Slowly, I lowered my head.

Standing on the other side of the fence was a little girl. She was just my size wearing and a cotton dress much like I was wearing. She stood looking straight at me. I pulled myself back up, shifted my weight, and stepped back. For a moment we stood silent, looking at one another. At last, I said, "Hello."

"Hello," she responded.

I felt the "shy feeling" coming. My mother had told me that if I kept on talking the feeling would go away. I searched my mind to find some little girl conversation to share in order to make a connection with the girl and to chase the shy feeling away. "Do you like to play dolls?" She had not moved at all and remained still.

She said, "I have never had a doll."

A question that had been asked to initiate play had gotten an unexpected answer.

Taken aback, I asked, "You have never had a doll?" My mind whirled in disbelief that such a thing was possible. Already backing away, a picture forming in my mind of dolls on shelves was already drawing me toward my house. I told my friend, "I've got lots of dolls…I'm going to ask my Mother if I can give you one."

At that, I turned and ran, ran, ran, yelling "Mama! Mama! Mama!" My heart pounded in my chest setting a cadence of hurry and urgency. I had to slow down to climb up the stairs, built to accommodate adults, but ran again across the porch and opened the screen door, darting through the opening where my mother knelt to catch me.

"Sandra, what's happened? What is the matter?"

I said to her, "I…just…met a…little girl…who has never…had a doll…. Can I give her… one of mine?" Mother held me for a moment, and then she whispered slowly in my ear in her soft Southern voice, "Let's go look at your dolls, and let's decide which one you would like to give her." Then, with her fingers on my shoulder, she led me to the place where my dolls were kept.

Kneeling down to my eye level, she said, "Little girls usually get baby dolls to start. Would you like to give her a baby doll?" I stepped up and chose a large baby and quickly turned away, running through the house and onto the porch. I heard the screen door slam behind me. My heart renewed its urgent cadence. Down the stairs and down the hill to where my new friend stood, waiting in stillness in the same place. I came close and prepared to hand the doll to her.

Suddenly, an arm came through the bars, and a little hand roughly snatched the doll out of my hand, pulling it back through the fence. Backing away in the same instant, the little girl, my little friend, turned, her doll in hand, and ran up a path, yelling, "Mama! Mama! Mama!"

I watched her disappear into a wooded area, not understanding what had happened.

Confused at her reaction, my first thought was, "*She didn't say 'Thank you',*" a shocking thing for a little Southern girl, but the lesser of the realities with which I had been confronted.

I never saw my friend again, although again and again I went to the spot where we had met. I had archived the location as one with a special meaning. Later, as time passed, I found my friend had left a gift with me. She had given me an ache in my heart. I ached because it seemed that I had plenty and because now I knew that there were little girls in the world who for some reason did not have enough. In the wisdom of childhood, I knew it was not right, and that it would never be all right with me. My world would never be the same.

That day in the life of a four-year-old child replays itself over and over. The short time with my friend has a special place in my life. From time to time, in my mind I see my friend again and feel her presence. Since that time, my life has been spent looking for a way to even the score—a treasure hunt for me and for my friend who has remained with me.

Instinctive Searching

The kind of treasure for which I have looked is not material, like dolls. The information that was needed concerned the big "why," the foundation for all the reasons why some had privilege and why some did not. Instinctively, the search has been for the conceptual information that would *even the score* for those who were limited from the first of life by lack of exposure to certain information

The process of finding the conceptual information is best described by a passage from the classic story "A Candle for St. Jude" (Godden, 1962, pp. 767-884). The discovery in this story started out in much the same way as my discovery unfolded for me. In this story, the ballet mistress, Madame Holbien, described the process of a discovery she had observed in her studio. The passage begins when Madame is surprised to witness a brilliant ballet written and danced by a student, Hilda, for whom she has a marked distaste. Hilda's partner in the dance is Lion, Madame's favorite former student who is now a professional dancer. The following passage from this story has deep implications about searching for conceptual information (Godden, 1962, pp. 840-842):

> Hilda has something Madame has not taught her and had it to a greater degree than Madame herself. She has a vision. She knows more than she knows...
>
> "How did you write this? What made you think of it?"
>
> "I don't know," said Hilda. "It came to me..."
>
> "That is right," Madame said gravely. "It came to you. You didn't make it up. That is what so many of them say. It came to you, it was vouchsafed to you," said Madame severely.
>
> "I found the Carlorossi *Fantasia and Variations*," Hilda said slowly. "They gave me the first idea of it. I thought they fitted. I showed them to Mr. Felix. He thought so, too. That is how it began."

Vouchsafed

That is how things happen sometimes. One can't honestly say, "I made it up." A more accurate statement is, "It came to me." For instance, during a short college lecture, I first heard of lects and dialects. The lects and dialects contained certain precepts and conceptual information. Not having time to pursue the information at that time, I went back a few years later and asked the professor if she remembered the lecture and knew the name of the reference. By the look on her face, I think she must have marveled that anyone remembered a lecture from that long ago! The truth was that I had never been able to get the subject out of my mind. Something was being vouchsafed to me that began in that college class on that day. The search had begun.

Her reference in turn referenced another book written by John Nist (1974), who wrote *Handicapped English: The Language of the Socially Disadvantaged.* The original idea for this treatment plan was found on the pages of Nist's book. Nist carefully outlines the childrearing conceptual information used by persons who spoke the highest lect, acrolect, or the standard unmitigated English. The conceptual information found in this type of English language allowed the children potential to develop normally; moreover, the information seemed to pass down through the language providing an atmosphere for successful development generation after generation. Other children were not so fortunate. They were born into other lects or dialects that lacked the rich conceptual language interactions and lacked the precepts that would consistently serve as guidelines for passing through developmental stages in an orderly way.

I knew that my friend from long ago probably wasn't the first generation to not have a doll—her plight was most likely a family legacy—transgenerational. I wondered as I read Nist, *If we know how families that understand certain conceptual information raise their children, why can't we find interventions that supply this conceptual information and fill in the gaps?* This question turned out to be an extraordinary question, which took more years to answer. Nathaniel Hawthorne (Readers Digest Association, 1985, p. 49) observes in *The House of the Seven Gables*, "As a general rule, Providence seldom vouchsafes to mortals any more than just that degree of encouragement, which suffices to keep them at a reasonably full exertion of their powers." So it was with my search. I never tired of the subject, and, little by little, the subject widened before me, giving me degrees of encouragement.

I began to hold on to articles that came across my path in my studies, things I just considered "useful." I gathered from many disciplines—psychology, sociology, linguistics, history, and something called "general semantics." Like the Carlorossi *Fantasia and Variations* which Hilda discovered in the process of envisioning her ballet, they seemed to fit, especially the linguistic information and the general semantic pieces.

Madame musingly continues as she watches a second time (Godden, 1962, p. 841).

> The ballet was in its first flush. Afterward must come the toil of its production when it would become real with properties attached to it: when, built up round its first conception, must come buttresses of decor, orchestration, dresses, lights. Now, it was itself, still visionary though fledged.

A Family Intervention Program

A Children's Psychiatric Hospital

The original program written for families displaying traits of transgenerational dysfunction was "fledged" at a children's psychiatric hospital in the form of a parents' manual called *Mindsets and Monkeyshines: The Rivendell Family Enrichment Manual* (Pate 1991), which was used for family intervention on an acute unit. The first fledged vision was buttressed by concrete exercises, which allowed the families to experience each concept in the family, finding their unique path for learning, thus allowing them to use their own family wisdom.

A structured community setting, described in the pages of *Uncapping Family Wisdom*, yields a stabilized background for learning. The participating families learn in a community with others, who like them, are also learning and taking graduated risks. The community provides the natural environment like that in which conceptual information is naturally absorbed by the privileged offspring in their family speaking patterns and in their communities, where the children are surrounded by people which speak the acrolect English.[6] The valued conceptual information in acrolect gives the language the ability to foster normal development due to the fact that the language most closely mirrors reality.

A Family Court Program

Later, the program was modified for use in a family-court setting to address the problems found in judicial settings with families exhibiting transgenerational dysfunction. Many times the communication in a family-court setting contains hearsay and is crisis prone. Many families in this arena do not have problem-solving skills and carry unresolved problems from past generational dysfunction. The distorted worldview found in the linguistic pattern of these families often brings chaos to the family dynamics and into the courtroom, which can result in the needs of the children being overlooked.

With the interventions described in *Uncapping Family Wisdom*, human developmental goals became the prime consideration in custody cases. The parents and/or guardians identified the developmental gains for their children and themselves. Working with an attorney *ad litem*, custody decisions were based on the willingness of the adults to change their pattern of conflict and make the development of their children their prime consideration.

A Treatment Center Program for Women and Children Affected by Domestic Abuse

Subsequently, at a residential treatment center for women and children affected by domestic violence and at in-training programs for staff in other centers, the program was modified into a treatment program called "Choosing Life." A recovery director and a staff of interns used the treatment program as a stabilizing agent for the overall activity going on in the center. The overall activity supported further therapeutic intervention in the form of individual, group, and family therapy for the residents and their children.

The Program in Private Practice

As changing times demanded new innovations for shortened hospital stays, another use developed. The program became a standard for interventions in a private practice setting for step-down care following mental health hospitalization. With modifications for the lack of a community in

6 This is not to say that communities that speak acrolect English are without dysfunction. Dysfunction can enter the environments of these families through substance abuse, mental illness, personality disorders, character disorders, and outside influences breaking through community and family boundaries.

private practice applications, the program was used for 20 years in individual and family therapy. The program was instituted for a family in need, and the program proved highly successful for extended family interventions.

The Program Reinforced by Research

The content and process of the program was further reinforced by research studies. These studies included

- A study comparing the language of males 18-23 of age at the Pulaski County Detention Center with males of the same age at a local university campus.
- Case study research entitled *Linguistic Legacy and Its Effects on Human Development*, which closely focused on four diverse cases in in-patient and outpatient study, using concentrated interventions based upon sociolinguistic, developmental, and general semantics conceptual information. These case studies follow the applications of the program in Part II of *Uncapping Family Wisdom.*

Six Reasons *Uncapping Family Wisdom* Principles Succeed

1. *Uncapping Family Wisdom* is enjoyable.

   Uncapping inert family wisdom is fun. Working with families who discover their grounding is very rewarding. Presenting the constructs which they can apply to family structure is like watering weeds—they spring right up, not waiting to be pampered, just releasing their stored energy. Even in different settings, the program retains a pristine quality and continues to refresh itself with different applications.
2. Research is important.

   The well-researched theories included in the program make a difference. New communities of families bring their own inert wisdom potential into the setting, using the acquired information to uncap their family wisdom and find unique pathways for their families. The information is not presented like the information was just always there but instead is always presented referring to process of the original research—in other words, as the information was originally discovered. The individuals and families realize that *they are part of* a discovery process that will be unique for their own families. Because the needed conceptual information was uncovered by researchers, and the researchers spent many years refining their skills of observation, today many people benefit from *their own* internal observations. Now the families themselves are the researchers, refining their skills at observation and discovering how the information can be used as precepts for finding the ultimate path for human development in their own family system.
3. Skilled facilitators lead.

In addition, the program stays fresh because the facilitators enter into the flexibility of the program by bringing their own knowledge and information about the special needs of the population that they serve. It would be difficult to facilitate the *Uncapping Family Wisdom* program without doing one's own work of examining one's personal family system, so the training of facilitators becomes an experiential endeavor. Periodic turnovers are common in many types of treatment centers. When the program is used as staff training in treatment centers, the systems become stable. For example, in one center, after viewing the results of the program in the resident population, a staff member came in and asked, "Can we [the staff] have therapy, too?" *Uncapping Family Wisdom* staff training for a formerly-resistant staff was quickly arranged.

4. Cross-disciplinary knowledge is the foundational strength of the program.

   As the program developed, information came together from across disciplines for effective interventions. The results of the process of multi-disciplinary cooperation were described in this way by Dr. A. Ward (1998), Professor Emeritus from the Department of Speech Communications at the University of Arkansas at Little Rock and a long-time consultant to the development of the program:

   > The careful balance necessary to perform studies that are in interdisciplinary scope, yet focused in application, takes great care and skill to construct... (A. Ward, personal communication, July 19, 1998)

5. There is a search for the cause of the cause of the cause of the cause of the cause.

   General semantic experts emphasize abstracting, which is discussed in depth in Chapter 2. Abstracting is at the foundation of the studies behind the treatment program; that is to always look for the cause of the cause of the cause of the cause of the cause. If one does not find that level, then one probably won't find the crucial, bottom-line solutions and will miss a large part of the process. Also, with a coordinated effort in treatment centers, the process allows different interventions to be going on at the same time, which allows for shorter treatment times, very important in today's allocation of time by managed care.

6. There is a goodness of fit.

   Toward the end of "A Candle for St. Jude," Madame understands that the ballet will remain new, because a life exists in the fit of the excitement and the choreography with the music. She can see that dancers will experience the excitement of the enchanted life of the ballet, which will make it new every time. The results are that she loses her two primary dancers who go away to dance the piece in bigger places, a destiny she understood from the first. The ballet, however, has made her gala a success, enlivened her remaining students, and touched the twilight of her career with triumph.

The life of *Uncapping Family Wisdom: A Program for Recognizing, Treating, and Reconciling Transgenerational Dysfunction* exists in the fit of the program with the environment that is carefully provided. Families can find their own wisdom in the framework and leave enlivened with their discoveries. Carefully planned communities, though artificial, still can do what communities were meant to do: provide boundaries, and form norms for the community, which will keep the families safe. In such a community, the latent wisdom can come forth.

Oracles

A Distinct Pattern

Transgenerational dysfunction does not exist in a vacuum. One of the reasons that transgenerational dysfunction is so evident at this time is that Western civilization is at a period of stagnation. In 1997, historians Strauss and Howe offered a persuasive prophecy about a new American era beginning just after the 2000 millennium. The authors looked back 500 years and uncovered a distinct pattern: modern history had moved in cycles, each one lasting about the length of a long human life, about eighty years. In these cycles were four eras, or turnings, arriving in the same order and each lasting about twenty years. The cycles may arrive a few years early or a few years late, but they have always come.

The first era was a "High," a period of confident expansion as a new order took root after the old was swept away. The last American High came during the years of 1946 to 1964. America became a global superpower, the middle class grew, and suburbs and interstate highways came into existence. Next came an "Awakening." The Awakening was a time of spiritual exploration and rebellion against the now-established order. From 1964 to 1984, riots, campus fury, war protests, black power, a divorce epidemic, environmental movements, and feminist movements came on the scene.

Next came an "Unraveling," an increasingly troubled era in which individualism could triumph over crumbling institutions. Strauss and Howe predicted that 1984 through approximately 2005 would be a time of high-tech individualism versus family values. Moralism would introduce cultural wars. There would be worries about crime, incivility, and cultural decay.

Last to come in the cycle was the "Fourth Turning," when society passed through a great and perilous time in history. The authors predicted that in 1997 there would be a period of unraveling which would last approximately eight more years. The next turning is similar to the former Fourth Turning between Armistice Day of 1918 and the Great Crash of 1929. Together, the four turnings embodied a rhythm of growth, maturation, entropy, and rebirth.

Enduring the Entropy and Preparing for Rebirth

The overview of history lends itself to the strong possibility for a coming of a period of crisis, foreseen for this time. A strong possibility is that, with the failing institutions and unvarying mindsets that are available, our culture will be unprepared to handle the coming problems. At this time, the questions that are being asked are very important, because the answers will come as a result of the crisis situations, which demand the answers. In this way, direction for the future will be found. The rhythms of history do not predict the outcomes of a time of crisis, just the timing and the dimensions; but the crisis itself makes society open to new paradigms that bring hope.

Other forewarnings came from the cultural historian and teacher, Jacques Barzun. He was born near Paris, France in 1907 and has remained at the center of American's intellectual thought for some six decades. The former provost of Columbia University, he was admired as the father of the Great Books curriculum. He wrote *Dawn to Decadence: 500 Years of Western Cultural Life to the Present*, a massive volume that summarizes cultural life in the West over the last half-millennium. He finished this book in his 91st year, looking back and writing about the changes he observed in society. Barzun wrote about current times, "There are ups and downs in this story. I think that we have arrived at one of the downs, which I call for convenience decadence, although the word has connotations that I do not share."

He did not mean that decadence was the end of everything, with everybody in a state of moral and intellectual decay. He was no prophet of doom; he looked at decadence as something that arrives at the end of great historical ages or the creative novelty that will burst forth from time to time when there are no real public goals. His work of philosophy stimulates an impulse to look deeper into the current trends of the world and how we got here. In an article by Mark Greenberg from the *San Antonia Express-News* (1998), Barzun commented:

> Institutions get caught. They forget their original purposes, or they no longer are able to fulfill them. Many people are discontented. There is moral relaxation, which is only an expression of being no longer guided by a general enthusiasm for anything....It's like being idle. And you are idle when you don't feel a public goal....When industry was booming in the early 19th century, everybody believing in progress, there was a kind of zest for life. All these matters which interest me are very difficult to judge accurately, and all I profess to do is to give a vision of these 500 years of history based on all that I have learned during my entire lifetime. I have seen the 500 years from 1500 or thereabouts to the present in Western Civilization as a unit with decadent characteristics. There have been decadences within the 500 years, short ones, and this may be a short one, too. But I think the signs are clear.

Uncapping Family Wisdom presents a new paradigm for these difficult times described by Stauss, Howe, and Barzun, giving clear directions on how to proceed with family systems that may have gotten caught in the societal changes and have a need to recapture an enthusiasm for possibilities for change at this time.

References

Barzun, J. (2001). *From dawn to decadence: 500 years of cultural life, 1500 to the present.* New York: HarperCollins.

Godden, R. (1962). A candle for St. Jude. In T. B. Costain & J. Beecroft (Eds.), *Thirty stories to remember.* New York: Doubleday & Co.

Greenberg, M. (1998, Spring). Interview with Jacques Barzun. *Arkansas Gazette.* Article from *The San-Antonia Express-News.*

Hawthorne, N. *The house of the seven gables.* Pleasantville, NY: The Reader's Digest Association, Inc., 1985.

Lyons-Ruth, K. (1995). Broadening our conceptual frameworks: Can we reintroduce relational strategies and implicit representational systems to the study of psychopathology? *Developmental Psychology, 6,* 121-143.

Nist, J. (1974). *Handicapped English: the language of the socially disadvantaged.* New York: Charles C. Thomas Publisher.

Pate, S. (1991). *Mindsets and monkeyshines: the Rivendell family enrichment manual.* Benton, AR: Rivendell Psychiatric Center.

Strauss, W., and Howe, N. (1997). *The fourth turning: an American prophecy.* New York: Broadway Books.

Ward, A. Personal communication to Oxford Graduate Research Council, July 19, 1998.

In Chapter 2…

The *Uncapping Family Wisdom* treatment program is built on the conceptual information found in the linguistic code of the families whose speaking pattern ensures developmental permissions. Nist spoke of *handicapped English*, not *handicapped people*. He saw all categories of people able to achieve and wanted them to be able to get on equal footing. Only the language some people spoke was not always attuned to the reality of situations and often overlooked the emotional needs of the users of the language. Nist in America, and Bernstein before him in England, studied the lects and dialects of English trying to foster success in educational potential. Neither person elevated one class or race over another but generously gave of themselves to try to find ways to improve the lives of their students. The search for a new paradigm began with the discovery that a population existed who spoke the Standard English language called *acrolect*, that is filled with rich conceptual information. The information found in this lect allows the children in this dynamic environment to develop normally; not only that, the information was passed on through the language and patterns of normal development and continued generation after generation. Nist attempted to isolate the conceptual information to enrich the lives of children caught in a cycle of poverty.

The search for the new paradigm sought to discover the baseline cause for inappropriate behavior considered all abstraction levels of possible intervention, and supplied missing conceptual elements, such as knowledge of developmental permissions. One case study discussed in this chapter illustrates a baseline cause that provided a direct intervention into an area of developmental arrest.

Although individuals as adults often have to take the responsibility to leave trauma-organized families, this does not eliminate the negative results of growing up without developmental permissions and without conceptual information. Many times treatment is necessary from a family system perspective. Care has to be taken to construct a program that bypasses shame found in families carrying some dysfunctional speech patterns as part of their linguistic heritage. Other components of the treatment supply human developmental permissions and conceptual language to fill in informational gaps—providing a way to uncap family wisdom by removing the transgenerational barriers. No family, whatever their background, can escape the possibility of transgenerational problems, because generations of positive development can be negatively affected by substance abuse, war, sudden migrations, or other unfavorable circumstances. The belief behind the paradigm of *Uncapping Family Wisdom* is that families, no matter what the structure, have an inherent wisdom that will come forth when barriers are removed.

CHAPTER 2

SEARCHING FOR A PARADIGM

Understanding any new paradigm calls for a common vocabulary to guide the way. Below are some useful terms that will serve as the beginning building blocks for ultimately uncapping dormant wisdom in families filling in gaps with a restorative treatment program.

Glossary

Abstraction levels: levels of exploration that lead to the ultimate cause of observed behavior to the prime intervention.

Conceptual information: information that supplies understanding from which changed behavior can originate. Conceptual information provides ideas that enrich reasoning abilities.

Developmental arrest: failure to advance in one or more areas of development.

Developmental permissions: approval for progress in the form of verbal or non-verbal affirmations given to children at appropriate times in normal human development.

Transgenerational dysfunction: patterns of dysfunction continued in a family system for several generations. An absence of conceptual information in the language of the family is related to a pattern of developmental arrest in the family. The pattern of developmental arrest can originate with cultural crisis, prolonged substance abuse in the home, or severe personal trauma.

Trauma organized: the interpersonal dynamics exhibited in family systems that incite emotional buildup and produce trauma for family members.

The little girl I encountered as a child was probably not the first generation that was lacking simple nurture, demonstrated by the fact that the child had not ever had a doll. Korzybski observes how language might play a part in giving structure, both good and bad, to future generations. "A language, any language, has at its bottom certain metaphysics, which ascribe, consciously or unconsciously, some sort of structure to this world" (Korzybski, 2000, p. 89). "Now these structural assumptions and implications are inside our skin when we accept a language—any language. If unraveled, they become conscious; if not, they remain unconscious" (Korzybski, 2000, p. 505).

Dysfunction, which comes in the form of structural assumptions and implications which do not reflect reality, continues through generations, if not unraveled. The dysfunction coming through language has been shown to be a statistically significant problem calling for transforming resolutions. The rising numbers of homeless, incarcerated, and trauma-organized families treated for abuse and domestic violence illustrate the necessity for a program that can help therapists recognize, treat, and reconcile transgenerational dysfunction. As Korzybski points out, there are structural assumptions and implications inside the skin of those born into a family experiencing transgenerational dysfunction. The younger generation has no recourse but to understand life as they hear it defined in the language of the family. How else would they understand life except to learn the views through the language that represents the views of the family as they have experienced life from their perspective?

The current theory of normal human brain functioning indicates that we have the capacity to choose how and what we think, and we have a capacity to adapt to new situations by making better choices (Diamond, 2002, p. 494). The subjective characteristics of our grammar, however, along with personal, social, and cultural biases, impede us from understanding and using the very information that could enable such a choice (Beck, 1979, p. 13). First, in order to make changes, we have to experience different perceptions and respond to reason.

We may assume that a person born and raised in a particular cultural belief system would think, feel, and behave differently than one born elsewhere, not because their brains differ, but because they internalize different cultural beliefs (Benjafield, 2007, p. 237). An adolescent male in Britain has different expectations than an adolescent male in Africa. People are conditioned by the language in which they are trained; but intelligence seems to be stable across populations (LeDoux, 2002, p. 31). Normal human brains exhibit relatively consistent form and function across cultures, but cultural belief systems differ, sometimes dramatically. Language identifies and defines cultural belief systems and represents a distinguishing group characteristic, directly affecting the thoughts, emotions, and behavior of the group (Adolphs, 2006, pp. 269-285). Browne and Keeley (2007, pp. 53-79) observe that even though humans share basic human emotions, they will react differently to stimuli based on culturally defined values. Knowing this, we can expect people to act in certain ways because of the way they have been acculturated.

This brings us to a search for solutions for those who have been affected by a family legacy or a culture bound by a limited view of the world. What the *Uncapping Family Wisdom* program will do is allow them to uncap their own family wisdom by evaluating what they consider best when given choices of ideas and alternate ways of viewing reality. If at all possible, they will accomplish this in a community deciding its own values with the help of the building blocks of families emerging into more healthy norms. This will, in turn, will enable the stabilization of their community.

Some problems have lasted through several generational cycles and are waiting for an opportunity for resolution. The resolution needed is not only for the individuals and families, but also for society that essentially needs more healthy families as the building blocks. What is called for is a method for dealing with serious problems in families. This method must be more than simply a hit-or-miss series of interventions into behavioral symptoms in the families, because deeper conceptual interventions are needed.

The Search for a New Paradigm

The search for a new paradigm began with the first discovery. The first discovery was that a population existed that spoke the English language in a certain form. The form of English is called *acrolect* and is considered to be the Standard English, the most correct version, which most accurately mirrors reality. Unlike the language most likely heard by the child met long ago, acrolect is filled with rich conceptual information that allows the children in the environment where this form of English is spoken to have a great opportunity to develop normally. Not only that, but the conceptual information appears to pass down through the language and provides an environment for successful development generation after generation. The basis of this linguistic pattern, acrolect, forms the framework for *Uncapping Family Wisdom.* The program provides individuals and families with conceptual information as a basis for expanded ideas that affect behavior and emotions. The program seeks to restore gaps in life skills that may have been affected by trauma in past generations.

The program transfers what one group, the speakers of acrolect, carries in their store of conceptual information to other groups, who may not have been exposed to the rich conceptual information. The conceptual information holds the possibility of more successful human development and richer family relationships. The semantic meaning gleaned from the acrolect gives developmental permissions for adults and children in the population who exhibit transgenerational dysfunction. The participants in the program are exposed not only to a new system of beliefs but also to new possibilities of thinking and behaving. The emotions could be affected. Bailey explains:

> Cultural belief systems and groups frequently overlap or contain subgroups, but a prerequisite set of beliefs usually determines membership. The rules they embody for the group, regarding thought and behavior, usually pass down from elder members and define the particular belief system. Because the rules and beliefs have direct impact on thought and behavior, they also have a dramatic effect on emotions (2008, p. 5).

Optimally, individuals and families are given an opportunity to learn in a protective community, so that the environment is like that found in an acrolect community. Barriers to shame are established by healthy community norms with appropriate behavior consistently modeled by the facilitator of the community group. Structured exercises allow the family to awaken their family wisdom and directly apply what they are learning. Classic research models of development are modified and used to teach and measure the application of the new concepts to individuals in the family.

Beginning at the End

When one searches for a paradigm, the end desired result of some sort of process is already in mind. In the case of searching for a paradigm to create a program like that found in *Uncapping Family Wisdom,* the desired end result is a way to electrify development in families that have been struggling with transgenerational dysfunction. The families are identified by a consistent conflict style and accompanying behavioral problems. Those who work with these families understand that structure is an important part of any program. The search will entail finding out what were the causes of the patterns of dysfunction that have continued though generations in families demonstrating transgenerational dysfunction. As an end result, the families will want to

- demonstrate the ability to discuss differences, instead of entering into conflict, and
- display the ability to have control over their thinking and emotions, rather than engage in inappropriate behavior.

Abstraction Levels

In between the desired positively-charged development and the presenting negatively-charged symptomology of inappropriate behavior are different levels of possible causes. These different levels are called "abstraction levels." To understand how the *Uncapping Family Wisdom* program works, one must understand abstraction levels. These abstraction levels allow the observer to discover the baseline cause for the presenting behavior. If the abstraction levels cannot be determined, the ultimate discovery of the cause of the presenting problems can have many false starts; or, the search may even stop prematurely. With interventions, circumstances may improve for a time, but the symptomology will most likely reappear.

Abstraction levels are used to look at a problem from different perspectives, to consider the different reactions observed, and to investigate the developmental aspects of the problem.

In treatment, abstraction levels are beneficial for three reasons:

- Interventions on different abstraction levels can be going on at the same time.
- An individual can understand what is underlying the behavior and emotion.
- Self-control can be learned by integrating a needed developmental permission.

The search for causes of behavior can supply conceptual information for the family and provide the basis for appropriate behavior and interaction within the entire family system.

In cases of generational dysfunction, the individuals in the family who experience a display of inappropriate behavior often find the effect of the behavior dynamic very powerful. Family members and those who treat the individual and observe the inappropriate behavior may have a high desire for the behavior to cease. If abstraction level applications are unknown, those who observe inappropriate behavior may respond in three ways:

- They may judge and distance from those exhibiting the strong affect of inappropriate behaviors.
- They may seek to modify the inappropriate behavior.
- They may look for reasons why the behavior continues to surface, but stop the process of discovery too prematurely to find the baseline cause.

Judging and Distancing

In the first response, when judging and distancing from the inappropriate behavior is the chosen process, the bars of prisons or "alternate locations" for those showing inappropriate behaviors may provide the needed boundaries for what is perceived as unacceptable behavior. Problems come with this response. Overcrowding in prisons and treatment centers may occur with a resulting early release back into society before treatment is complete. Persons confined by boundaries of separation or confinement may stay at a low stage of moral development, obeying only to avoid punishment or to receive rewards. Negative learning may occur, which can lead to even more violent actions or the new learning of ways to avoid compliance with behavioral standards. Transgenerational dysfunction is common in cases of recidivism. In these cases, if these dynamics of dysfunction are left unattended, the dysfunction can continue into further generations unchecked by the intervention which could protect future generations.

Modifying Behavior

The second possible response is to actively try to modify the inappropriate behavior. While in some cases, behavior modification may have a lasting positive change in at least one area of life, problems may occur in cases involving dysfunction coming through the generations. All the reasons for the behavior may not be uncovered. In a behavior modification program, behavior may improve in response to the rewarding stimulation of the positive responses to appropriate behavior or punitive responses to inappropriate behavior. Regression may take place as situations change and the stimulus of positive responses to appropriate behavior or punitive responses to inappropriate behavior is no longer present. The locus of control in the individual may remain on the outside; that is, the rules for appropriate behavior remain on the outside and are not internalized in an individual's code of ethics. The "rules" remain externalized, belonging to authority figures and are only obeyed if the reward is considered worthwhile or the punishment severe enough to avoid.

Stopping Prematurely

The third possible response is to look for the reasons that unsatisfactory behavior continues to surface. Those attempting to intervene may suspect that something, identified by inappropriate individual and family dynamics, lies behind the cause and effect of transgenerational dysfunction. Direction about how to proceed may not be available, so the searching will stop prematurely, without finding the ultimate cause that could bring a possible long-term solution for the family system. When investigation into the process of unsatisfactory behavior stops, the following may happen:

- The conceptual information that ultimately might equip the individual to change inappropriate behavior to appropriate behavior remains unknown.
- The integration of systematic conceptual information in mental and emotional processes also remains unknown.
- Behavior might indeed change in one area; but, depending on the discovered precursors for the behavior, the criteria for an overall, more permanent solution, which might affect many behaviors, remains undiscovered.
- While the unsatisfactory behavior may stop for a time in one member of the family, the family system may be accustomed to the inappropriate behavior. The very same behavior or a variation of the behavior may crop up in another family member. This dynamic is a fact that is well known in family systems therapy.

So, the search for potential bottom-line cause or causes can have many false starts when judging and distancing, attempting behavior modification, or discontinuing investigation prematurely without searching for the ultimate cause. When searching for diagnosis the ultimate contributing causes must be discovered for the highest order of intervention and the most lasting change to occur. To find the most accurate cause of inappropriate behavior, abstraction levels can be considered.

Finding the Cause of the Cause of the Cause of the Cause of the Cause

In order to get to the very bottom of the problems, the cause of the troublesome behaviors that are observed may entail following a trail through several abstraction levels. Abstraction level processing is involved in many of the interventions found in this program. Following through several abstraction levels will allow one to reach a baseline cause that determines the ultimate cause in a line of several causes. The process leads to a baseline cause for a particular behavior. When a baseline cause is determined, another order of reasoning abilities can be incorporated. For instance, those different levels might be illustrated in an abstraction-level pyramid like this:

observed behavior

the cause

the cause of the cause

the cause of the cause of the cause

the cause of the cause of the cause of the cause

the cause of the cause of the cause of the cause of the cause:

____

Baseline Cause

The Importance of a Baseline Intervention

If one does not follow through to the baseline cause for beginning an intervention, especially in cases of generational dysfunction, the bottom line to problems that could be identified more completely is not uncovered and reasoned through to the observed effect. The ultimate cause and effect of behavior is not understood or treated.

The partial discoveries in abstraction levels are often helpful to change and can be used for intervention, but an early *partial* discovery intervention may not uncover the need for conceptual information that has to be understood for a more permanent change to take place. With the baseline intervention, the conceptual information gives the individual the capacity to internalize the knowledge needed to solve his or her own problems and master a range of behavioral patterns. Other levels that may be used for intervention could keep the locus of control externalized in authority figures, while the internalization of the locus of control of behavior is the paramount goal.

An Example of a Baseline Intervention

Take the case of Jim, for instance. He was asked to go to therapy by an older aunt with whom he lived. He would occasionally rage and had shattered some very expensive objects in a family vacation home and some in his aunt's home. There were some clues in the history that marked these behavioral incidents as a suitable investigation into transgenerational patterns of dysfunction. A suicide/homicide had occurred in the family two generations back. There were two cases of substance abuse in the next generation and multiple divorces among several individuals in the family. The family system, which appeared to be losing its stability with every succeeding generation, was becoming trauma organized with lack of self-control and raging behaviors. Trauma organization toward behavior that was chaotic was evident in the actions of family members.

If the episodes in Jim's history were diagrammed, we could begin with the results of Jim's observed behavior and trace a cause and effect path down to the potential original cause. We could observe psychological, biological, and behavior patterns. Here is how the abstraction diagram would appear:

***observed behavior*: shattering of objects**

***the cause*: acting out feelings of rage (adrenalin surge—anger turned out)**

***the cause of the cause*: emotion—mix of feelings (anger turned in)**

***the cause of the cause of the cause*: shame-perceived inadequacy (depression)**

***the cause of the cause of the cause of the cause*:**
irrational response to verbal stimuli (helplessness)

the cause of the cause of the cause of the cause of the cause:
arrested psychosocial development
Baseline Cause

To understand the process let us look at Jim's case. One day in therapy the baseline cause was discovered. Jim was sitting on the sofa in the office. Jim was not good at small talk, and the therapist had realized that Jim did not have very much ego development, a sure sign of developmental arrest. The therapist had decided to "lend him his ego" by talking about different things, bringing in his thoughts and feelings and, generally, sharing his process of forming conclusions. Jim was listening intently, gathering in terms that described feelings and the logic of the therapist. Sometimes he would ask Jim if he agreed with what he was saying, bringing Jim into the conversation and provoking thought. Suddenly, as the therapist spoke he used a regional idiom to describe his activity, which could have been construed as a racial slur. The therapist noticed Jim wince. He understood that Jim did not come from a family who talked in this manner nor was he familiar with the term, since the idiom normally was used in another part of the country. The therapist in "lending him his ego" had made a verbal slip that not only was inappropriate, but not at all in character for him.

By that time, the appointment time was almost over; and, after talking a little longer, the therapist said goodbye to Jim. After thinking about the interaction, the therapist determined that he had probably heard the idiom in his childhood, maybe even when he was at Jim's stage of ego development. When he was being relaxed and casual, letting Jim listen to him think out loud, the idiom had surfaced. He decided that he would begin the next session with a discussion of his use of the term and Jim's reaction.

When Jim returned for the next appointment, the therapist told him that he had something for which he would like to take responsibility. He discussed the comment and told Jim that he had visited his hometown a week before he saw him last week and had been around people who might use that type of language. The therapist explained some of the nuances which made the idiom more understandable. He explained that whatever or wherever the source, using that kind of language was inappropriate and completely out of character for him. He explained that he wanted to take responsibility for the remark and asked Jim to please excuse that remark.

Jim was silent for a moment then asked, "How did you do that?"

The therapist questioned "How did I do what, Jim?"

Jim said, "You just said you were sorry, without wallowing."

The therapist told Jim that he knew that everyone makes mistakes and that he had made a mistake. He repeated that everyone made mistakes. The therapist explained that he did not even know what happened, because it was not something he would normally say, so he had decided that the best solution for his discomfort was to take responsibility for the behavior. The therapist explained that he knew how to separate what he did, his behavior, from who he was—his character formation. He explained that because he had decided to take responsibility for the mistake, he kept his sense of personal power and self-worth intact by deciding to self-discipline himself. The therapist explained that if he had not said anything, Jim would certainly have a reason to make judgments, form opinions, and perhaps even lose respect for him. The therapist stated, "We both knew I made the comment, and the comment was an inappropriate thing to say. I know that it is all right to make mistakes, as long as I take responsibility for my mistakes, so that is what I did."

Jim had gotten what he needed. He saw someone make a bad mistake, saw the person take responsibility for the mistake, saw him separate the mistake from who he was and who he knew himself to be. Jim did not realize something else that had happened: Jim had seen someone model the permissions needed to master the second stage of Erikson's psychosocial development. The second stage of Erikson's psychosocial development deals with autonomy versus shame and doubt. The main struggle for a child at that age of development is "Is it acceptable for me to rely on my judgment and find out that I can do many different things? Will I be shamed and always doubt if I am doing the *right* thing if I become *too independent?"* The child needs to explore and experiment, to make mistakes, and to test limits. Corey comments on Erikson's views:

> If children are allowed the freedom to select meaningful activities, they tend to develop a positive outlook characterized by the ability to initiate and follow through. However, if they are not allowed to make some of their own decisions, or their choices are ridiculed, they develop a sense of guilt over taking the initiative. Typically, they withdraw from taking an active stance and permit others to make decisions for them (Corey, 1986, pp. 23-24).

Now, Jim had seen someone model that it is permissible for someone to make a mistake and take responsibility for the mistake, something he had not seen in his family of origin. What Jim could have received at the ages of one through three in learned responses received from his parents in their conceptual language was unavailable to Jim. In fact, the language in Jim's family *denied* this developmental permission along with the mature executive functions Jim needed for monitoring his personality that accompany this permission.

Jim had little experience with evaluating the language and the assumptions of his language which he had inherited. For every mistake, he might have reprocessed old messages such as, "You are stupid." Like others in his family, he had just integrated information, especially this type of subjective, shaming-value statements stated as truth. Without the full benefit of the use of mature executive functions, which could mediate the truth of shaming-value statements, he often felt helpless and frustrated. LeDoux (2002, p. 96) observed this in similar families, "They tended not to question the factual basis of information, the logic of assumptions, or the reasonableness of conclusions, nor did they have the acquired grammatical framework to do so." Jim was blind to other possibilities such as the fact that a discriminatory subjective response, instead of a rational response, to an emotional stressor was affected by his lack of a normal psychosocial developmental permission. Without this permission, he was blind to other, more rational possibilities. To learn how to handle the unsatisfactory behavior which had brought him into therapy, he needed to

- advance in development by integrating a developmental permission,
- acquire conceptual information that would allow him to manage the strong feelings and the behavioral reactions to the strong feelings which he experienced, and
- learn to manage the shame.

Jim learned conceptually how to be objective about a making a mistake, how to separate the lack of perfection from his self-worth, and how to take responsibility for his actions. He learned that when he thought and acted rationally, he could bypass the shame that came with inappropriate behavior. In short, he not only learned to take responsibility for his mistakes but also learned to feel proud of the way he handled himself when taking responsibility for any mistakes.

After this event, Jim did not come back to therapy. His parents reported that the older relative with whom Jim lived disclosed that Jim had stopped raging and had ceased the destructive behaviors. The verbal and non-verbal patterns, which powered the tendency toward a developmental arrest, were uncovered in the family communication pattern. Jim's father was later treated for the same developmental arrest as Jim.

The psychosocial arrest in this family system was due to a faulty communication pattern passing down through the language of the family system. The negative communication pattern was passing on the inclination for developmental arrest. Permission was needed in the form of a positive answer to the question, "Is it all right to make a mistake and learn from my mistake?" In Jim's family there had been no room for mistakes. There was a missing developmental permission. At the appropriate time in normal human development, permission for making and correcting mistakes had not been encouraged with verbal or non-verbal affirmations. In fact, the developmental permission had not been known or given at all. In their formative years, the children in this family had learned the ritualized concrete thinking of their ancestors, in this case blurred by substance abuse. In their family system, they learned "ineffective cognitive habits and grammatical inaccuracies" (Benjafield 2007, p. 231). Benjafield argues that the rigid, culturally-biased misperceptions can be inherited from "generations of unscientific, misinformed, poorly-educated elders." In this case, all of the family members were intelligent and college educated, but the biased misperceptions continued due to a culture of substance abuse in the family. Although there might have been some substance-abuse intervention, the dysfunction was still in the family system and did not change until the problems of the family system of arrested developments were addressed.

In Jim's family the standard was perfection, which resulted in Jim's inappropriate raging behavior. Some of the members of this family system self-medicated with alcohol to deal with the emotional pain. If continued, this pattern would likely have led to further declining development for future generations. Fortunately, the baseline cause of the effects or symptoms was observed and uncovered; then developmental growth occurred throughout the family system.

Not all cases are this straightforward or permanent, but the episode does point out the fact that a grain of information which seems basic to trained people can often prove exceedingly valuable. The abstract levels of the intervention enabled a full uncovering of the causes of the inappropriate behavior and an intervention into the baseline of the causes.

Understanding the Paradigm

Jim's case demonstrates many parts of the paradigm. Understanding the need to find the cause of the cause of the cause of the cause of the cause in order to find the developmental problems that underlie transgenerational dysfunction is a beginning step. Next, an enrichment program is needed that unravels, filters, and questions the assumptions and implications found in the personal language by which individuals are raised. The program quickly allows the family members to fill in conceptual gaps in abstraction levels, to expose the baseline cause of behavior, and to supply missing developmental permissions to modify behavior.

The Treatment Program Formed from the Paradigm

The treatment program that was formed from the paradigm is fully outlined in Part II, Chapters 6-11. Included in the program are self-evaluative instruments and structured exercises which serve to integrate the needed conceptual information. The components of the paradigm for the *Uncapping Family Wisdom* program include

- Developmental permissions found in the speech patterns of families with a linguistic code that mirrors reality form the structure.
- The use of a community setting, where information can be assimilated much like conceptual learning is attained in an optimal society environment. Norms set by the therapist facilitator in the treatment environment provide safety for the community and bypass shame.
- Self-evaluative assessments for each family that uncover actual semantic errors which are coded in the family's speaking pattern and contribute to arrested development and family conflict.
- Self-evaluative assessments for each family which reveal the individual human developmental gains found in their family systems.
- An application of management and leadership technique which is directly applied to the management of the home environment.

- A clear identification of shame-based issues, so that the individuals in the family system can receive developmental permissions.
- Specific instructions on how the family can modify and control behavior in their family.
- Recognition of the members of the family system as an entity, which has become an important building block for constructing a healthy society.

In short, the program supplies human developmental permissions and conceptual information to fill in the gaps of unlearned material. The method unravels and filters by indirectly questioning the assumptions and implications found in the personal language by which individuals were raised. The program uncovers unconscious static rules, often unspoken, that keep individuals from achieving stages of basic human development. In addition, the conceptual information and its application provides dynamic views of individual and family potential, electrifies development, bypasses shame, and modifies behavior. Finally, family wisdom is uncovered in the family system itself.

The Importance of Conceptual Information

The Basic Formula

Transgenerational Function = (+) Human Development Permissions
(+) Conceptual Information

Transgenerational Dysfunction = (–) Human Development Permissions
(–) Conceptual Information

The basic formula displays the difference between the natural orders of both function and dysfunction. The necessary components must be there for natural human development. Transgenerational function occurs when a person is in contact with parents who give permissions to pass through developmental stages. The conceptual information must be available for transgenerational function, so that gaps will not occur in living skills. Affirmations for every stage of development will be presented in Part II, Chapter 8.

Transgenerational dysfunction, on the other hand, comes when there is a lack of needed human developmental permissions and gaps in conceptual information that make acquisition of daily living skills difficult. Most therapeutic foster parents are very familiar with the behavior of children who have missed developmental markers because of the lack of permission from their biological parents or others who were raising them. Therapeutic foster parents also are familiar with children who lack conceptual information with which to form good decisions for daily functioning.

References

Adolphs, R. (2006). What is special about social cognition? In J. T. Cacioppo, P. S. Visser & C. L. Pickett (Eds.), *Social neuroscience, people thinking about people* (pp. 269-285). Cambridge, MA: MIT Press.

Bailey, C. E. (2008). Semantically mediated cognitive integration of frontal lobe and limbic processing in *Homo sapiens*: uncertainty, evolution, grammar, and accurate cognition. *Cognitive Sciences* 3(1): pp. 85-144.

Beck, A. T. (1979). *Cognitive therapy and the emotional disorders.* Madison, CT: International University Press.

Benjafield, J. G. (2007). *Cognition* (3rd ed.). Canada: Oxford University Press.

Browne, M. N., & Keeley, S. M. (2007). *Asking the right questions: a guide to critical thinking* (8th ed.). New Jersey: Pearson Prentice-Hall.

Corey, G. (1986). Theory and practice of counseling and psychotherapy. Belmont, CA: Wadsworth, Inc.

Diamond, A. (2002). Normal development of prefrontal cortex from birth to young adulthood: Cognitive functions, anatomy, and biochemistry. In D. T. Stuss and R. T. Knight (Eds.), *Principles of frontal lobe function.* New York: Oxford University Press.

Erikson, E. (1963). *Childhood and Society* (2nd ed. rev.). New York: W. W. Norton & Company, Inc.

Korzybski, A. (2000). *Science and sanity: An introduction to non-Aristotelian systems and general semantics* (5th ed.). Brooklyn, NY: Institute of General Semantics.

LeDoux, J. (2002). *Synaptic self: How our brains become who we are.* New York: Russell Sage Foundation.

In Chapter 3...

The language into which a person is born affects his or her views of reality. While the future of the person is not determined, the language has an effect on how the person perceives the world. Psycholinguistics point out adaptive and maladaptive language and consider its effect on psychological adjustment and human development potential. Sociolinguistics, with studies of speech codes, has pointed out how whole levels of society can establish adaptive or maladaptive speech patterns, which can unknowingly dictate convention, systems, rules and regulations.

Information about three different speaking codes, acrolect, mesilect, and basilect, was used to change ideas about how best to understand students and the world from which they come. Now, these same ideas are being used to expose families to conceptual information, which clarifies the ways of viewing the world around them and aids in their communication with one another, leading to a reduction of conflict in the process.

Speaking patterns in families contain certain conceptual information. The degree of conceptual information available in the language of the family varies. Conceptual information is very important because permissions for childhood development are found in the language of the family. Conceptual information provides ideas that enrich reasoning abilities. In turn, the enriched reasoning provides ideas that establish options for behavior in the family unit and determines the range of functioning for the family. The conceptual information given through the speaking pattern found in the family system also determines the world view of the family. In turn, an expanded world view opens the options of behavior for the family and the potential for human development in the family.

In the areas of conceptual information, any absence or void that exists may cause early developmental arrests, which may continue into succeeding generations. Families who do not have the proper conceptual information cannot naturally transfer to the next generation needed information on how children develop morally, socially, cognitively, and psychologically. People caught in this cycle do not know of options and may be perplexed or at a loss of what to do.

Another way of describing the difficulty of combining linguistic ideas and information about human development is

- the absence of correct conceptual information can be found in the communication pattern of many families.
- the passing down of information, coded in the family language, leads to further dysfunction in succeeding generations of many families. Unless intervention is available, conceptual information missing in the speaking pattern of the family causes developmental arrest in the offspring of the family and causes further developmental arrest in the succeeding generations.

The *Uncapping Family Wisdom* treatment program allows the participants to evaluate their own family speaking pattern and supplies information and skills which are missing. Exposure to an organized plan that incorporates conceptual information from the fields of neuroscience and linguistic studies can influence the changes needed for developmental gains in families. In the process, individual needs, family needs, and community development needs can all be addressed.

CHAPTER 3

LANGUAGE AND LECTS

To better understand the information in this chapter, terms from the specialized vocabulary of linguistics and some other terms of interest to the study are defined. These terms will enable understanding of a new paradigm for solving difficult problems in family interventions, where successful interventions were previously considered rare or impossible.

Glossary

Acrolect: the lect or variation of language generally found in highly educated families who speak the English language. Acrolect is considered to be the Standard English. This lect has conceptualizations which allow optimal human development.

Mesilect: the average and most heard variety of English. The lect is value-laden and roles are carefully defined. Mesilect is thought to reflect a desire toward upward mobility. Mesilect is considered a true lect, as opposed to a dialect, and can be found in middle class society.

Basilect: the restricted language generally found in families with low levels of education. The static nature of the language challenges advancement. Basilect is prone toward semantic error and is considered a dialect of substandard English.

General Semantics: a term, attributed to Albert Korzybski, which is a general overview of the structure and meaning found in language. General semantics highlights semantic errors intrinsic to the English language. Semantic errors are ways of speaking which do not reflect reality.

Speech Codes: the study of how language spoken by groups in society can establish adaptive or maladaptive speech patterns that can unknowingly dictate convention, systems, rules and regulations. Language is thought to highly influence a notion of reality for its speakers.

Linguistics: the scientific study of languages. The study of languages is from a historical and comparative point of view or from a descriptive and structural point of view.

Psycholinguistics: the study of adaptive and maladaptive language and its effect on psychological adjustment.

Societal Decay: a process whereby a culture loses its cohesion in the forms of morals, values, roles, and responsibilities. A moving away from formerly-set standards of customary behavior.

In this chapter of *Uncapping Family Wisdom*, the knowledge base will be expanded to include some information from the field of general semantics. Commenting on current events, Charley Reece (2007), writer of *National Perspective*, a nationally syndicated column, observes how politicians manipulate the public with their play on words. He stresses in a column that names and labels do not alter the act that is happening, because words are a set of symbols humans use to communicate with each other. He observes that the word *symbol* is never the same as the actual thing.... He says, "That is the lesson of general semantics, a subject all adults should study. All of the manipulation of our minds is done, for the most part, with words, whether the motive is political, commercial, ideological or religious."

Reece's opinion regarding the importance of the study of general semantics was reinforced when linguists, semanticists, neuroscience psychologists and psychiatrists, and other mental health professionals began to also connect language use with problems that hinder childhood development. Imagine the effect on a developing child who is growing up in a home where language has been used inappropriately in a way that does not actually reflect reality! Many times the ability to question the use of language by objective observation is not a known factor to many people. Because most people do not understand how to objectively observe the family language, the potential for harm remains out of the awareness of the parents, who continue to reason and use language the way their own parents reasoned and used the language. In many families, the speaking pattern is the means whereby transgenerational dysfunction is passed down the family line.

In *Science and Sanity*, the semanticist Albert Korzybski (2000) wrote about seven different speaking errors found in the English language, stating that language influenced not only thinking, but also all of human behavior. The language system that Korzybski isolated was a dynamic language, not a static language which kept past dysfunction in the present, causing stress and anxiety. At the time of his writing, he felt that language directly affected our nervous systems. He felt that if language habits were immature or distorted, behavior was also less than mature. He commented that words could make people "unsane" to various degrees. Korzybski never used the word insane because he felt the term was out of touch with reality. Unsane referred to the various ways we speak and behave which fall on a continuum of sanity.

Korzybski also introduced a new term, "time-binding" and defined man as a "time-binder." What did Korzybski, mean about man being a time-binder? Beavers (1977, p. 53), an important contributor to the science of modern cognitive psychology, observed

> He meant that each generation could conceivably begin where the last left off, (and) culture could progress by learning and remembering without re-experiencing.... Time-binding refers to the capacity to have a past, a present, and a future as a part of one's self-awareness, and to be able to focus on these at will.

Neuroscience, Psycholinguistics and Sociolinguistics

In order to understand the *Uncapping Family Wisdom* treatment program, we need to delve further in order to increase the knowledge base to include some information taken from the field of neuroscience, psycholinguistics, and sociolinguistics. The information in this section is especially important because of the inclusion of the work of Basil Bernstein and John Nist, observers of the effect of language. This pioneering work on class and language changed the course of education (Charap, 2000). Their individual studies of family language opened the way of understanding the impact of the linguistics for different noticeable parts of society. Their studies were designed to aid families, especially children, caught in a cycle of poverty—not to prove superiority of one class over another (Campbell, 1997). The original studies were used to educate teachers on how to enrich the language choices of the students in order to enlarge their conceptualization of reality. Information needed to understand how to remove the barriers which block family wisdom is gleaned from these studies.

Here the work of Bernstein and Nist, based on scientific observation, will be directly applied to a treatment program for families. The *Uncapping Family Wisdom* program will supply the optimal conceptual information that can be used as part of a systematic intervention into the language that negatively affects human development in childhood. Language that negatively affects human development is frequently a result of transgenerational factors. Failure to intervene can result in a lifetime of problems for the adults and a continuation of blocked development in future generations.

"*Uncapping Family Wisdom*" means just what it implies. The family wisdom is inherent—the wisdom just needs to be uncapped. The wisdom is often unavailable due to the language used in the home, which affects the well being of the individuals in the family line. True wisdom is accompanied by a freedom from disquieting thoughts and feelings. Wisdom has a cognitive, emotional, and, most likely, a behavioral effect. In the case of Jim (Chapter 2) searching for the cause of the cause of the cause of the cause of the cause led to correction of several problems in thinking and affective components. The cause of the cause of the cause of the cause of the cause was a missing psychosocial developmental permission that was not provided in the family language. Only when he asked for and learned another method for addressing the cognitive vacancy of development that had caused his family difficulty for generations, could he change his behavior. Jim's behavior was greatly altered due to the fact that his complete thinking and affective processes were impacted by a new reasoning, only possible with the newfound developmental permission. He could now reframe the situation, understanding what response was possible using a different language pattern. He now understood the reason for his disquiet. The applied wisdom and self-evaluations uncapped his wisdom to find peaceful ways to guard his previously undefended, fragile self.

New and Older Ideas in Agreement

Neuroscience Contributions

In neuroscience literature, more and more attention is being given to what is called "evolutionary perspectives." Keller and Chasiotis (as cited in Bailey, 2007) discuss how humans tend to want to gravitate toward positive rewards. They observe, "From an evolutionary view, this makes a lot of sense, because the unfamiliar may represent a potential danger, while the familiar has at least theoretically been evaluated and found to be safe. We tend to do what is familiar and stay safe."

Asking an individual, especially a child, to make a change outside of the system puts the child in danger of negative feedback. The systems were formed as a whole, and to break out of that whole would be very difficult indeed for a child. In the *Uncapping Family Wisdom* program the emphasis is on changing the family system to make change safe for the children. For change to take place, the program must make sense to the adults. The adults must feel in control, keeping the control centered in the family unit while the family is in the community and hearing the same information as other families. The adults must decide on safety issues for their individual family units, perhaps in an individual family session with a mental health provider.

Generations of dysfunction can be very powerful. Shame can keep dysfunction stable over generations. Irrational thinking usually passes down through many generations, and, in part, because of our tendency to gravitate toward the familiar, carries into adulthood and away from the unfamiliar (Benjafield, 2007, p. 386). Humans have a tendency to experience rewards, or gratification, for sticking with the familiar, and punishment, or anxiety, for venturing into the unfamiliar.

Rich conceptual information is not available to all families, leaving some children at risk. Benjafield describes their plight in this way:

In childhood, we not only learn the ritualized concrete thinking of our ancestors, but we also inadvertently learn ineffective cognitive habits and grammatical inaccuracies, faulty assumptions, coincidences imagined as cause-effect conclusion, superstitions, myths, magical thinking, and rigid, culturally biased misperceptions handed down from generations of unscientific, misinformed, and most often poorly-educated elders (2007, pp. 321, 333-334).

Charles Bailey (2007, p. 27), a neuro-psychiatric researcher, states that if intervention is not present, children have little experience with which to evaluate different concepts, and they uncritically absorb whatever they encounter with no regard for its rational usefulness or accuracy.

To correct these tendencies in families, the *Uncapping Family Wisdom* program builds conceptual information into the written intervention processes. Healthy conceptual norms lead to good mental processes, which can provide a safe community environment where the wisdom can be uncapped by the family unit. The methodical introduction of the information allows families to make gradual systemic changes based on conceptual information.

Psycholinguistic and Sociolinguistic Ideas

Sociolinguistics has to do with the culture where we live. Much more is going on than meets the eye. As was discussed in Chapter 1, every 80 years our Western civilization appears to pass through four turnings of social change (Strauss and Howe, 1997, pp. 7, 177-253). When we enter periods of societal decay, where our culture is losing its cohesion in the forms of morals, values, roles, and responsibilities, we have to look on different levels to determine solutions in order to understand what is working and what is not working. Many families become symptom bearers of the regression of society and are at a loss of what to do. This is a prime time for intervention. During times of societal decay, individuals, families, and communities are easier to access and easier to change than society at large; moreover, during times of regression, a strengthening of individual, family and community can impact society in positive ways.

The work of psycholinguistics has served to point out adaptive and maladaptive language and its effect on psychological adjustment. Sociolinguistics, with their studies of speech codes, have pointed out how whole levels of society can establish adaptive or maladaptive speech patterns, which can unknowingly dictate convention, systems, rules, and regulation. Sociolinguistics, which came into the science of sociology in the 1970s, highlights the social impediments to learning and the role that communication plays in reinforcing class structure.

Basil Bernstein

The new ideas of the sociolinguistics were upsetting at first. In September 2002, Professor Mary Douglas, referring to John M. Charap's obituary of the English sociolinguist, Basil Bernstein, in *The Guardian*, explained the problem in this way:

> At that time, the link between humans and speech acts was taken to lie within the individual psyche. To propose the social structure as the governing factor was revolutionary.... The real stumbling block for the linguists was his [Bernstein's] favourite word, "code." They could talk about language as a code, but not about "speech code." Paradoxically, the critics in sociolinguistics suspected him of bias against the underprivileged, a bizarre perversion of his attitude.... He was also suspected of determinism, cultural or linguistic...a complete misunderstanding. When works from seminal writers are read, we can understand that their points were argued in varying degrees. Political jealousies, protection of previously-held positions, and narrow classifications of subject boundaries were often involved. Today, the works of seminal writers can be gleaned for their innovative discoveries, and the rest can belong to history. Bernstein's work is notable because he looked at the differences in speaking patterns and vocabulary of three groups of families: the aristocracy, military classes, and the English working classes. He never intended to imply that any groups of humankind involved were doomed to stagnancy; he just reported his observations about the language that led to stagnancy. Bernstein (1969) was concerned about the effect of language on human development. He was concerned that those children in certain populations
>
> - would be the victims of a limited presentation of the common language and become seekers of social solidarity in preference to the realization of individual achievement and personal fulfillment;
> - would be trapped in limiting, rather than an exploring, conceptual instruction and unable to cope with ambiguity and ambivalence;
> - would become skilled at surviving by having a closed sense of communication that consisted of reading facial expressions, bodily gestures, and intonation patterns, rather than what was actually being said;
> - would grow up to have a poor command of cause and effect; or
> - would be exposed to authoritative modes of social control rather than a request model; therefore, they would choose power instead of language as a means of exercising influence over the behavior of others.

Look carefully at Bernstein's concerns. How current do these problems seem? How does this pattern compare to gang-related behavior today? How many are in counseling today, as a result of being impacted by adults who grew up in this manner?

How can we intervene in these dynamics? By looking carefully at the language of the family system using assessments that allow clients to evaluate their families in a different, non-threatening light, deep interventions can be made. By examining how the influences of society have affected their family view, members of the family can decide for themselves what is right for their own family system. Families can and do incorporate new ideas. When the incorporation is done in a community setting with other families making their own choices, strong communities can evolve. Even in a private practice setting, therapists, in addition to addressing behavior and using a variety of techniques, can reveal societal and sociolinguistic factors that can be considered in a systematic way.

John Nist

Along with Basil Bernstein, John Nist, an American, sought to intervene with children who were less advantaged, partially because they were trapped by the language spoken in their environment. He did not question the intelligence of the children but wanted to expand their conceptual world so they could adapt and succeed in an academic setting. He saw too many children becoming disadvantaged by the language spoken around them. He referred to *handicapped language,* not *handicapped children.* Nist studied the language of the children who had been deprived by their language environment and called the malady *culturally disadvantaged.* He did not mean that they were less intelligent, just that they had not been exposed to different types of conceptual information. He saw their possibilities and desired to help (Nist, 1974, p. 80).

The dialect language they spoke, basilect, had a distinction of what he called "segmented reality" (Nist, 1974, pp. 129-131). Reality was not consistent due to the lack of conceptual information. The responses of the children often seemed reactionary, and the interactions in the families were often reactions to reactions. There were gaps in their information base. The children who were born into these families had much to overcome and had little conceptual information about how to be successful.

He also observed the two lects of those who spoke Standard English, one which insured the successful raising of children generation after generation and the other that held on to values and roles that they felt would insure upward mobility.

Anthropological psycholinguistics, particularly the work of Whorf (Whorf, 1956), stated that the language one spoke shaped one's personal experience of the world. In other words, language defined reality for the speakers. "Modern linguistic determinism" (sometimes called linguistic relativity) refers to the idea that the language we use *to some extent* determines the way in which we view and think about the world around us. Linguistic relativity means that thought is merely affected by or influenced by our language, but determinism does not mean that language determines thought or that language and thought are actually identical. According to Margolis et al. (2008), linguistic determinism is the subject of spirited debate.

The vehicle for transmitting culture is language. Nist (1974, pp. 144, 200) classified the variance in the language of the disadvantaged. The language of the socially disadvantaged excelled in communicating information about concrete subjects and stereotypical social situations, but the language was deficient in expressing abstractions and subtle distinctions of feelings. The process of events was not expressed; therefore, the process of events, in all probability, was not understood. Nist's observations point out a lack of understanding of cause and effect and a limited feeling vocabulary.

Linking the information on linguistics to developmental tasks is imperative if parents are to learn how to give permission to develop to their children. The formation of language and the concepts in the language occur simultaneously with the developmental stage formations for children. In early stage formation, the children receive information on trust, personhood, initiative, and conscience building. In all probability, if the developing child is denied stage development permissions by use of an inherited style of speaking, there will be a developmental stage arrest in early childhood.

Acrolect, the Language of the Advantaged

According to Nist (1974, pp. 74-75), the acrolect speech pattern is the most prestigious within the language. Speakers of acrolect English tend to be well educated, culturally advantaged, socially adroit, and highly competent in performance. Speakers of acrolect have very extensive vocabularies and can switch cultural and functional levels of usage. These speakers have a freedom and skill in communicating and switching to different abstraction levels and tend to take their time to plan what they are about to say.

Nist and Bernstein looked at the child-rearing practices of families who spoke acrolect. They observed the dialect of the families to be a very dynamic speech pattern that had developmental permissions built into the structure. Rhetorically, acrolect is an interactive language with unrestricted codes, not limiting the thinking process of individuals. The speech of the acrolect class is generally free of so-called grammatical errors and stylistic lapses, which violate mood, tone, or attitude. Speech patterns show an extreme sensitivity to the immediate context situation (the here and now) and tend to keep emotive function at a pleasant level, usually positive in mood, tone and attitude. There are generally not as many rules about what one can say, and much feedback is available to the speaker. For these reasons, Nist and Bernstein viewed acrolect as the "standard" version of English because the normal use of the language was not a cause for interpersonal stress.

Mesilect, the Language of the Middle Class

According to Nist (1974, pp. 76-80), mesilect was considered the most pervasive version of language speech variety. He observed that speakers of mesilect tend to have no more than a high school education, tend to be neither very culturally advantaged nor socially adroit, and tend to be only fairly competent in performance. The vocabulary is inadequate for the conversational demands needed for all societal levels of language use. In mesilect, there tends to be conversational variety. Generally, mesilect is full of mistakes caused by attempting to overcorrect. A speaker of mesilect seems to have a "speech monitor" in his or her psyche that causes "overcorrection" of language in order to possibly achieve the standards which might advance their social standing. The lect is full of stylistic lapses that violate mood, tone, or attitude; that is, the non-verbal communication and communication about the communication do not always serve the purpose of the verbal communication. Speakers are not sensitive to the immediate context, sometimes taking something out of context. The language is inadequate in public gatherings and can step up emotive function to an unpleasant level, whether positive or negative in mood, tone, and attitude.

Speakers of mesilect operate fairly skillfully in the three most informal styles of discourse—intimate, familiar/casual, and consultative. Families who speak mesilect foster interpersonal methods of learning. Mesilect may appear in personal letters but, except in fiction, it is seldom found in published form. For speakers of mesilect, role obligation and differentiation of roles are very important. Mesilect emphasizes positional modes of control over personal appeals: this means that a role in the family gives a person more power, and requests usually are made in the form of an order, not a request. The manner of speaking demands a restricted language by role and authority rather than a freer style of interaction.

Basilect, the Language of the Socially Disadvantaged

Nist observed (1974, pp. 80-84) that basilect constituted a form of cultural deprivation and social disadvantage. Usually, speakers of basilect are not high school graduates. The language is very poor in both competence and performance. The vocabulary is restricted. Basilect has a confusing blend of intimate, familiar/casual, and consultative styles with the result that its speakers tend to look upon persons who used more sophisticated language as outsiders who might be suspect. The style of talking is insensitive to the immediate context situation and insensitive to the subtleties of feeling accompanying the conversation. The lect is generally inadequate in public gatherings and has a strong tendency to step emotive function up to an unpleasant level, usually negative in mood, tone, or attitude.

Families who speak basilect fostered hierarchical methods of learning, with emphasis on authority and status, and develop closed rather than open systems of communication. Power and control are the preferred modes of control as compared to the positional and role controls of the mesilect speakers, or the personal appeals mode of the acrolect speakers.

Nist's Conclusions Concerning the Lects

According to Nist, the varying lects impact the structure of society. Looking at the languages from a psychosocial position, acrolect, mesilect, and basilect give different levels of developmental permissions, with basilect causing the most difficulty in developmental advances. As more and more persons in basilect family systems lose developmental permissions, the family systems lose their structures. Stigma is attached to this mode of speaking, and others consider the dialect substandard. Adults who want their children to get more out of life recognize the stigma and long for pathways to success. As a way out of the stigma, they seek answers through advanced education.

The acrolect English has important conceptual information built into the language pattern. These concepts have developmental permissions that enable the parents to raise children who can experience a high degree of development in a nurturing environment. Because of the conceptual language that is being passed down in the family speaking pattern, the process of high levels of development tend to continue generation after generation.

The Work of Ruby Payne

Dr. Ruby Payne is a leading expert on the mindsets of the poverty class, the middle class, and the wealthy class in the United States. Her workshops for educators, employers, policymakers, and service providers have allowed these professions to intervene in situations in the school population, which would have been poorly understood otherwise. The following, used with Payne's permission, is a portion of her model.

The following pages provide a very practical application of the information regarding the different lects in the English language.

Hidden Rules among Classes

Hidden rules are the unspoken cues and habits of a group. Distinct cueing systems exist between and among groups and economic classes. Generally, in America, that notion is recognized for racial and ethnic groups, but not particularly for economic groups. There are many hidden rules to examine. The ones examined here are those that have the most impact on achievement in schools and success in the workplace.

But First...A Little Quiz

Take the quiz on the next few pages, putting a check mark by all the things you know how to do.

Could You Survive in Poverty?

Put a check by each item you know how to do.

- ❑ 1. I know which churches and sections of town have the best rummage sales.
- ❑ 2. I know which rummage sales have "bag sales" and when they are.
- ❑ 3. I know which grocery stores' garbage bins can be accessed for thrown-away food.
- ❑ 4. I know how to get someone out of jail.
- ❑ 5. I know how to physically fight and defend myself physically.
- ❑ 6. I know how to get a gun, even if I have a police record.
- ❑ 7. I know how to keep my clothes from being stolen at the Laundromat.
- ❑ 8. I know what problems to look for in a used car.
- ❑ 9. I know how to live without a checking account.
- ❑ 10. I know how to live without electricity and a phone.
- ❑ 11. I know how to use a knife as scissors.
- ❑ 12. I can entertain a group of friends with my personality and my stories.
- ❑ 13. I know what to do when I don't have money to pay the bills.
- ❑ 14. I know how to move in half a day.
- ❑ 15. I know how to get and use food stamps or an electronic card for benefits.
- ❑ 16. I know where the free medical clinics are.
- ❑ 17. I am very good at trading and bartering.
- ❑ 18. I can get by without a car.

Could You Survive in Middle Class?

Put a check by each item you know how to do.

- ❑ 1. I know how to get my children into Little League, piano lessons, soccer, etc.
- ❑ 2. I know how to properly set a table.
- ❑ 3. I know which stores are most likely to carry the clothing brands my family wears.
- ❑ 4. My children know the best name brands in clothing.
- ❑ 5. I know how to order in a nice restaurant.
- ❑ 6. I know how to use a credit card, checking account, and savings account—and I understand an annuity. I understand term life insurance, disability insurance, and a 20/80 medical insurance policy, as well as house insurance, flood insurance, and replacement insurance.
- ❑ 7. I talk to my children about going to college.
- ❑ 8. I know how to get one of the best interest rates on my new-car loan.
- ❑ 9. I understand the difference among the principal, interest, and escrow statements on my house payments.
- ❑ 10. I know how to help my children with their homework and do not hesitate to call the school if I need additional information.
- ❑ 11. I know how to decorate the house for the different holidays.
- ❑ 12. I know how to get a library card.
- ❑ 13. I know how to use most of the tools in the garage.
- ❑ 14. I repair items in my house almost immediately when they break—or know a repair service and call it.

Could You Survive in Wealth?

Put a check by each item you know how to do.

- ❑ 1. I can read a menu in French, English, and another language.
- ❑ 2. I have several favorite restaurants in different countries of the world.
- ❑ 3. During the holidays, I know how to hire a decorator to identify the appropriate themes and items with which to decorate the house.
- ❑ 4. I know who my preferred financial advisor, legal service, designer, domestic employment service, and hairdresser are.
- ❑ 5. I have at least two residences that are staffed and maintained.
- ❑ 6. I know how to ensure confidentiality and loyalty from my domestic staff.
- ❑ 7. I have at least two or three "screens" that keep people whom I do not wish to see away from me.
- ❑ 8. I fly in my own plane or the company plane.
- ❑ 9. I know how to enroll my children in the preferred private schools.
- ❑ 10. I know how to host the parties that "key" people attend.
- ❑ 11. I am on the boards of at least two charities.
- ❑ 12. I know the hidden rules of the Junior League.
- ❑ 13. I support or buy the work of a particular artist.
- ❑ 14. I know how to read a corporate financial statement and analyze my own financial statements.

The first point about this exercise is that if you fall mostly in the middle class, the assumption is that everyone knows these things. However, if you did not know many of the items for the other classes, the exercise points out how many of the hidden rules are taken for granted by a particular class, which assumes they are a given for everyone...

...Several explanations and stories may help explain parts of the quiz.... The bottom line or driving force against which decisions are made is important to note. For example, in one school district, the faculty had gone together to buy a refrigerator for a family who did not have one. About three weeks later, the children in the family were gone for a week. When the students returned, the teachers asked where they had been. The answer was that the family had gone camping because they were so stressed. What had they used for money to go camping? Proceeds from the sale of the refrigerator, of course. The bottom line in generational poverty is entertainment and relationships. In the middle class, the criteria against which most decisions are made relate to work and achievement. In wealth, it is the ramifications of the financial, social, and political connections that have the weight. Being able physically to fight or have someone who is willing to fight for you is important to survival in poverty. Yet, in middle class, being able to use words as tools to negotiate conflict is crucial. Many times, the fists are used in poverty, because the words are neither available nor respected.

> The one deep experience that distinguishes the social rich from the merely rich and those below is their schooling, and with it, all the associations, the sense and sensibility, to which this education routine leads throughout their lives.
>
> As a selection and training place of the upper classes, both old and new, the private school is a unifying influence, a force for the nationalization of the upper classes.
>
> C. Wright Mills, *The Power Elite*

One of the biggest difficulties in getting out of poverty is managing money and just the general information base around money. How can you manage something you've never had? Money is seen in poverty as an expression of personality and is used for entertainment and relationships. The notion of using money for security is truly grounded in the middle and wealthy classes.

The question in the quiz about using a knife as scissors was put there to illustrate the lack of tools available to those in poverty. Tools in many ways are one of the identifiers of middle class—from the kitchen to the garage. Therefore, the notion of maintaining property and repairing items is dependent upon having tools. When they are not available, things are not repaired or maintained. Often, students do not have access to scissors, pens, paper, pencils, rulers, etc., which may be part of an assignment.

One of the biggest differences among the classes is how "the world" is defined for them. Wealthy individuals view the international scene as their world. As one told me, "My favorite restaurant is in Brazil." Middle class tends to see the world in terms of a national picture, while poverty sees the world in its immediate locale. Several fourth-grade poor students told us when they were writing to the prompt, How is life in Houston different from life in Baytown? (Baytown is 20 minutes from Houston), "They don't have TVs in Houston."

Hidden Rules Among Classes

	POVERTY	MIDDLE CLASS	WEALTH
POSSESSIONS	People.	Things.	One-of-a-kind objects, legacies, pedigrees.
MONEY	To be used, spent.	To be managed.	To be conserved, invested.
PERSONALITY	Is for entertainment. Sense of humor is highly valued.	Is for acquisition and stability. Achievement is highly valued.	Is for connections. Financial, political, social connections are highly valued.
SOCIAL EMPHASIS	Social inclusion of people he/she likes.	Emphasis is on self-governance and self-sufficiency.	Emphasis is on social exclusion.
FOOD	Key question: Did you have enough? Quantity important.	Key question: Did you like it? Quality important.	Key question: Was it presented well? Presentation important.
CLOTHING	Clothing valued for individual style and expression of personality.	Clothing valued for its quality and acceptance into norm of middle class. Label important.	Clothing valued for its artistic sense and expression. Designer important.
TIME	Present most important. Decisions made for moment based on feelings or survival.	Future most important. Decisions made against future ramifications.	Traditions and history most important. Decisions made partially on basis of tradition and decorum.
EDUCATION	Valued and revered as abstract but not as reality.	Crucial for climbing success ladder and making money.	Necessary tradition for making and maintain-ing connections.
DESTINY	Believes in fate. Cannot do much to mitigate change.	Believes in choice. Can change future with good choices now.	Noblesse oblige.
LANGUAGE	Casual register. Language is about survival.	Formal register. Language is about negotiation.	Formal register. Language is about networking.
FAMILY STRUCTURE	Tends to be matriarchal.	Tends to be patriarchal.	Depends on who has money.
WORLD VIEW	Sees world in terms of local setting.	Sees world in terms of national setting.	Sees world in terms of international view.
LOVE	Love and acceptance conditional, based upon whether individual is liked.	Love and acceptance conditional and based largely upon achievement.	Love and acceptance conditional and related to social standing and connections.
DRIVING FORCES	Survival, relationships, entertainment.	Work, achievement.	Financial, political, social connections.
HUMOR	About people and sex.	About situations.	About social faux pas.

The discussion could continue about hidden rules. The key point is that hidden rules govern so much of our immediate assessment of an individual and his/her capabilities. These are often the factors that keep an individual from moving upward in a career—or even getting the position in the first place.

What Does This Information Mean in the School or Work Setting?

- Assumptions made about individuals' intelligence and approaches to the school and/or work setting may relate more to their understanding of hidden rules.
- Students need to be taught the hidden rules of middle class—not in denigration of their own but rather as another set of rules that can be used if they so choose.
- Many of the attitudes that students and parents bring with them are an integral part of their culture and belief systems. Middle-class solutions should not necessarily be imposed when other, more workable, solutions might be found.
- An understanding of the culture and values of poverty will lessen the anger and frustration that educators may periodically feel when dealing with these students and parents.
- Most of the students that I have talked to in poverty do not believe they are poor, even when they are on welfare. Most of the wealthy adults I have talked to do not believe they are wealthy; they will usually cite someone who has more than they do.

—Payne, R. (2005, pp. 37-45)

Psycholinguistic and Sociolinguistic Application to the *Uncapping Family Wisdom* Program

Bernstein and Nist concentrated on educational interventions in the past, as does Payne today. Instruction was given to teachers on how to intervene in handicapping language, which prevented their students from realizing their full potential, was an attempt to change the lives of children and enhance their futures.

Uncapping Family Wisdom takes another route, another venue for intervention. The program allows the possibility of psychosocial interventions with the entire family in a community with established healthy norms, previously unavailable to these families. The program provides rich conceptual ideas found in other language patterns. Participating families may have lacked exposure to these conceptual ideas if they were not found in the family speaking pattern. The conceptual ideas contain dynamic developmental permissions, which foster normal human development, appropriate cognitive responses, and affective responses in the family system.

One important element of the family intervention is that adults as well as children are allowed to pass into higher stages of development. Developmental permissions come from the conceptual ideas found in the program and the environment created by the maintenance of healthy community norms by a facilitator. These interventions with the adults in the family are very important for permanent changes for the family system. Many times, children who are attempting to pass through developmental stages will appear impudent, arrogant, or presumptuous to an adult parent who does not understand human development and has not passed through the developmental stage the child is attempting to master. Unless the adults in the family are allowed to pass through the developmental stages first, permission for the children to pass through the stages will, most likely, not be forthcoming in the family system. When administrating the program, the goal is to build a strong family system of strong individuals who know and exercise the choices which will bring the best long-term consequences to all family members. In addition, if problems do arise, the family will have an opportunity to experience counseling and will be more likely to seek help from other counselors.

Building a Community for *Uncapping Family Wisdom*

The *Uncapping Family Wisdom* treatment program presents the conceptual information in acrolect that was gleaned from psycholinguistic and sociolinguistic studies. The subject of these studies was the families in the English culture that appeared to have a generational linguistic legacy which contained rich conceptual information.

The role of the facilitator is to create a safe environment, expose the family to new information, and, if asked, assist the family. Most families do well on their own. They just need the opportunity to learn in the specially-structured environment with material which opens their mind to possibilities. Instead of simply falling into an old pattern of dysfunction, due to ignorance of conceptual information that has been unavailable to them, the individual families need an opportunity to use their own family wisdom to decide their family legacy. The *Uncapping Family Wisdom* treatment program uses the information to allow the family an opportunity for positive self-evaluation of the family unit so they can adapt the program to their family. The specifics of the program will be discussed in Chapters 6-11.

References

Bailey, C. E. (2007). Semantically mediated cognitive integration of frontal lobe and limbic processing in *Homo sapiens*: uncertainty, evolution, grammar, and accurate cognition. *Cognitive Sciences* 3(1):85-144.

Beavers, R. (1977). *Psychotherapy and growth.* New York: Brunner/Mazel, Inc.

Benjafield. J. (2007). *Cognition* (3rd ed.). Canada: Oxford University Press.

Bernstein, B. (1969). Elaborated and restricted codes: an outline. In Lieberson (Ed.), *Explorations in Sociolinguistics* (pp. 126-135). Bloomington, IN: Indiana University.

Campbell, J. (1997). *The Sapir-Whorf Hypothesis.* Retrieved March 21, 2006 from http://venus.va.com.au/sugestion/sapir.html.

Charap, J. (2000, 27/12). Obituary, *The Guardian.* Retrieved 2/1/2006. from http://www.guardian.co.uk/obituaries/story/0,3604.373772,00.html.

Douglas, M. (2000, 27/12). Obituary, *The Guardian*. Retrieved 2/19/2006 from http://www.guardian.co.uk/obituaries/story/0,3604,373772,00.html.

Korzybski, A. (2000). *Science and sanity: An introduction to non-Aristotelian systems and general semantics* (5th ed.). Brooklyn, NY: Institute of General Semantics.

Margolis, E., & Laurence, S. "Concepts," *The Stanford Encyclopedia of Philosophy (Fall 2008 Edition)*, Edward N. Zalta (Ed.).

Mills, C. (1956). *The power elite.* New York: Oxford University Press.

Nist, J. (1974). *Handicapped English: the language of the socially disadvantaged.* Springfield, IL: Charles C. Thomas Publisher.

Payne, R. (2005). *A framework for understanding poverty* (4th ed.). Highland, TX: Aha! Process.

Reece, C. (2007). The lesson of general semantics. December 24, 2007, *The Benton County Daily Record*, p. 5A.

Strauss, W., & Howe, N. (1997). *The fourth turning: an American prophecy.* New York: Broadway Books.

Whorf, B. (1956). *Language, Thought and Reality.* Cambridge, MA: M.I.T. Wiley.

In Chapter 4...

Self-reflexiveness refers to the ability to analyze words by linguistic means, taking into account that words not only refer to objects but also to our attitude toward these objects. Self-reflexiveness allows individuals and families to objectively observe their own language and to understand their conflict style. Using the self-reflexive process affords us the opportunity to step back and look at family language, allowing objective understanding of how language affects our views of reality and affects potential development. Taking an objective look at the legacies of language and how human development is affected by language can enlarge our idea of the dynamics of human development.

To replace legacies which are not useful, more adaptive options are available in the *Uncapping Family Wisdom* program. Individuals can choose to use other ways of speaking which can bring more satisfying emotive reactions and cooperation in the family. With the program, family members can look objectively at the individual developmental patterns of family members in order to understand how language has affected views of reality and development.

"True age" is the vast collection of all previous developmental ages that may or may not match a chronological age and may provide evidence of developmental interruptions in more than one age level. Linking the information on linguistics to developmental tasks is imperative if the parents are to learn how to give developmental permissions to their children; moreover, the parents can simultaneously receive these permissions themselves. Developmental permissions supply the approval for progress in the form of verbal or non-verbal affirmations, the cues that signal others that they are lovable and capable.

In normal human development, these affirmations are given to children at appropriate times, allowing the development of feelings and mental states that accompany developmental changes. In cases of developmental arrest, the potential for development can be affected by childhood trauma, the lack of basic physical needs being met, or denial of permission to develop due to the linguistics and/or semantic style of speaking in the family. Patterns of arrested development are sometimes passed on to the next generation.

Several ways of looking at language from different perspectives lead to a similar conclusion. Considering our language, learning to understand what we are saying, and learning to control what we say certainly will enable developmental advancement. One focus of the therapy method found in *Uncapping Family Wisdom* is to teach conceptual information that provides developmental permission to children using principles found in acrolect, the Standard English. The exercises and evaluations are a type of guided interplay, which both parents and their children may have missed at an early age.

CHAPTER 4

LINGUISTIC LEGACIES AND THEIR EFFECT ON HUMAN DEVELOPMENT

Most people give little thought as to how the language a child hears can affect his or her future in a dramatic way. This chapter relates how a person can begin to think about language and begin to understand how language can heal the past and change the future for individuals and families. For now, the discussion is only on the opening up of meaning which will illustrated in this chapter, but applied later in the exercises and illustrated in case study research which will come in Part II of the *Uncapping Family Wisdom* program. The following terms may be helpful.

Glossary

Affirmations: verbal and non-verbal cues that signal to others that they are lovable and capable. In normal human development these affirmations are given to children at appropriate times allowing the development of feelings and mental states that accompany developmental changes (Clarke and Dawson, 1989). See *Affirmations* on pages 150-159.

Guided Interplay: describes the interactions when a parent gives and the child receives conceptual information regarding developmental permissions. The term can also describe the interactions between a facilitator and the families attending where verbal and non-verbal interactions allow developmental permission. Guided interplay is active during the time when the structured exercises in *Uncapping Family Wisdom* are being adapted to the family.

Self-Reflexiveness: the ability to analyze words by linguistic means, taking into account that words not only refer to objects but also to our attitude toward these objects (Johnson, 1995, p. 155).

True Age: a way of looking at true developmental ages in moral, cognitive, psychosocial, and social categories within the chronological age measurements.

Developmental Permission: any permission in the form of verbal or non-verbal affirmations that supplies the approval for progress in development.

Table 4.1—The Effects of Semantic Interventions on Development over Four Months

Analysis of Moral Development				
Stages of Development	**Period of Treatment***			
	Beginning			**End**
	Months 1	2	3	4
Stage 6 People think civil disobedience is acceptable in order to protest unjust laws that violate universal ethics. The principle of right and wrong becomes more important than the unjust law.				
Stage 5 Individuals have a commitment to the democratic process for making and changing laws, as well as to social behavior contract and individual rights.				
Stage 4 Individuals obey because of duty and responsibility. They obey to keep social order of national system together.				
Stage 3 Individuals obey out of loyalty to families and other groups such as church, teams, etc. They obey to preserve relationships. Behavior norms are important part of how people personally think individuals should be.				
Stage 2 Individuals obey to get rewards. Rules for how to behave remain on the outside. The individual does not internalize rules.				
Stage 1 Individuals obey to avoid punishment. Rules for how to behave remain on the outside and are not internalized by the individual.				
Semantic Interventions	**Allness**	**Dead-Level Reckoning**		

*The period of outpatient treatment for this patient was 4 months.

said to let others know that we believe they are lovable and capable. In normal human development, these affirmations are given to children at appropriate times allowing the development of feelings and mental states that accompany the developmental changes. Basically, developmental permissions supply positive affirmations to the following questions.

- Can I learn to trust myself to get my needs met?
- Can I be an autonomous person in my own right?
- Can I have personal initiative?
- Can I learn to get along with others?

In the absence of these permissions human development is difficult. Clarke and Dawson (1989, p. 290) state, "Affirmations act as permissions to grow and change, embracing developmental gains in moral, cognitive, social and psychosocial development. When we offer developmental affirmations to children, we offer powerful support that strengthens their ability to accomplish their developmental tasks successfully." Clarke and Dawson saw that the unfinished business[7] from any prior developmental period will continue to demand to be addressed again and again, until the child resolves the issue satisfactorily. The unfinished business can be resolved by receiving "permissions," which are verbal or non-verbal affirmations, making developmental conceptual information understandable for each individual.

Uncapping Family Wisdom recognizes the necessity for developmental permissions but seeks to supply the permissions for all members of the family, understanding that the adults may not have had the basic developmental permissions that affect family cohesiveness. A complete summary of affirmations identified by Clarke and Dawson are included in Chapter 8, pp. 150-159.

Human Development Potential

Human beings develop in many ways. Four categories of development, which have been extensively researched and observed, are moral, cognitive, social, and psychosocial development. Beginning in early childhood, arrests in development can affect potential if the basic permissions needed to develop the self are not forthcoming. Sometimes, the basic developmental permissions in childhood are interrupted by childhood trauma. The developmental permissions can also be affected when the basic needs such as food, clothing, and shelter take precedence in life. Sometimes the basic developmental permissions are denied by the language, in the linguistics and/or the semantic style of speaking, preventing natural development in the adults and children. Cases of arrested development are sometimes passed on to the next generation. Then, stored somewhere in family dynamics, the potential for full development in one or more areas may wait generations for an opportunity to come forth.

Parents may not set out to harm the children under their care, but linguistic legacies, fears, and over-cautionary statements can interfere with natural human development. The speaking

7 *Unfinished business* in this text refers to developmental stages that have not been resolved. Permissions are given by parents to further growth through developmental stages. If parents do not give age-appropriate permissions, the normal growth process through the developmental stages might not occur. If permissions are not received, developmental arrest occurs. Developmental arrest issues can often be resolved in various long-term therapies.

patterns often control the family dynamics and are passed down through succeeding generations. All too often, parents do not realize that they are hindering their children's development. The parents themselves may have waited all their lives to receive the same permissions they need to offer their children.

Same Transgenerational Developmental Levels in Family Members

In the case of Jim in Chapter 2, we saw that the father was in need of the same permissions as the son who was in therapy. These situations are found in cases of transgenerational dysfunction. In these cases, the farther the chronological age has advanced past the optimal time for development, the more the unattractive defense mechanisms have solidified, making treatment difficult. (On page 54, see Correlation of selected defense mechanisms with global assessment of mental health. Defense mechanisms are listed according to mental health maturity levels.) In addition, adults who have not had the advantage of normal development may actually have negative feelings toward family members who want to experience full personhood. Educating and allowing the dominant adults to experience the joys of self-understanding and self-actualization can move them away from power and control dynamics fueled by negative emotions and can rescue them from a life of loneliness and conflict.

Table 10.1. Correlation of selected defense mechanisms with global assessment of mental health.

	Assessment[b]				
Defense[a]	*Haan (1977)*	*Vaillant (1977)*	*Battista (1982)*	*Vaillant (1985)*	*Bond (1983)*
Psychotic defenses					
Denial (of external reality)	Not rated	Not rated	Not rated	Not rated	Not rated
Distortion (of external reality)	Not rated	Not rated	Not rated	Not rated	Not rated
Immature defenses					
Passive aggression (repression)	Defending	n.s.	n.s.	− −	−
Acting out	Not rated	−	n.s.	− −	−
Dissociation	Defending	n.s.	−	− −	−
Projection	Defending	−	n.s.	− −	−
Autistic fantasy	Not rated	−	−	− −	Not rated
Devaluation, idealization, splitting	Not rated	Not rated	Not rated	Not rated	Not rated
Neurotic (intermediate) defenses					
Intellectualization (isolation)	Defending	n.s.	+	n.s.	n.s.
Repression	Defending	n.s.	n.s.	n.s.	n.s.
Reaction formation	Defending	n.s.	Not rated	n.s.	n.s.
Displacement	Defending	n.s.	n.s.	+	n.s.
Somatization, undoing, rationalization	Not rated	Not rated	Not rated	Not rated	Not rated
Mature defenses					
Suppression	Coping	+ +	+	+ +	+
Altruism	Coping	n.s.	n.s.	+ +	n.s.
Sublimation	Coping	n.s.	n.s.	+ +	Not rated
Humor (playfulness)	Coping	Not rated	Not rated	+ +	+

a. Terms from DSM-III-R.
b. Symbols: n.s., not significantly correlated with mental health; + or −, positive or negative correlation, $p < .05$ (Pearson product-moment coefficient) or $r > .25$; + + or − −, positive or negative correlation, $p < .001$

Reprinted by permission of the publisher from *THE NEW HARVARD GUIDE TO PSYCHIATRY*, edited by Armand M. Nicholi, Jr., M.D., p. 203, Cambridge, Mass.: The Belnap Press of Harvard University Press, Copyright © 1988 by the President and Fellows of Harvard University.

Moving Toward a Brief Therapy Mode

Analytical therapists have long known how to discover and treat these developmental interruptions. Over sometimes long periods of time, they may indirectly supply developmental permissions as they respond and interact with their patients. In the *Uncapping Family Wisdom* program, the initial discovery of developmental permissions and treatment are accomplished in a systemized way in order to maintain a brief therapy mode. The self-knowledge acquired in the program can be carried forward in further therapies whenever problems surface, speeding the course of therapy.

The conceptual information gained in the program will lead to insight into other world views and supply understanding from which changed behavior can originate. The conceptual information provides pathways to ideas that enrich reasoning abilities.

General Semantics of the Family

Hidden barriers unique to every family contribute to the lack of permissions needed for development. Blocking mechanisms are coded into the verbal and non-verbal language code that individuals have inherited through the family-speaking pattern. These blocking mechanisms are many times out of the awareness of family members and will affect parent-child interplay and interrupt development in the children, unless the structural assumptions and implications can be discovered. A self-diagnostic assessment used to uncover hidden developmental barriers in the speech patterns of the family systems was discovered through observation in linguistic research. In families who speak acrolect, a pattern of permissions for positive developmental achievements was found in their language patterns. These families are successful in giving developmental permissions and activating potential for development in their family systems. Using the observational material garnered from the population that speaks acrolect, the families in the *Uncapping Family Wisdom* program will clearly see what objectives their individual family can incorporate. Empowered by what they are learning, the adults and the children can develop together in a safe environment. As they participate in the structured family exercises, safe in the structure that is provided, interacting successfully for the first time often brings hope into the family unit. The importance of family dynamics becomes evident and the families usually gravitate toward the positive choices found in the conceptual language of the program. The assessment and intervention are discussed in detail in Chapter 7.

The Effect of Linguistics on Developmental Tasks

Linking the information on linguistics to developmental tasks is imperative because language conception for a child is occurring during the same time as developmental stage formation. The language and non-verbal interplay will largely determine the permission and potential for normal development. Miller and McNeill (1969, p. 714) found that a normal child, not impaired by hearing loss or speech impediment, will begin to say words at about one year of age. By 1½ years of age, the child will begin to form simple two-word and three-word sentences. By four, the child will have mastered nearly the entire complex abstract structure of English. In a little more than two years, between four and six, the child will acquire full knowledge of the grammatical system of the native tongue in a process of guided interplay with adults interacting with a child. This time frame covers the period when early childhood development gains are at their prime and parental interplay has an important role in development. One source of guided interplay is parental speech and another source of guided interplay is parental reaction to a child's speech. The child is receiving information on trust, personhood, initiative, and conscience building.

In some families, however, language is formed differently and with a different effect. Three things can happen:

1. A child can be denied stage developmental permissions by the form of language spoken in the environment of the child and the absence of healthy guided interplay. As a result, there may be a developmental stage arrest.
2. The dynamics of the interpersonal communication patterns in families can lead to trauma for the members, and the families can become trauma organized. (Bentovim, 1992, pp. 66-67)
3. A developing child in a trauma-organized family system may not develop a feeling vocabulary needed to vent feelings. These children miss out on developmental achievement that could have been learned through guided interplay with their parents.
4. A developing child in a trauma-organized family system may not develop mature defenses and use defense mechanism that cause problems for the child and cause problems for others.

Notice in the Correlation of Selected Defense Mechanisms, the psychotic defenses that are natural in infants, but are replaced by higher-level immature defenses that begin to appear normally at 3-5 years of age, are followed by intermediate (formally called "neurotic") defenses. The mature defenses can be developed as cognitive thought comes in dominance to soothe the earlier defenses which are feeling based; however, in trauma-organized families, the systems are essentially *action systems* not involved with thinking and talking (Bentovim, 1992, p. xi).

Needed conceptual interactions may be missing in the development of children due to trauma, emotional unavailability of parents, or the transgenerational dysfunction legacy; but the conceptual information can be introduced cognitively and integrated later in life. The *Uncapping Family Wisdom* program addresses transgenerational problems with radical interventions in a sheltered community setting.

Carroll also acknowledges in his book *Language and Thought* (1964) that the conceptual information could be introduced and integrated in later life. He describes the knowledge of concepts as learned responses, which are mostly out of our awareness. He observes that the concepts are learned indirectly in the interplay between a parent and a child. He states that conceptual information that is integrated determines how well a person gets along with others, the potential quality of family relationships, and even how much income a person may accumulate during a lifetime. If the interplay has been interrupted, Carroll outlines the "constructs" that could be introduced to identify errors in family language and to build conceptual information.

Constructs

The constructs Carroll named are reason, faulty reasoning, problem solving, and persuasive speech. He describes these constructs in the following way:

- Reason is thinking, aided by language. If the descriptions and skills which language provides are not available, reasoning will prove difficult.
- Faulty reasoning is a failure to test one premise or idea against another. Faulty reasoning involves a setting up of improper equivalencies between terms, because of an uncritical acceptance of premises. For instance, a person can state his or her opinion or judgment as if the opinion or judgment was not a subjective view but a rational fact. The acceptance of an opinion or judgment as fact is a false premise. To use a false premise in an argument can lead to faulty reasoning.
- Problem solving is the manipulation of concepts. The solving of a problem involves taking different concepts found in conceptual information and working with the concepts to find out how to solve a problem.
- Persuasive speech has an emotionally toned connotative meaning. Both emotions and thought are used in persuasive speech.

Using Concepts and Constructs to Understand Human Development

Since reasoning is thinking aided by language, language enhances the ability to think by introducing different perceptions into thinking. Since different concepts make up conceptual information, the concepts discussed here are different perceptions of human development found through observation in research. In order to fill in gaps in development, information regarding these human developmental concepts is necessary to form a base of conceptual information. Presenting the developmental conceptual information of moral, social, cognitive, and psychosocial development can broaden the understanding of human behavior when working with families who have missed developmental opportunities due to trauma, the emotional unavailability of a parent, or a generational legacy. Family members can learn conceptual information terminology which provides the constructs that enable effective reasoning. The terminology can help in describing and understanding what is seen in a person's own development and also in the developmental makeup of others in the family system.

As more information regarding development is revealed, the ability to understand the behavior of others will be enhanced. One way that understanding basic human development will aid problem solving is that members of the family will learn that problems can be viewed differently by others. These different views bring up different feelings to others in the family and influence their behavior. Learning how to make decisions by first having consideration for the feelings of others, rather than only using rational, cognitive statements to make decisions, is an important tool for improving communication in the family. Members of family systems will often discover that lack of consideration for the feelings of others is usually the root cause of much family conflict. After the Stages of Development are learned, the attention of the family is needed to test for any faulty reasoning which was present before the new information on communication and development was integrated. The causes of current conflict can now be identified in an organized way.

The *Uncapping Family Wisdom* program uses the exercises and evaluations in the program as a type of guided interplay, which the parents and the family may have missed out on at an earlier age. The interventions for developmental arrests are administered in a controlled environment with structured exercises. The interventions are transparent to the participants, providing protection from shame. The family knows what the therapist is doing before anything is done. The result is that intervention gets to the root cause of developmental arrest—the lack of developmental permissions.

Three important characteristics set intervention apart in *Uncapping Family Wisdom*:

- The program furnishes a "feeling" vocabulary, which takes into consideration the concept of cause and effect.
- The guided interplay between the parents and other family members is carefully structured and monitored for safety.
- The instruction and guided interplay between the facilitator and the community allow the participants to observe the setting of norms to structure a safe environment.

Guided Interplay in Direct Behavioral Applications

In the *Uncapping Family Wisdom* program, in one important exercise, business leadership and management skills are applied to a family's own household. This interplay is a practical application of the well-tested management concepts that were learned in the program. In this interplay, the family learns new concepts and practices the semantic-relational skills learned earlier in the program. Often, the family authoritarian leader is especially impacted, and changes begin to take place, increasing understanding of the practical aspects of life. The skills are not just learned, they are immediately put to use.

Acquiring personal life-management skills is usually exhilarating and affirming to the families. Applying management techniques to the family system is usually new and interesting for the individuals in the family. By the time behavior modification is connected with development and semantic information in the program, the family unit understands how inappropriate behavior limits choice for the individual involved in the behavior dynamics and for the family affected by the behavior. Most importantly, the behavior modification now is accomplished not through a power-and-control dynamic, but through an understanding of cause and effect and internalized locus of control. This means that the former power-and-control defense mechanisms are no longer necessary, and a person's behavior has become his or her own responsibility.

References

Bentovim, A. (1992). *Trauma-organized systems: physical and sexual abuse in families.* London, UK: Karnac Books.

Carroll, J. (1964). *Language and thought.* London, UK: Prentice-Hall.

Clarke, J., & Dawson, C. (1989). *Growing Up Again.* New York: Hazelden Press, Inc.

Johnson, K. G. (1995). Critical thinking for survival in the 21st century. In G. Sawin (Ed.), *Thinking and living skills: general semantics for critical thinking.* Concord, CA: International Society for General Semantics.

Korzybski, A. (2000). *Science and Sanity: An Introduction to Non-Aristotelian Systems and General Semantics* (5th ed.). Brooklyn, NY: Institute of General Semantics.

Miller, G., & McNeill, D. (1969). *Psycholinguistics: the handbook of social psychology, Vol. 3.* G. Lindzey & E. Aronson (Eds.). Reading, MA: Addison-Wesley Publishing Company.

In Chapter 5...

Time-binding is a process in which one can use experiences in one time span to learn valuable information upon which to build for the future. Burton Miller's training of underprivileged women in the 1960s was, for him, the memory of a lifetime. His experience is a prototype for a new, different kind of intervention with families who exhibit symptoms of transgenerational dysfunction. The program was highly successful due to his entrepreneurial positioning for the benefit of the poor. He brought in general semantics to teach the women cause and effect. He helped them understand how they fit into the whole. This chapter discusses a similar process of the *Uncapping Family Wisdom* program which ideally uses a specialized community environment. The group facilitator uses languages patterns and non-verbal physical applications that offset the intensity and shaming that can occur in families. As the program progresses, the direct and indirect verbal and non-verbal interventions serve to prepare the families for direct teaching on shame and its effect on human dynamics. This application will occur toward the end of the program.

The program teaches families how to erect needed boundaries individually and in the nuclear and extended families. The families learn where they fit into the overall picture of families, communities, and society. The facilitator and the assistants honor family boundaries and trust the process of the program to guide the families. They place their trust in the latent wisdom that is present and waiting to be released in the family system.

Trauma-organized families know little about conceptual ideas, such as the need for community boundaries, family boundaries, family norms, or human development and permissions. The families become reactionary to the environment around them. *Uncapping Family Wisdom* is a program that will benefit all families at their levels of adjustment, but especially families which are recognizable as being trauma organized.

The structure of the program ensures a continued bypassing of shame will occur. There is a careful setting of community norms. The building of family cohesiveness is a primary goal so that individual autonomy in an atmosphere of respect will provide additional protection from shame.

CHAPTER 5

PREPARING THE ENVIRONMENT FOR THE *UNCAPPING FAMILY WISDOM* PROGRAM

The background information that is needed for the content of the *Uncapping Family Wisdom* program has been discussed in past chapters. Chapter 5 provides a bridge from the background information that is needed to understand the important interventions in the formal program. The actual program begins in the next chapter.

Below are some terms which will bring clarity to our discussion, as the process of the program is discussed, and the formal content is presented.

Glossary

Shame—an all-or-nothing experience in which the possibility of there being any value in a person is lost. Feelings of total worthlessness flood the victim from head to foot. A belief prevails that other people can see how bad one is, with a feeling that there is no possibility of redemption (Birchmore, 1997).

Time-Binding—refers to the unique capacity to pass the products of our creativity from one generation to the next. Through language, other symbol systems, and artifacts, we can use minds and nervous systems from miles and centuries away. One generation can begin where the last one left off (Berleth, 1992, p. 105).

Trauma-organized Families—knowing little about such conceptual ideas as the need for community boundaries, family boundaries, family norms, or human development and permissions, the families become reactive to the environment around them (Bentovim, 1992).

The *Uncapping Family Wisdom* program has been used successfully for many years with individuals, couples, and families in private practice settings, staff trainings, and retreats. The most dynamic change and utilization, however, occurs in a specialized community environment. This specialized community setting is necessary and effective in working with what Bentovim (1992, p. xxi) calls "trauma-organized" families. In the community environment, a trained group facilitator uses language patterns that offset the intensity and shaming that can occur with families who have not had the benefit of such a community.

Healthy norms assure that safety is a built-in component in the specialized environment. The process uses non-verbal and verbal guided interplay, which are so important in creating peak learning experiences needed to spark development. In a healthy community environment, learning with others can occur naturally. For those who have existed in a decaying society without healthy norms, an environment of enrichment changes perspectives and behavior.

As we begin, taking a closer look at the dynamics, environments, and historical impacts that influence trauma-organized families will aid in understanding the inherent problems.

Understanding Trauma-Organized Families

A social worker in Eastern Arkansas describes her trauma-organized families in the following words:

> Because the area is so dangerous, I am driven to and from work. I am watched as I walk into the building in the morning and back to my car at night. My clients are children being raised by grandparents or single mothers, many of whom are on drugs.
>
> My clients cry: "If I only knew my father." Many of these children have serious problems and are in danger of harm to themselves or others. All industry has left the area. I think the culture has collapsed.

Some families may come from communities which are "toxic" with numbers of trauma-organized families. If we understand this segment of the population, we can get a clear picture of why a structured program and environment is needed. It is important to understand how families become trauma organized. The families usually have been handling problems that could have been stopped by community boundaries, if an organized community with appropriate norms had existed. Sometimes, the families have been blamed and stigmatized when their families began to show the strain of handling stressors coming from the lack of community boundaries, which let in harmful influences like drug dealing. The missing community boundaries, added to the stressors coming from their family heritage, are overwhelming to the family units. Knowing little about such concepts as community boundaries, family boundaries, family norms, or human development and permissions, the families become reactive to the environment around them. At the end of the downward spiral into trauma-organization, physical abuse and sexual abuse often enter into the experience of families. In his work with trauma-organized systems, Bentovim (1992, p. xi) explains:

> It is not a question of the individual creating the system, or the system creating the problem. Events in the lives of individuals create "stories" by which they live their lives, make relationships, initiate actions, respond to actions, and maintain and develop them. Abusive traumatic events have an exceptionally powerful effect in creating self-perpetuating "stories" which in turn create "trauma-organized systems" where "abusive" events are reenacted and reinforced.

Bentovim (1992, p. xvi) describes levels of trauma organization and the way events in the lives of the trauma-organized systems are connected from the individual, to the family, to the professional, and beyond to the societal and cultural levels. He observes that trauma-organized systems are essentially action systems not involved with thinking and talking.

Cultural Influences in Trauma-Organized Families

In addition to trauma that occurs in the family in the current generation, some families have lost their structure several generations ago due to cultural impacts on the family. The families were unable to give their offspring developmental permissions, because their own developmental permissions were denied by a culture. Sometimes, when families are observed, behavior seems unusual; but when attempts are made to understand what happened to families in a particular cultural setting, the behavior may become more understandable. In some cases, when consideration is given to what has happened to the family on a cultural level, the population as a whole needs to address the influences that have negatively influenced the family. In addition, the conceptual language that was missing needs to be restored to these families. Then, at that time, responsible behavior can be expected to follow.

As van der Kolk, McFarlene, and Weisaeth (1996, p. 407) observe,

> Culture is supposed to render life predictable. When the cultural defense mechanisms are lost, individuals are left on their own to achieve emotional control. Traumas that occur in the context of social upheavals, such as revolutions, civil wars, and uprootings, create profound discontinuity in the order and predictability that culture has brought to daily life and social situations.

An example of denied developmental permissions by cultural influences is the effect of slavery on the African-American community. The civil rights enactments that came approximately one hundred years later in the 1960s are an example of the need for cultural adjustments. Even today, in certain parts of the country, the evidence is still seen that although outstanding progress was made in many families, the mere legislation and enforcement of laws did not change the future of some families. Some individuals, especially college-educated ones, picked up conceptual language, sometimes in a less formalized, more haphazard way than is revealed in the *Uncapping Family Wisdom* program. Still, today, the conceptual language that is needed to reflect reality more accurately and provide optimal developmental permissions is not available to all families. In these cases, the families lack important tools to use to overcome the years of denied developmental permissions which have come through cultural influences and sometimes through family legacies.

Wars and migrations have a similar effect. Children born into a traumatic environment may be unable to freely pass through developmental stages and acquire the permissions necessary to live life to its fullest. There are many documented stories of *grandchildren* of survivors of the Holocaust who missed developmental permissions. Raised by adult children of survivors who were emotionally unavailable to them due to massive losses of loved ones and survivor guilt, the third generation is often unable to find normalcy with parents whose thoughts are often stuck in past memories. These children are now in a situation of trying to make their sad parents happy. But intervention into the family system is possible and may restore the family wisdom that was interrupted by cultural trauma, thus preventing the cycle from continuing into the future.

A Success Story

We have been talking about a sort of negative time-binding where individuals and families had only negative experiences from the past upon which to build. What we want to do in the *Uncapping Family Wisdom* program is to experience a positive time-binding intervention. Time-binding is an important concept in that aids us in thinking about things in history that have been helpful and which contain process and content that still are important today. We can learn from the experience of others as they became creative in working through problems. Kodish and Kodish (2001, p. 27) describe time-binding in the following way:

> We do this (time-binding) among ourselves as we communicate. We do this across generations so that each generation of humans has the potential to start off where previous generations ended. We utilize the experience of the past as we develop the present and future.

The story about to be told is about an experience of time-binding that occurred in Chicago in the 1960s. In 1949, Burton Miller was first exposed to general semantics, which was discussed in Chapter 4 and will be introduced in the *Uncapping Family Wisdom* program in Chapter 7. He brought the methods of general semantics into a project he undertook in Chicago a few years later. Miller began working with women of various ages who were considered unemployable and who thus had no opportunity for advancement in life. The only training they could expect was some possible training in a remedial program that would lead to a low-income job with no future advancement opportunities.

Here is where time-binding comes in. This particular piece of history is important today because we can learn from Miller's successful experiences, avail ourselves of what is useful, and seek to replicate some of the experiences. From what was accomplished in a different time and different place, we can begin to create new experiences. Not only can we learn what was done in the past, we can also add to the experience by making an adjustment to a style of family-system intervention that will prepare groups of people today to time-bind prime healthy information to pass on to future generations. You see, Burton Miller did not just change the lives of a group of women; he changed the lives of their families and the families that came after them. What was done at that time has many valuable implications for what is needed for today. The *Uncapping Family Wisdom* specialized environment and material can lead a family and a community toward conceptual information of what is considered normal in human relationships and community interaction.

The Times of Our Lives

It all started when his future partner, Robert Laskow, became a principal owner of three electronic data processing service bureaus. Burton Miller's educational background and vocation were not in social service. He had attended Northwestern University and for a time had worked in a clinic at University of California, Los Angeles (U.C.L.A.) for children who were, as the term was then, "emotionally disturbed." Miller was busy working as a stockbroker with an old securities firm, but never could forget his days at U.C.L.A. working with the children. Laskow had received a B.A. and a law degree from Harvard, and had a continuing interest in social problems. Laskow had also authored a course in computer programming at LaSalle Extension University, while he was practicing law.

As time went by, Miller and Laskow gravitated toward a common avocation of education. Their common interest was the new field of data processing. In 1963, the two men from Chicago bought an almost defunct data processing service firm. They did not know it yet, but this was the start of something big. This move toward the data processing world would take them far from their beginnings as they focused in on the narrow field of key punching IBM cards.

The position of key punching was an essential step in the ever-emerging field of automatic data processing. Data processing in the 1960s was a glamour job staffed by well-trained sophisticated personnel. At that time, as the computer age was coming into being, there was a high demand for key punch operators with 8,000 job openings in the Chicago area. The occupation of keypunch operator paid well, $66 to $100 dollars a week, a great deal of money in those days. Key punch operation was a prestige activity associated with complex and tangible data processing machines, not far down the line from the "electronic brain" of those times. The key punch operator was a critical employee, because an error on the operator's part could conceivably start a chain of events causing the loss of thousands of dollars.

Because there was a shortage of data processing operators, Miller and Laskow together opened a training center on The Loop in Chicago. At first, when they started to work with key punch training, they had no idea it might prove useful in relation to the unemployed. Miller and Laskow had merely developed a new approach to data processing instruction, heavy on actual practice and light on mathematical theory—the reverse of the conventional method. Miller and Laskow observed that the 8,000 job openings for key punch operators matched the 8,000 figure for the unemployed in Chicago at that time. Since applicants with a skilled academic background were scarce, Miller and Laskow turned toward the unskilled.

They established the Institute for Technological Training to train the "unemployable" who were then on what was called "relief rolls." In the new school, Miller became Director of Training and Laskow became Director of Placement. Visiting with the Public Aid Director with the State of Illinois, they agreed not to charge anything for training until the student had been successful in a new job for 30 days. A win-win situation was in store for the county, which stood to gain $5,000 a year for every student trained in key punch operation and placed into employment.

The program was a grand success and fifty women were placed after the first training. General semantics was an important part of the program. General semantics is the study of words and their effects on individuals and cultures. Wanderer expands on the definition:

> General semantics is the science and art of how we operate in the world around us. We take note of the kinds of assumptions we make, the way we see things, the way we use words and symbols, the role of our self-concept in our relationship with the rest of the world, and some of the kinds of bias and distortion that plague all of us in the way we listen, the way we think, and the way we operate.

The women changed their outlook on the static positions they had inherited in their environment and began to think in dynamic ways. Looking back, Burton Miller today says that the success of the program was due to the fact that the training dealt with the whole person, not just the learning of a skill by merely practicing at the machine. The women literally got on-the-job training. The role and position of the key punch operator was explained, and the work was placed in the context of what went on before and what happened after the cards were punched. An effort was made to make each woman feel that she was not going to be just another cog in the wheel, but an intricate part of the whole. They punched a time clock in and out just as they would in their future work, and the upscale offices were kept immaculate as was befitting to the position the women were to fulfill. The students also received three hours of instruction a day on the fundamentals of good grooming, proper attitudes for job positions, and business etiquette, all qualities expected on the job site. They were not trained in a vacuum, but had a view of the whole process around their new positions as data processors. Burton Miller remembers:

> The result of such an approach was that not one head was raised from the intense concentration upon the work and practice taking place at that time. Motivation to master the work came not only from the intrinsic glamour of data processing at that time, but also from treating the student as an individual and giving her support at every step of the way. From grooming instruction to group problem analysis, each woman gained personal insight into herself. I came to realize that, all too often in our society, we tend to treat the symptoms rather than the cause of a problem. We can eradicate some of the causes, if we try. Not all of them, but some of them. I don't think it was just the training, I don't think we taught them as much as we exposed them to what they needed to know. I think the success was due to exposure. We just gave them exposure on all levels, and they could take it from there.

There were secondary effects to the training in the lives of the women. First, the effect on the children of the women who were exposed to learning was profound as they saw their formerly-unemployed mothers acquire self-confidence and dignity. The importance of the exposure to the working processes and the changed demeanor of the parents gave the families a growing sense of respect and a new forecast for their future. Second, the exposure to the actual employment situations and learning where the job position fit into an overall picture allowed the women to obtain important conceptual information indirectly and integrate the information into other parts of their life. As women who were previously considered unemployable became responsible citizens, their lives were transformed. They had respectable positions with possibilities for future advancement.

The *Uncapping Family Wisdom* Environment

The idea that exposure was the key for these women is similar to the ideas presented in the *Uncapping Family Wisdom* treatment environment. The exposure to the conceptual language with its dynamic processes goes hand in hand with the private family self-evaluations and exercises, which allow the family to identify needed changes in thoughts and feelings in order to advance in life. Teaching the women how their job fit into the overall workings of the system is similar to the cause and effect lectures that teach families in the *Uncapping Family Wisdom* treatment program that they can impact society for good.

When working with people in the *Uncapping Family Wisdom* program, two different qualities in the program are important. These qualities are process and content, which, in this case were very specialized. We saw how Miller and Laskow provided the content of the training that was the skill training and the instruction. The process of the program was having the women in an actual office setting in the Chicago Loop to provide a real work environment, having them "clock in," just like they would on the job, and letting them see for themselves how their job fit in with the office process.

Up to this point, most of what has been discussed regarding the *Uncapping Family Wisdom* program has been the background of the content of the program. Future chapters in Part II will include the application in the form of exercises and self-evaluations. The content is fundamental and very important; however, it could be lost without understanding and learning the equally important process of the program.

Understanding the Process of the Program

The Holding Environment

William Pinsof in *Integrative Problem-Centered Therapy: A Synthesis of Family, Individual, and Biological Therapies* (1995, p. 407) integrates self-psychology with family systems therapy. Pinsof's ideas, integrated from different therapies, provide for a safe, warm environmental envelope known as a "holding environment." A safe holding environment is imperative in creating an *Uncapping Family Wisdom* community environment.

The idea of a warm, nurturing, and empathetic therapist was a large and controversial step for psychoanalysis and also for some engaged in family therapy. The facilitator of an *Uncapping Family Wisdom* project, however, moves past just nurturance toward an outright display of confidence in the abilities of the participants. After presenting information, the facilitator backs away to allow the family to apply the information in their own way to the family system. If the family wants the help of the *Uncapping Family Wisdom* facilitator or any of the assistants, they will have to ask. Some families will ask, and some will feel prepared to proceed alone.

The program environment is very structured. The therapists may be challenged by the process of the program which involves a hands-off policy with the families. Just like all group work, the facilitator and the assistants will have to stay back, trust the process, and allow these important processes to occur:

- the bypassing of shame,
- the setting of community norms, and
- the building of family cohesiveness and individual autonomy in an atmosphere of respect.

Bypassing Shame

Shame is a barrier to process. From the time the families enter the community setting, shame prevention is in effect. One important alternate part of the program is the administration of the program within a supportive, controlled community setting, with the community acting as a large group and the family acting as a unit within that group. This type of intervention is so helpful because many of the families with generational dysfunction have no sense or experience of community.

When asked, many people today agree that our society is in a state of decay. Although many families are affected to some degree, some families appear to be the symptom bearers of this decay and often are poorly understood. Since these families have probably not experienced a community with knowledge of established, civilized norms for the members, they are especially vulnerable to shame. Shame in a community is a special worry appearing as an overwhelming, debilitating feeling that one may have done something wrong, improper, or immodest, perhaps even out of one's awareness. In some families, the very language use often includes shaming in direct and indirect communication; therefore, addressing the potential for shame is critical to continuing treatment, attendance, and participation in the program meetings. For this reason, special forethought is given to techniques designed for sidetracking shame.

To begin, shame is introduced as a visitor in the community and is seen in shaming language styles and non-verbal interactions. The nature of shame is exposed and the families attending are alerted that a community norm will include the *absence* of shaming at all times.

The program is structured so that all family units are learning the same thing at the same time with the same exercises. No one is put in the position of knowing less than others. No competition is possible; because, since they reflect the unique dynamics of the individual family, the exercises are different for each family. During the program, the facilitator draws attention to his or her own mistakes and models self-acceptance and appropriate, mature defense mechanisms. The families soon learn that it is all right to make a mistake, and they learn how to take responsibility for a mistake.

During the program, the families complete all the assessments and then share the information with the facilitators or assistants. This is just the reverse of how things are usually done with the facilitator in an evaluative position. Although shame has been mentioned and described from the first, in the last meeting, after the family-speaking patterns have been isolated and the family members have acquired tools to deal with their feelings, shame is openly discussed and diffused in an objective matter-of-fact manner.

Setting Program Community Norms

Understanding the pressures placed on the families, the therapeutic facilitator acts to focus the community on norms needed for safety and structure. The facilitator draws on the wisdom found in the community to set the standards. With needed norms in place, the family can relax in the supportive environment, acquire missing conceptual information, and evaluate their personal progress. In this way, beginning with the entry into the program, shame is sidetracked by the community norms, the program structure, and the power given to the family to evaluate themselves. The families can see that others are learning and acquiring information at the same time.

The facilitator will need to be well trained to adopt an interplay style with the families similar to the style a knowledgeable parent adopts with children in early developmental stages. The facilitator respects the process of the families and guides the families into choices rather than telling the families what is "right." Attention-seeking behavior is expected and met with kindness and acceptance. The facilitator recognizes that acceptance of the least attractive behavior, or acceptance of the lowest person in the pecking order, will instill trust in the new community. The community is well-structured and controlled by norms introduced in the introductory lectures and instructions. This mimics the type of healthy environment into which many persons with acrolect speaking patterns are born.

The families learn where they are in the overall picture of things. They come to understand the parts of a culture—the society, the community, the family and each individual member—and what the appropriate norms are for the each part. Care is taken that each family member understands that he or she is an intricate part of a whole community. The individuals and the family unit understand how they impact the whole.

Building Family Cohesiveness and Individual Autonomy in an Atmosphere of Respect

So much is learned in communities. Healthy unified communities have cohesion, especially those communities that have acrolect patterns in the language of the families. The community norms are well known and in agreement with the norms of other families in the community. The parents share healthy legacies revealed by conceptual norms that foster human development. These norms are known because of time-binding in past generations. These families have examples that model where to begin in caring for children. Using the conceptual norms found in healthy communities, the process of the *Uncapping Family Wisdom* program

- allows parents to evaluate the individual developmental levels found in their family system;
- demonstrates how family-speaking patterns affect human development;
- allows each family to identify conflict patterns by using general semantic measures; and
- exposes families to leadership styles that stress cooperation and respect.

References

Bentovim, A. B. (1992). *Trauma-organized systems: physical and sexual abuse in families.* London, UK: Karnac Books.

Berleth, D. R. (1992). Survival depends on caring, sharing. In K. H. Johnson (Ed.) *Thinking creatively: a systematic, interdisciplinary approach to creative critical thinking* (p. 150).

Birchmore, T. (1997). *Shame and group psychotherapy.* Retrieved 10/12/2006 from http://www.birchmore.org/index.html. Englewood, NJ: Institute of General Semantics.

Kodish, S. P., & Kodish, B. I. (2001). *Drive yourself sane: using the uncommon sense of general semantics.* Pasadena, CA: Extensional Publishing.

Miller, B., Personal communication, March 12, 2004.

Pinsof, W. (1995). *Integrative problem-centered therapy: a synthesis of family, individual and biological therapies.* (p. 407). New York: Basic Books.

van der Kolk, B., McFarlene, A., & Weisaeth, L., Eds. (1996). *Traumatic Stress: The Effects of Overwhelming Experience on Mind, Body, and Society.* New York: The Guilford Press.

Uncapping Family Wisdom

Part II

PART II

UNCAPPING FAMILY WISDOM: RECOGNIZING, TREATING, AND RECONCILING TRANSGENERATIONAL DYSFUNCTION

Using the information we received in Part I, we are now ready to make actual application. This is where the *Recognizing, Treating, and Reconciling Transgenerational Dysfunction* program begins, as the self-evaluative exercises reveal the beginning place for individuals and families participating in the program. Building on the information in Part I, Chapters 6-10 will present the *Uncapping Family Wisdom* program. Four case study research investigations will be followed.

Before looking at the actual program, information about the type of research used for the four case study research investigations is in order. While it will be helpful to know how the individuals were studied, it is not necessary that you comprehend everything about the research, process or content, to understand the mechanics of the program which are plainly presented. The charts provided in the case study research material should clarify how the program impacts individuals and families using the various interventions in *Uncapping Family Wisdom.*

For those who are more research oriented, the following information may be of interest. The type of research chosen for the process for the case investigations is called "case study research" (Yin, 1994). Case study research is helpful in depicting contextual conditions and not just the phenomenon of study. The purpose of this book is not to present the research in its fullness, but to build upon the research. That is what the work you do will accomplish—the work will build upon another level of research. The research, the twenty-year use of the material, and the programs which have been written from this material are presented here to be built upon. Since intervening variables are difficult to control in working with families displaying characteristics of transgenerational dysfunction, the case study research method allows the researcher to look for patterns rather than immediate cause and effect relationships.

An important difference in case study research is that case studies generalize to theory, not populations. Yin (1994, pp. 30, 31-32, 36) notes, "The investigator's job is to expand and to generalize theories (analytic generalization) and not to enumerate frequencies (statistical generalization)."

The case study research benefits from the prior development of theoretical propositions to guide date collection and analysis. The prior theoretical propositions in this study were built upon

- the linguistic observations of Bernstein (1969) and Nist (1974);
- the general semantic theory of Korzybski (Ward, 1987);
- the cognitive development observations of Piaget (1971);
- the social development theory of Selman (1976b);
- the psychosocial development theory of Erikson (1963); and
- the moral developmental theory of Kohlberg (1981).

Chapter 6 presents the characteristics of a strong family. Actually, the characteristics contain conceptual information used to parent children by adults who were found to be speaking the acrolect grammar. The conceptual information was also learned from the community in which the children lived. Many of the characteristics were isolated by Beavers (1977) in his work.

The remaining chapters, then, include information about the process of conducting an *Uncapping Family Wisdom* program and present the beginning of four real-life therapeutic interventions in the case study research. At this point, learning to recognize, treat, and reconcile transgenerational dysfunction in a structured program will begin. So you can see how the programs actually worked in different settings. Throughout the rest of the book, some chapters will periodically refer to the ongoing process of the four case study research investigations. The final graphs of each individual study will show his or her progress over a varying period of treatment. The measurements are gathered from the four types of development and the semantic interventions determined by the family speech pattern. The comparison of the beginning and the progress of each individual diagnosis is seed for future studies. You will want to notice the difference in developmental arrest(s) for various diagnoses. For instance:

- How often does a particular developmental arrest(s) in the individuals with certain diagnostic labels in this study compare with a developmental arrest(s) in the individuals you encounter with the same diagnostic label?
- Can you expect more semantic errors with certain diagnostic labels, or a few semantic errors used with more intensity and/or more often?

Past experience with this program has revealed that people learning how to administer the program soon get caught up in the interventions personally, ending up in a study of their own family system. That fact gives assurance that the program works both with professionals and those seeking service, bringing stability to the overall community. The chapters in Part II are

Authors whose contributions are pivotal to the interventions found in Part II in the *Uncapping Family Wisdom: Recognizing, Treating, and Reconciling Transgenerational* program are listed in the reference lists that follow the chapters.

References

Beavers, R. (1977). *Psychotherapy and growth.* New York: Brunner/Mazel, Inc.

Bernstein, B. (1969). "Elaborated and Restricted Codes: An Outline." In Lieberson (ed.), *Explorations in Sociolinguistics* (pp. 126-135). Bloomington, IN: Indiana University.

Erikson, E. (1963). *Childhood and society* (2nd ed. rev.). New York: W. W. Norton & Company, Inc.

Kohlberg, L. (1981). *Essays on moral development. Vol. 1. The philosophy of moral development.* New York: Harper & Row.

Korzybski, A. (2000). *Science and sanity: an introduction to non-Aristotelian systems and general semantic (5th ed.).* Brooklyn, NY: Institute of General Semantics.

Nist, J. (1974). *Handicapped English: the language of the socially disadvantaged.* Springfield, IL: Charles C. Thomas Publisher.

Piaget, J. (1971). *The Construction of Reality in the Child* (M. Cook, trans.). New York: Ballantine (original work published in 1936).

Selman, R. (1976b). A developmental approach to interpersonal and moral awareness in young children: Some educational implications of levels of social perspective-taking. In T. C. Hennessy (Ed.), *Value and moral development.* New York: Holt, Rinehart & Winston.

Ward, A. (1987). Introduction to general semantics. In J. Butler (Ed.), *Insights into communication: Course syllabus for speech communication* (4th ed.) Scottsdale, AZ: Gorsuch Scarisbrick, Publishers.

Yin, R. (1994). *Case study research.* Thousand Oaks, CA: SAGE Publications.

In Chapter 6...

The information found in Chapter 3 finds a direct application in the *Uncapping Family Wisdom* program presented in this chapter. Along with the program that is presented, four case study research investigations begin. The *Uncapping Family Wisdom* model is influenced by linguistic research and other family therapy and attachment therapy models including those of Beavers, Bowen, Bowlby, Madsen, and Pinsof.

The relationship of the facilitator and the families is unique. The facilitator provides a safe, holding environment and only enters family boundaries when invited in by the family. The interventions are concrete and action oriented, but they are powerful in their indirect and nonverbal forms, which appeal to insight therapists. Many interventions that occur in the process of the program are really rational family decisions which are made after information is understood and assimilated.

The characteristics of a strong family listed in this chapter were gleaned from the observation of families who were successful generation after generation in rearing children who passed though each of the expressed stages of normal human development. These families speak acrolect, in a cultural environment where Standard English is the language choice of the parents. The adults raise their children in ways that appear to promote normal human development generation after generation. The families in the *Uncapping Family Wisdom* programs are exposed to new information in a specialized environment much like the environment in which families in an acrolect community would learn. The families are each invited to self-evaluate their own family to discover new conceptual information and new direction for their family. The program is structured in an information-building mode to give the families confidence in their ability to help themselves. Structure and encouragement stimulate the families to take risks. The knowledge that others are doing the same gives them hope which comes with being a part of a vibrant community. Each family is learning and growing and is aware that others are also learning and growing.

Personal responsibility of the individual family member is presented in this chapter for the first time and will grow in importance in the program. With the introduction of an exercise on fairness and responsibility in a family system, the family members begin to see themselves as part of a whole and begin to understand how their individual behavior affects the entire family, moving the individuals away from any egocentric position. Hierarchal problems are intercepted by showing the adults respect and teaching fairness in the family. As data is collected from within the family, the family decides where to begin. The families are given a goal sheet that promotes cognitive awareness in the individuals, which will boost their ability to excel in educational, social, and vocational environments in the future. The community becomes a place where individuals and families can use their skills together to improve their life for themselves and others.

Chapter 6 begins with the first exercise in the *Uncapping Family Wisdom* program, called "Characteristics of a Strong Family." The exercise is used to administer the program to families in a community setting.

CHAPTER 6

CHARACTERISTICS OF A STRONG FAMILY

The twelve characteristics of a strong family listed in this chapter were gleaned from the observation of families who were successful generation after generation in rearing children who passed though the expected stages of human development, because the children in these families received developmental permissions from the parents. Below are some terms to aid in understanding the process:

GLOSSARY

Self-differentiation—a dynamic in which each member in the family can have his or her own thoughts and feelings. Having these personal opinions is not threatening to other members of the family. Failure to self-differentiate from family-of-origin members at the expected age can cause problems in building future family relationships.

Acrolect societies—societies which contain families who speak a language that normally allows expected human development to occur.

Warm holding environment—a peaceful, safe environment in which people can heal.

Attachment—refers to the degree of being attached to another by affectionate regard. Once established, the degree of attachment behaviors or lack of attachment behavior is self-reinforcing and persistent.

Successful passage through childhood development stages is important. Due to the self-differentiation of the child from the parents, the passage allows flexibility in each generation. In the acrolect speech pattern, these permissions are built into the language that is spoken around children; that is, the positive permission for development is usually heard by individuals in the home and community.

Family Psychotherapy Models

To understand the *Uncapping Family Wisdom* program model, the context of the program within historical models is important. By looking at historic ideas and more current thinking about family dynamics, the program's formation for addressing difficulties in family dynamics can be better understood. Although the information in the program came from a linguistic source as observed by Monfils (1987), much of the material in this chapter is implied in family psychotherapy practice.

Robert Beavers

More than any other, the Beavers Model (1993, pp. 73-103) puts forth many of the characteristics used as a basis for the foundation for the *Uncapping Family Wisdom* treatment program. Beavers describes families as healthy, midrange, or dysfunctional. He describes healthy families as open systems that interact with the outer world. He notes the appropriate boundaries between individuals in the family and the boundaries between generations. He describes clear roles, rules, and expectations, so any confusion because of mixed messages is avoided. Finally, he describes how families allow the expression of emotion and respond empathetically to those emotions.

The first unit of the *Uncapping Family Wisdom Participant's Manual*, the Characteristics of a Strong Family, contains some aspects of Beavers Model and fuses the aspects with other conceptual information derived from societies which spoke acrolect. Beavers (1977) believes that a growth-oriented model, rather than change-oriented model, is a more sensible focus. Of course, change comes after growth, and a higher level of adjustment is possible.

Murray Bowen

Murray Bowen (1978) discusses generational dysfunction in relationships which can be projected into the spousal relationship and the parent-child relationship in current relationships if the individual has not differentiated from their family of origin. He notes that self-differentiation from the family of origin leads to freedom from early pathological dynamics. A person can differentiate from the dysfunctional dynamics of the family of origin and can make a healthy decision to change the dysfunctional interactions of the family of origin. The person can have more normal interactions in current relationships, can be free from early pathological dynamics, and can stop the generational dysfunction from passing down to future generations.

Using Bowen's discoveries, the conceptual information found in the Characteristics of a Strong Family unit can go a step further by looking at what information was missing as multigenerational passages of dysfunction came down the family line. Families in the *Uncapping Family Wisdom* program discover this information in a protected environment and begin to understand the underlying pressures on their family. They see the pressures have occurred because their family did not know the constructs (now listed in the program) that underlie paths toward rational thinking and emotional stability. Missing constructs supply the tools for rational thinking and emotional stability that allow development to occur.

William Pinsof

William Pinsof (1995) is noted for his use of a warm, holding environment in which his clients can heal. He also observes transgenerational trends. In his *Integrative Problem-Centered Therapy: A Synthesis of Family, Individual, and Biological Therapies,* transgenerational investigation into the family system is a fourth screening to uncover childhood wounds which can become transgenerational problems. The first strategic screen is an attempt at intervention; a second screen includes an exploration of emotions; and a third screen incorporates a psychopharmacological assessment. If the first three interventions have not worked, Pinsof then goes on to individual therapy of family members. He believes the therapeutic relationship created in the self-psychology of Heinz Kohut can help heal childhood wounds, which maintain some of the conflicts that manifest in the family dynamics. A search for diagnosis continues through the therapy after different interventions prove unsuccessful.

Like Pinsof, *Uncapping Family Wisdom* uses the idea of a warm, holding environment. The community setting becomes the warm, holding environment in which the participants can heal through structural self-evaluation by the families and changing family dynamics.

Debra Wesselmann

Debra Wesselmann (2007, pp. 113-130) compares family system and attachment models. She observes that both models hold the view that styles of attachment and interpersonal behaviors within families, once established, are self-reinforcing and persistent (Bowlby, 1989, pp. 119-136; P. Minuchin, 1974, pp. 289-302; S. Minuchin, 1974; Van IJzendoorn, 1992, pp. 76-99) even across generations (Bowen, 1978; Van IJzendoorn, 1992, pp. 76-99). With these observations in mind the *Uncapping Family Wisdom* program provides information on relating in a protective environment. In the protective environment, individuals have built-in opportunities to try out different, more adaptive styles of relating that are self-reinforcing. Good feelings accompany self-differentiation, when permitted alongside attachment to the family group. The program allows interventions into transgenerational factors immediately, with periods of psychoeducational intervention followed by family self-evaluations.

Using the information that is given, the family evaluates their status and selects their own path. The program assumes that many of the problems come from societal impacts and immediately invites the families to find out how their family has been impacted by society. For a time, this process takes the blame for the problems from the individuals, until they have more information with which to address the problems they find in the family. At this time, responsibility for family discord becomes a family goal with choices that will build the self-esteem of the family.

The program maintains that, given the right conceptual information, within a consistent holding environment, the family can gain confidence in their successes and work toward healing their family. The holding environment is a protected community environment offering security, but it can also exist in an office environment created for a family intervention of this type.

As a result of self-evaluation in the areas of semantics, development, leadership style and family management, each family chooses its own way in the warm, holding community environment. The environment is an exposure to acrolect, the highest form of interaction that is found in linguistic research. The style of the units in the program has a rhythm of education, intervention, practice...education, intervention, practice...which is self-reinforcing to the families. As they apply acrolect conceptual information directly to their family unit, the family members experience the pleasure of change and also understand the "why" of the changed circumstances. The *Uncapping Family Wisdom* therapist aids the family unit in healing the wounds. Unidentified wounds maintain the conflict in the family. Throughout the therapy interventions with the other participants in the community environment, the therapist also aids the family in checking emotional, psychological, and biological reactions. Being in a protected specialized environment where others are learning enhances the stabilization of the individual, family, and community as a whole.

In future meetings, the families will identify specific development that is being arrested in the family line, will establish a basis for pointing out family semantic patterns for controlling conflict in the family, and will begin to fill in conceptual gaps that will enhance their range of reasoning abilities.

The Relationship between the Facilitator and the Families

In Salvadore Minuchin's structural therapy model, *Families and Family Therapy (1974)*, he recommends that the therapist join the family. The therapist-facilitator for the *Uncapping Family Wisdom* program will seek to join the family by being in the same community with the family. The facilitator and the assistants ask permission to enter the family boundaries, but only if a family appears to need help; and then they exit the family boundaries as quickly as possible. The program takes the place of the intimate therapeutic relationship.

Like Minuchin's intervention style, the interventions are concrete and action oriented; however, many interventions in this program are most powerful in their indirect and non-verbal forms, which appeals to insight therapists, who prefer an analytical approach. Like the Montessori educational system, the family members learn from interacting with the program and the environment furnished with the program more than by interacting with the facilitator. Many interventions occurring in the process of this therapy are actually rational family decisions which are made after information is understood and assimilated. The *Uncapping Family Wisdom* program prepares families to enter more conventional types of therapies as people with some normal exposure to conceptual information, *rather than* trauma-organized individuals with severe problems too difficult for an individual therapist to handle alone. For a definition of "trauma organized," see the Glossary in Chapter 2.

Consideration of Past Problems

Uncappping Family Wisdom shares an objective with Madsen and Nichols (1999) as described in *Collaborative Therapy with Multi-Stressed Families*: the objective of moving away from trying to identify and correct old problems. In fact, *Uncapping Family Wisdom* views the old problems as merely symptoms of a possible chronic lack of developmental permissions or a void in the family system's information base. Any resistance, difficulty, or general dysfunctions are, more likely, signs of a shame base and the need for safety. Bypassing shame is an important part of the intervention in the *Uncapping Family Wisdom* program. Research into linguistic dialects highlights terms that describe types of resistance and the presenting worldview and can yield insight into what makes any defenses necessary for the participants.

Many defense mechanisms will be seen in participants of the *Uncapping Family Wisdom* program settings. They are evidence of dysfunctional language patterns and development. For this reason, families are given broad-based entrées into their problems, which are

1. a mastery of the dynamics of their specific, semantic family-conflict pattern, and
2. an evaluation of the developmental permissions needed for their family to achieve self-reliance.

In other words, the mastery of the conceptual information of their own semantic family-conflict pattern and the needed developmental permissions will create a wide path of knowledge regarding social/emotional intelligence and more dependence on rational abilities. This mastery allows emotions to grow quiet because an "adult" part of the personality is forming and is now taking control of situations with the use of rational thinking.

The Uncapping Family Wisdom program differs from other therapies because the program observes the family unit from a family-in-environment perspective. The family-in-environment perspective includes the family's place in a community and the family's place in the overall society. The exercises in the program are designed to expand the worldviews outside of merely intra-family dynamics, so the family members can understand how society has affected the family and how the family can affect society. In Chapter 5, we discussed the work of Burton Miller with the women in Chicago. He stated that an important factor in the success of the program was explaining the place of the workers in the overall picture of things. In the program, families learn that any changes in the family will affect the family, the community, and the society at large. Community building becomes a definite focus, especially toward the end of the program, because the participants now have so much to give back to the community. With several *Uncapping Family Wisdom* programs going on in the same city at the same time, an effect on the local society can be expected.

Case Study Research

Four different case studies from inpatient and private practice environments serve to show the adaptability of the program for different populations. The case studies show the presence of the general semantic variables and the effects of linguistic legacy on human development. The results will be summarized in Chapter 12.

Case Study Research #1—Amy

Amy was a 14-year-old female who was admitted to a residential treatment center under the auspices of the Department of Human Services. The patient was physically small and well groomed. Her manner was private, determined, self-contained, and forthright. The patient showed signs of separation anxiety from her mother.

The patient claimed that her brother-in-law had raped her in the living room of her parents' home while her sister slept on another sofa and her parents were in their bedroom. All parties involved including her stepfather, mother, brother-in-law, and two sisters insisted, "Amy is crazy. Nothing happened." According to the patient, she had escaped in her small truck, and her boyfriend's mother had given her protection for the night and called the authorities the next morning. Medical attention was not sought.

Amy's mother had come far from her beginnings of poverty. She was a tall, attractive woman who had a job as an executive secretary at the Chamber of Commerce in a small town. Her husband, Amy's stepfather, chose not to participate in therapy at the hospital and, as a result of the alleged incident and the patient's resulting hospitalization, was reported to be hostile toward the patient. During hospitalization, Amy's mother continued to say in front of the patient and privately that nothing had happened. She repeatedly told Amy to tell the truth. Privately, she related that Amy had hallucinations and had always been "a strange child."

On the unit, the patient was in a population of adolescents with conduct disorders. She appeared to be uninfluenced by their negative behavior and appeared to have nothing in common with them. She simply did her chores and followed the program. In a group she faded into the background and appeared emotionally constricted. The nurses observed she constantly cried for her mother in an unusual manner, like a little child. Somatic complaints were reported in the charting. In individual therapy, she disclosed a very simple life of driving her truck, being with her dog, going to school and going to her job. She had a boyfriend, but was not sexually active. Her psychological testing revealed some schizoid personality disorder characteristics (*DSM-IV-TR*, 2000, p. 696).

The personnel at the Department of Human Services and the prosecuting attorney were convinced the patient was telling the truth. The prosecuting attorney and the case workers were supportive, which was comforting to Amy. The patient related she was glad others believed her. The prosecuting attorney disclosed to the staff that he strongly suspected the brother-in-law and one brother were into heavy drug trafficking and he felt the patient was in danger.

The hospital staff also believed the patient. While in the hospital, Amy did not exhibit any behavior that would make the staff feel she was untruthful. Most of the staff felt the personnel at the Department of Human Services had brought her in for protective reasons, hoping hospital staff could persuade her to go into a foster placement, in addition to treating the anxiety the child was manifesting.

As discharge planning was scheduled by the staff, the patient was adamant about wanting to go home. The mother was less interested, but wavered, seemingly concerned about the appearance she would make if she openly rejected her daughter. The therapist felt an urgency to find an escape route for the patient in case things became too difficult at home from any pressure being put on the patient to drop the charges. The patient was firm about pressing charges and held on to her story about what had happened with her brother-in-law. The mother was still in denial about the possibility of events; the sister and brother-in-law shared the stepfather's hostility. The patient was determined to go home, even if she would be going home into this situation.

Case Study Research #2—Kay

The subject, Kay, a 32-year-old woman, who participated in case study research was invited in to assist in the writing of this report. She decided to own her psychiatric labels at the beginning of therapy, so anything which was reported in this study was no surprise to her. She was asked if her story could be used and what name she would like to be called in the report. She replied "I want to use my own name. I'm the one who did all that work, why should someone else get the credit?" For her protection and because of the maladjustment still surrounding her in her family system, her real name was not used. She was a valuable contributor from whom much was learned about the experiential side of the process of therapy. Her personal contribution to this case study research is quoted several places in the study.

The referral for the patient came from the attorney *ad litem* for Third District Circuit Court. The judge and the attorney *ad litem* were troubled about some elements of the case. The client, a 31-year-old female whose name was Kay, had been fighting for continued custody of her two children. The court had granted her custody, and the attorney working to guard the rights of the children knew she needed help. Her former husband, the father of her children, was a minister, highly educated and in command, but he had the traits of antisocial personality disorder (*DSM-IV-TR,* 2000, p. 701).

The minister was well respected and powerful in his religious community. Few people knew his well-kept secret—he had been married five times. The children in the family were troubled, one child manifesting the characteristics of the father and one manifesting the characteristics of the mother.

Being the child of two alcoholic parents, Kay had difficulty in parenting her children. She had been hospitalized one time previously, and over the next six years of treatment, she was hospitalized on two other occasions. Her diagnosis was borderline personality disorder (*DSM-IV-TR,* 2000, pp. 706-710) and multiple personality disorder, later called dissociative identity disorder (*DSM-IV-TR, 2000,* pp. 526-529).

During six years of treatment, the destructive dynamics of the family interactions were observed. Her former husband was a master at knowing how to "work the system." He set up insulting and degrading dynamics and watched while Kay acted out her outrage. He quietly set up these dynamics in view of others who observed her out-of-control behavior without understanding the provocation for the behavior. After one such incident, he appealed for custody of the children and was granted custody due to her hospitalization. He quietly and calmly watched Kay being tortured by the loss of her children and the helplessness she experienced from his power over her life. However, after observing the situation for some time, his superiors in his church began to understand the situation and relieved him of his position as minister.

Now free from any restraints, year after year, his manipulative persecution atrocities continued. For instance, Kay had no job skills and worked for a minimum wage, barely able to pay her rent. He sued her for child support and received a substantial part of her salary. He was highly educated, was not employed, and was supported by his new wife.

Kay's childhood history was filled with extreme verbal and physical abuse from both of her alcoholic parents. Kay's first move toward therapy came when she attended a workshop sponsored by a mental health facility. She listened and read the participant's manual from the workshop carefully. A few weeks later during therapy, she told the therapist she was going to believe the manual was true and the therapist was telling her the truth. In this way, the patient began to form a system of belief regarding what was normal, a structure upon which she could build in the future. The system of belief regarding what was normal represented an important "leap of faith" for this individual, who had searched through self-help books for the answers to her complex problems. The decision to form a belief system also represented an establishment of trust in the therapist and the program. She also now began to believed that she could internalize a whole system of thinking she so desperately needed.

Coming from a background of chaos and still in a present state of family organizational chaos, Kay learned to form boundaries around herself to organize the chaos inside before she could move away from the dysfunction. She had two important positive strengths that brought her comfort:

- She believed in God, though she was extremely afraid of Him. As she grew to understand that she could move past punitive expectations and learned not to relinquish control of her life, her faith furnished her security. She shared her faith with others and acquired a support group for the first time.
- She was also very intelligent. Most of her intelligence had been used for survival with little left over for development. An important focus of therapy was the freeing of these positive qualities to develop her inherent personhood.

Over the period of six years of treatment, all sorts of chaotic events continued. Rather than focus on these during therapy, the therapist and the client decided to accept them as normal for the current circumstances of her life. They also decided to continue to plow ahead with the organized program, in which the client had placed her faith. The chaotic events were tied into established paradigms in the program, so the client could understand what was happening in her life. She began to get the conceptual structure she needed for skill building. The client needed the conceptual structure for skill building in order to create her own interventions into the chaos. After all, she understood the methodology of the chaos far better than anyone.

Case Study Research #3—Charles

Charles, who was 45 years old, came to a seminar with his third wife, Susan, who was interested in getting help with their blended family. He was a forceful person, in appearance and manner. His first marriage had been to an older woman, fourteen years his senior. The second marriage was to a woman named Nina, with whom he shared a biological daughter, Liz, age seven, and a 16-year-old son, Matt. Nina was now married to James and they had one child together, Brent. Charles' third marriage was to Susan who had two children, Toni, a fourteen-year-old girl, and Lane, a ten-year-old boy. Over a period of the next four years all of the adults and children in these families came into treatment with the therapist. Charles, who had initially recommended that every one of these people get therapy, did not enter therapy himself until four years after the family members had become involved in therapy.

As time passed, it became apparent Charles played an important role in each one of the individual cases. He was the main father figure for most of the children. He was a powerful man, an executive in a large merchandising establishment. He appeared to have narcissistic personality disorder traits (*DSM-IV-TR*, 2000, pp. 714-717). He raged when he was irritated and was especially cruel to the male children in his care when they neared puberty. He adored Liz, his biological child who loved but was very afraid of her father. He continued to father Toni, even after he and her mother separated. He was a strict and strong father figure and very important to the otherwise fatherless children.

Over a period of four years, Charles was invited to several sessions with different members of his family. The therapist was careful not to shame or blame him, seeing his involvement, both financially and relationally, as critical to several children and adults, even though at times his behavior was very harsh and inappropriate with the children. The dynamics of the various relationships were discussed with him, along with the feelings of the family members in treatment. He came to the sessions and listened, never voicing an opinion; however, he did change some behavior at the therapist's request.

One day Lane, who was in treatment at the time, was on a ferry ride outing with Charles, Susan, Toni, and Liz. The family was alone on the top deck. Charles was talking on his cell phone, began to rage, and then slung the cell phone out over the railing of the boat.

The therapist had taught Lane to put his hands up in front of him in a stop position as a boundary to signal to say inwardly, "Look at Charles have his emotions." In this way the child was to detach from the violence and not feel responsible for the raging behavior. But, instead of repeating the message inwardly, Lane made the statement aloud.

The family froze and, after a minute, all spontaneously laughed. After another minute Charles laughed, too. People observing the family's laughter began to laugh also. Charles told those with him that he knew who had told him to say that and called the name of the therapist. The fact that Charles paused and waited, then laughed, probably meant he had successfully divided his emotions from his sense of self and was able to give in to the positive defense mechanism (the ability to see the humor in this situation). This was unusual behavior for him. The united front of the laughter coming from the majority of the family system had broken through. Most of all, Lane had finally successfully kept himself safe and had formed a boundary from the raging for the first time.

The following Monday morning, Charles called the therapist and told her what had happened. He asked how much of Lane's problems were his responsibility. The therapist told him approximately 90%. Charles replied, "Maybe I need to make an appointment." He made the appointment and entered therapy.

In cases where violence, power, and control issues are involved, and/or when problems with addictions are present, the dysfunctional family system has to change before the powerful person will change. In this case, the process for this family took over four years before the system became healthy enough to unify in addressing the inappropriate behavior of a powerful member. Humor, a powerful, healthy defense mechanism, combined with nonjudgmental truthfulness, was used to defuse the situation and prompted Charles to enter therapy, where he disclosed experiencing sexual abuse when he was entering puberty.

Case Study Research #4—Paul

Paul, 42 years old, was court ordered into treatment for sexual abuse of his daughter. Paul displayed signs of antisocial personality disorder (*DSM-IV-TR,* 2000, p. 701), narcissistic personality disorder (*DSM-IV-TR*, 2000, pp. 714-717), and sexual addiction (*DSM-IV-TR*, 2000, p. 234). His daughter, who was now living with her aunt, had disclosed this abuse to a teacher at her school. He participated in therapy for four months, and his extended and nuclear family joined him in treatment. Incest had been common in his family of origin. Paul had molested all his sisters, and he continued this pattern by molesting his young teenage daughter. His thinking was so twisted he honestly thought the provocation came from her.

In treatment, as openness replaced the shame of the family, the family decided on safety measures to assure the children in this family would be free from the childhood abuse inflicted on all of the adults in the family in their childhood. Paul came to understand that he was actually acting out the abuse he had received at a tender age. Through questioning, Paul began to know and understand his acting-out behavior. He recognized that during the molestation of his daughter, he remembered the details of his own abuse. In treatment, he learned to handle his own behavior and agreed he could never be alone with a child again. He acquired the skills to say, "Please, do not leave your child alone with me. I was abused as a child, and I may repeat that abuse." Also, at a family meeting that he called, Paul addressed all the children in his family and the extended family, telling them he was not to be alone with them and to leave the place if the possibility of being alone with him was imminent. He never asked or attempted to be alone with his daughter. His family reported that he continued to warn everyone about his dysfunction in a responsible way.

Meanwhile, the female members of his nuclear family met and gained "entitlements." His daughter became very assertive in his presence, and the women formed a strong bond to assure safety. Paul respected the assertiveness of the women and began to see them as people with feelings, capable of being hurt, as he had been. In other words, he began to show important signs of empathy. The consensus of the family was that the women were involved and consistent in providing a safe family environment; therefore, they were not concerned about any safety issues concerning Paul.

The police were urged to consider the welfare of Paul's adolescent daughter, since she had become quite independent with her aunt and stepmother. She had passed the point of being a victim of her father; but, determined to get a conviction, the police working with the case disregarded any progress made in therapy. The daughter loved her father very much, although she had decided not to be a victim. Her father, in spite of his dysfunction, supplied other important needs.

The therapist was concerned Paul's daughter would lose her main source of income and security and would be sent back to her mother in Oregon. The mother had several sexual partners and no permanent relationship. The boundaries of her home appeared to be open with people coming in and out, not a good atmosphere for a child, especially one who had been sexually abused. The court had originally given Paul custody due to the mother's neglect and her lifestyle.

Paul had a strong support group in his church. All the members in the church knew of his background and were willing to support the family with strong boundaries and accountability.

Summary of the Beginning Case Study Research

With this variety of cases, we observed different pathologies, and people were in treatment for various amounts of time. All were exposed to the same material and all were active in their own self-evaluations of positive achievement and of areas where they felt they could use some help. The Characteristics of a Strong Family are directly derived from the observations of acrolect childrearing practices first mentioned in Chapter 3. These characteristics were presented to the families in the case histories as the beginning point for the program. The information found there was not available to them within their family system or within the society from which they came.

The explanation of the role of society in the lives of the family members will help to move shame and blame away from the families themselves. Later, when family members have some integral conceptual information, the program will shift toward personal responsibility to impact the society positively as individuals, as family units, and as a community as a whole. The participants in *Uncapping Family Wisdom* groups can recognize that the ability to understand and live these characteristics lies latent inside of them and within their own families. By understanding the characteristics of a strong family, the participants are enabled to grow in knowledge of themselves, their family system, and their world views. At this same time, they will learn the missing content, the characteristics of a strong family, and will learn directly and indirectly from the process of the meeting environment.

Facilitator's Guide for Participant's Manual

The facilitator can use information from this chapter as well as from Chapter 3 to prepare the twenty-minute instruction, which will precede the family exercises and discussion. The facilitator must take care to consider the population of the families attending and what background information will be useful.

Ideally, the facilitator will be sharing a meal with fifteen families eating at individual tables, sized according to the number of family members. The facilitator may visit for a brief time with all the families and eat with a different family each time. Depending on the size of the group, a number of assistants will be present for any families who might need assistance. A group of 15 families will need a therapist facilitator and two trained assistants. The ideal time to begin the instruction is when the meal is nearing completion. After the meal, a binder, pens or pencils, along with the exercises are placed on each table in the custody of an adult. By putting an adult in charge, the facilitator will be showing respect and establishing hierarchy in a small way with the parents who, when the family begins to self-evaluate, will need the affirmation because they will be a part of the family group participating in the exercise.

The instruction begins with an explanation of terms and how the terms relate to the experiences of the exercises to follow. The end of the instruction period is a good time to clear up the disposable dinnerware and take a restroom break. After the break, people will be at ease and prepared for a relaxed time together with their family. The enjoyment of eating together, the tone of the lecturer, and the unhurried break will enhance the possibility of a relaxed family time. The facilitator and the assistants can use this time to watch for family tensions and be ready to assist, if needed.

When the family time together begins, the families are asked, "Would you like to see how society has affected your family?" Before any evaluation begins, explaining the application of Nist's work (and other interventions that will come later) starts the process of bypassing shame by moving the blame and cause away from the family. The locus of control will then be moved to the participants and into the boundaries of the family. From a sociological perspective, the question eases entry into the family boundaries, because indirectly someone has said, "It is not all your fault." Now the family can relax and free up a natural curiosity as they enter the self-evaluation.

The twelve characteristics introduce the twelve levels that will be covered in all the interventions. The twelve characteristics will also point out the content and processes needed to enter into the application of these characteristics in the unique family systems. The material from the *Uncapping Family Wisdom Manual* follows.

Moving Into the Meeting Environment

Objectives *(1 hour and 30 minutes)*

1. **Introduction of Characteristics of a Strong Family Organization by the Facilitator (25 minutes)**

   Exercise 6-A. Self-Evaluation of Strong Family Characteristics

   The participating individual or family member will evaluate their own family organization.

2. **Introduction of Fairness and Responsibility in a Family System (20 minutes)**

   Exercise 6-B. Self-Evaluation of Fairness and Responsibility

   The participating individual or family member will evaluate fairness and responsibility in their family system.

3. **Polling the Family (15 minutes)**

   Exercise 6-C. Collection of Data from Family Members

   An adult member will lead the family discussion and collect the information from the family members.

4. **Break (10 minutes)**

5. **Introduction of Plan of Action Worksheet (20 minutes)**

   The family will select one item to work on from Exercise 6-D.

   An adult member will lead the family discussion by reading across the goal headings and allowing the family members to fill in the spaces. Only one exercise will be completed, and the project will go home with the family.

Facilitator's Guide for Characteristics of a Strong Family Worksheets

> ***Facilitator's Note:* Introduce the first exercise with the information below.**

"Each family has a family system. A family system is the way things work in your family. All families are unique in their own way. Some families contain a mother, father, and children, but many families are composed differently. No matter what the size of your family happens to be, it is very important to begin to think of yourself as having a complete family. When parents divorce or become separated for other reasons, part of the grieving process is the feeling that an important part of the family is missing. There is a hole in the family and everyone feels the missing element. The family must shift roles and restructure the family organization, so that the family can begin to feel whole again. Care must be taken that children not move into adult roles that are too big for the children to fill. No matter how large or how small your family is, you can organize it into a healthy, functioning unit. Some roles in blended families and stepfamilies are difficult to understand, and single parents face their own unique problems; nevertheless, a strong, unique family organization can be formed.

"If you are single, without other members in your unit, consider yourself an important element of society. You can be a very important energy source to a single-parent family in need of a big brother or sister for their child. You can choose a career with duties which would be difficult for a parent with childcare responsibilities to assume. You can fill an important place in society.

"As all of you go through this manual and learn new organizational and parenting skills, the best foundation to build upon is a positive attitude toward how your family is constructed right now. You must build upon a foundation of reality, not on how it used to be or how you wish that it were constructed, but just what reality is at this period of time. A confident attitude and recognition of your own family's 'specialness' is contagious and very beneficial to your children.

"Let's begin."

> ***Facilitator's Note:* Now read and explain the information about Exercise 6-A. Use information in Chapter 3 in the *Uncapping Family Wisdom* text to fill in interesting additions to the written information. Give the families twenty minutes to gather the information, and then have them place the information in their family binder.**

> ***Facilitator's Note:*** **Introduce the exercise with the following information.**

"Now take a bird's eye view of your family and take one statement at a time. An adult will ask the other family members if the family, as a working unit, knows how to do what is mentioned in each statement. Which adult would like to record the answers of the family? Just have a simple discussion and vote. *Circle* those areas the family unit knows how to do when working as a team, and *put a check* by those areas about which the family feels they can learn more. You may see that not many will know at this point how to do many of the skills as a family, although you may use the same skills regularly in other places. This exercise is just to help you understand how society has affected your family. We will complete this exercise again at the end of the program to see how much your answers have changed and to show how much you have learned."

Exercise 6-A

Characteristics of a Strong Family

1. **Strong families know how to work as a team.**
   The family members are committed to one another. The family as a whole is committed to seeing that each member reaches his or her potential. The family as a whole is committed to seeing that no individuals in the family suffer, so that other members of the family can have an exclusive right to reach their full potential.
2. **Strong families know how to set clear goals and are committed to the goals.**
   Many individuals may know how to set goals, but goal setting might be more difficult within the family. We will talk about a special way of thinking to help set goals and look for things that may be getting in the way of family unity.
3. **Strong families tend to have communications that are clear.**
   There is no difference between verbal and non-verbal messages. The family members have developed listening skills and each family member can express what it is they want and expect to be understood.
4. **Strong families can respect differences.**
   Differences in viewpoints are not regarded as disloyalty to the family beliefs. In contrast, each individual is able to freely comment, reporting on what he sees and feels and what he hears.
5. **Strong families operate under constructive forms of leadership and share most decision-making responsibilities.**
   Each member of the family is free to express an opinion and therefore share in the decision-making process.
6. **Strong families know how to show appreciation.**
   This involves being able to recognize the positive aspects of others and to let them know that these qualities are valued. It also means that individuals in the family feel comfortable about receiving compliments themselves.

7. **A strong family feels safe.**
   They have developed a reasonable set of rules to offset problems involving power and control. Discipline is built into the family organization, and when something upsets the balance of the family, the control rules go into operation. The family uses the rules as boundaries and becomes creative within these boundaries.
8. **Strong families own their own problems and do not blame them on others.**
   Individuals in the family know how to take responsibility for their own problems and how to enable the family to solve them.
9. **Strong families use change as an opportunity for learning.**
   They see the world as constantly changing and view problems as an opportunity for individuals to stretch and grow. They learn to cope with temporary frustration.
10. **Strong families can demonstrate openness and trust because they know and use problem-solving techniques to handle conflict in the family.**
    The family knows how to take into consideration how reality is viewed by each family member. The emotional impact of any decision on each family member is also considered.
11. **Strong families have strong external boundaries between the family and the community norms. Community rules may be unsafe.**
    They understand the pressures that society places upon family boundaries, and they maintain the boundaries through family loyalties. They can identify external cultural problems that impinge upon the family boundaries and face them openly. The family moves the power of control into their family when the society is not holding firm boundaries of safety.
12. **Strong families understand the importance of having a positive family climate.**
    When respect is lessening and hostility seems to be growing, these families seek outside help in the form of counseling and/or support groups.

> ***Facilitator's Note:*** **Now is the time for the facilitator and any assistants to walk around and be interested in the process. The facilitator should not enter the family boundaries when the family is conversing comfortably within the structure. If you or an assistant observe a family in crisis, ask the family if you can help. The facilitator and assistants should treat the family with respect and use the least possible intervention. The facilitator can rephrase a question or go to a process question if there is a problem in content; or, the facilitator can clarify a content question if the problem is in process. That is, if a disagreement is on the content of what is being said, ask "Is there something about how the answer was stated that concerns you?" If the disagreement is about process about the way something is done, ask "Do you agree with what we are talking about?" Make sure everyone understands and agrees on the content and process of the problem that has arisen. After all the facts are clear, allow the family unit to decide on what can be done. Remember, you are modeling proper behavior; and by your actions you are setting up the norms of the community.**

Fairness and Responsibility in Families

> ***Facilitator's Note:*** **Instructions for introduction of the Areas of Fairness and Responsibility in the Family.**
>
> **The program is now introducing the ideas of fairness and responsibility in the family system. This will become a recurring theme, as more and more conceptual information is absorbed by the families. As, with this meeting, the end of the program is nearing, keep the atmosphere light, and use your body movement to give energy to the group. Give every family member a copy of Exercise 6-B. Read the two paragraphs below to the group and have them complete the exercise.**

In the STEP approach to parent-child relationships, Dinkmeyer and McKay (1997) discuss how the democratic system has impacted the ways families relate to one another. Many different segments of the population are demanding equal treatment under the law, and this attitude has extended into our families. Parents who were raised in a more authoritarian time may protest the idea of equality in the family.

What is needed is a balanced view that takes into consideration the experience of the parents and the need for children to develop self-respect and independence. There are different areas of responsibility, which are important for unity in a family system. Let's check areas of responsibility in which every family member is equal.

Exercise 6-B

Areas of Fairness and Responsibility in the Family

Look at the areas of responsibility that are listed. **Circle** the ones that you feel the family does well as a team. Put a **check** by the areas that you feel need improvement.

- ❑ *Respect*
- ❑ *Trust*
- ❑ *Concern and caring*
- ❑ *Understanding one another*
- ❑ *Listening*
- ❑ *Focusing on assets rather than faults*
- ❑ *Openness in sharing of thoughts and feelings*
- ❑ *Commitment to common goals*
- ❑ *Right to select independent goals*
- ❑ *Supporting and accepting one another*

> ***Facilitator's Note:*** **Now, using Exercise 6-C, it is time for an adult in the family to poll the family's answers from Exercise 6-B. Have everyone pass his or her sheet to the designated individual to take a census poll of what the family thought were areas in which the family takes equal responsibility and the areas that could use some improvement. Let the family choose which area they would like to work on first.**

Exercise 6-C

Polling the Family

In which areas does the family take equal responsibility and which areas could use some improvement?

Respect	circled ______	checked ______
Trust	circled ______	checked ______
Concern and caring	circled ______	checked ______
Understanding one another	circled ______	checked ______
Listening	circled ______	checked ______
Focusing on assets rather than faults	circled ______	checked ______
Openness in sharing thoughts and feelings	circled ______	checked ______
Commitment to common goals	circled ______	checked ______
Right to select independent goals	circled ______	checked ______
Supporting and accepting one another	circled ______	checked ______

What area would the family like to work on first?

____

____

____

Facilitator's Guide to Plan of Action Study

Facilitator's Note: **The following exercise can be used if time permits. This exercise will be reintroduced later due to the rich cognitive goal-setting method. To demonstrate Exercise 6-D, the facilitator can model the exercise in front of the class asking different family members what they think. The facilitator and assistants can help those who need assistance, remembering always to ask before coming into the family boundaries.**

Many families do not realize the tremendous support and encouragement that can result from working together toward family and individual goals. By developing a system for goal setting, everyone stands a better chance of reaching or realistically evaluating their goals. The family will use the sample goal sheet to work on one area from Exercise 6-D.

Use Exercise 6-D to begin to set family goals. ***Make sure that everyone in the family sees the Plan of Action Worksheet*** and understands how the family is going to proceed. Now decide what the plan of action is for your family. Some suggestions for plans of action that others have used are

- to become a strong team,
- to have better relationships, and
- to have a peaceful family.

Exercise 6-D

1. Choose a plan of action of your own, or use one of the above suggestions. What is the plan of action for your family?

   ____

2. Put the family's plan of action in the first column.

3. Put the area of family responsibility that the family chose during Exercise 6-C in the first goal space. Have a family member read the heading above each goal and work across the page following the headings.

   - Steps to goal
   - First step and when will you take it?
   - What barriers might get in your way?
   - How will you overcome the barriers?
   - How will you check your progress?

4. Just do one goal at a time and take twenty minutes to work on that goal, answering the questions found in the headings on the chart. Work across the page being careful to listen to all the possible answers from different members in the family.
5. It is normal to get stuck at times. Assistants will be coming by to see if anyone needs help.

The goal-setting method in Exercise 6-D begins a type of processing that can ensure success for the adults and especially for the children who probably have not seen or heard anyone process information in this way. The exercise will be reintroduced in a later chapter to ensure that this goal-setting method is integrated into the thinking pattern of family members. Those families with transgenerational addictive problems will not be familiar with the process and may need help when they can't answer the following questions:

"What barriers might get in your way?"

"How will you overcome these barriers?"

"How will you check your progress?"

These questions have to do with knowledge of cause and effect and information about long-term consequences. These processing skills are natural in a community of acrolect speakers and are absorbed in early childhood development. As addressed in Chapter 7, many of the families here will have members with developmental arrests from early childhood. A person with a generational problem with substance abuse may not know what to do when barriers have a possibility of getting in the way, and that person may need help. For now, the process of learning about cause and effect and long-term consequences is beginning.

Facilitator's Note: **End the first meeting by having the families each tell what their family has learned and how they might apply the information to their family. Have one member of the family (perhaps the smallest child) give the family report. Encourage and compliment the families by telling them how you feel ("I'm impressed!"). Tell them how much you enjoyed being with them. The goal sheet from Exercise 6-D can be carried home, and the goal sheet can become part of a welcoming report from each family for the next week. Have extra charts available next week for those who may forget their charts. Remember the value of having the family process toward goal setting in this way? When an opportunity arises, begin to bring this processing method into the interactions that you have with the families. The way of processing what Exercise 6-D teaches can carry over into school and employment settings.**

Plan of Action Worksheet

Plan of Action	Goals	Steps to Goal	First Step: When will you take it?	Barriers to Goal	How will you overcome barriers?	How will you check progress?

References

American Psychiatric Association. (2000). *Diagnostic and Statistical Manual of Mental Disorders, Text Revision* (4th ed.). Washington, DC: Author.

Beavers, W. (1977). *Psychotherapy and growth: family systems perspective*. New York: Brunner/Mazel.

Beavers, W. (1993). Measuring family competence: The Beavers systems model. In F. Walsh (Ed.), *Normal family processes*, 2nd ed. (pp. 73-103). New York: Guilford Press.

Bowen, M. (1978). *Family therapy in clinical practice*. New York: Aronson.

Bowlby, J. (1988). Developmental psychiatry comes of age. *American Journal of Psychiatry*, 145, 1-10.

Bowlby, J. (1989). The role of attachment in personality development and psychopathology. In S. I. Greenspan & C. H. Pollack (Eds.), *The course of life:* Vol. 1. Infancy (pp. 119-136). Madison, CT: International Universities Press.

Dinkmeyer, D., Sr., McKay, H., and Dinkmeyer, D., Jr. (1997). *The parent's handbook*. Bowling Green, KY: STEP Publishers.

Haley, J. (1963). *Strategies of psychotherapy*. New York: Grune and Stratton.

Madsen, W., and Nichols, M. (Eds.). 1999. *Collaborative therapy with multi-stressed families: from old problems to new futures*. New York: Guilford Publications, Inc.

Minuchin, P. (1974). Families and individual development: provocations from the field of family therapy. *Child Development, 36*, 289-302.

Minuchin, S. (1974). *Families and family therapy*. Cambridge, MA: Harvard University Press.

Monfils, B. (February 1987). Parenting methods of the acrolect. Paper presented by faculty member in Family Communications in the Department of Communications at the University of Arkansas at Little Rock.

Pinsof, W. (1995). *Integrative problem-centered therapy: a synthesis of family, individual and biological therapies*. New York: Basic Books.

van IJzendoorn, M. (1992). Intergenerational transmission of parenting: A review of studies in clinical populations. *Developmental Review, 12*, 76-99.

Wesselmann, D. (2007). Treating Attachment Issues through EMDR and a Family Systems Approach. In F. Shapiro, F. W. Kaslow, & L. Maxfield (Eds.), *Handbook of EMDR and family therapy processes*. Hoboken, NJ: John Wiley & Sons, Inc.

Yin, R. (1994). *Case study research*. Thousand Oaks, CA: SAGE Publications.

In Chapter 7...

Different sources are reviewed from which various ideas about language and the distortion of language came. Augustine, a fourth-century scholar, looked at the linguistic legacy of the Hebrew language. Fabre d'Olivet, an eighteenth-century linguistic historian, believed there were common elements in all languages. Count Albert Korzybski, a Polish semanticist, observed seven peculiarities and distortions in the English language that caused confusion and developmental problems.

Several authors referred to the "structural violence" found in particular uses of language. A discussion of structural linguistic violence in society and family can increase understanding of the necessity of intervention in faulty societal, community and family language. A misuse of language is a significant factor in creating political oppression and economic and social discrimination. Exposing the nature of verbal abuse highlights the impacts on societal, community, and family levels. We inherit useful and faulty language patterns that can influence either cooperation or conflict in the family. This chapter isolates the semantic aspects (first introduced in Chapters 3 and 4), which prove frustrating in family interpersonal communication.

The use of affirmations can be a means with which to strengthen the abilities of children to accomplish developmental tasks successfully. Missing affirmations in family speaking patterns can cause developmental difficulty in the family. Developmental arrests from any prior developmental period demand to be addressed again and again until the child resolves the issue satisfactorily. Healthy family linguistics can provide age-appropriate affirmations needed for childhood developmental needs.

Case study research continues in this chapter with semantic evaluations for the four investigations. Case study research provides insight into interventions where linguistic legacies have been affecting human development. The tables containing the analysis of linguistic legacy on human development expand the recognition of the different evaluations for each case study research investigation.

Chapter 7 utilizes the exercises in "Communication Barriers in Family Dynamics," which provide the information for semantic intervention into the language patterns of the families participating in the *Uncapping Family Wisdom* program.

CHAPTER 7

COMMUNICATION IN THE FAMILY SYSTEM

The emphasis in Chapter 7 is on recognizing the semantic aspects of inherited family speaking systems that might frustrate family members. Semantic factors that frustrate family members can lead to conflict and transgenerational dysfunction. The linguistic legacy and general semantics information in Chapters 3 and 4 aid families in understanding their family speaking pattern as they apply the conceptual information described in this chapter.

Historical Ideas on Language

The search for clear language unmixed with distortion is not new. People may marvel at the ways language can be used to tear down, build up, pacify, and soothe; however, few really understand the underlying principles that can be found in family speaking patterns.

In the past, some authors have considered the strength and weakness of language. One of these was Saint Augustine.

Augustine

Augustine was a fourth-century scholar, a church official, and a prolific writer. He discussed the Hebrew language, which was the language of Abraham, the historical father of the Jewish people, and attempted to trace a history of the language that Abraham passed on to his descendents.

Ancient myths, including an ancient story in the Hebrew writings, spoke of the confusion of languages that, according to Jewish tradition began at a place called Babel. In *The City of God* (1950, pp. 534-537), Augustine wrote that Hebrew was the "pure" language that existed before the confusion of the languages at Babel and that afterwards Hebrew was the only language not mingled with confusion. In his writing in the fourth century, Augustine believed that this language was passed down the ancestral line to the tribe of Heber, the grandson of Noah, from whom the language derived its name. Later, Abraham was born into the Hebrew language that preserved the ancient writings of the Old Testament.

Fabre d'Olivet

Writing during the time of the French Revolution (around 1789), Fabre d'Olivet (2002) was a linguistic historian who had an interesting idea. He introduced the concept of La Langue, as the common, unified, and creative core of purity found in all languages. He thought that all languages (*langues*) still had at their center a true, unadulterated, universal pure language. He thought a universal language had existed but was now scattered through all languages, affecting the purity of the universal language.

Albert Korzybski

Albert Korzybski's work, *Science and Sanity: An Introduction to Non-Aristotelian Systems and General Semantics* (2000, p. 753), contains very essential information to the training goals in the *Uncapping Family Wisdom* program. He was the semanticist who, as discussed in Chapters 3 and 4, introduced the importance of time-binding information for future generations. Korzybski wrote from the perspective of knowing eight different languages himself. He looked at the peculiarities of the English language and pointed out some identifiable patterns of speaking which did not reflect true reality. These identifiable speech patterns served to "kick up" the emotional level in conversations, which caused conflict. He pointed out that if a person were born into an English-speaking society, he or she might be exposed to seven different problem areas that in turn might lead to communication problems. These areas of speaking errors are labeled as follows:

Polarization—A kind of communication that causes conflict because the communication implies that only two choices are available to the speakers.

"Intensional" Orientation—The coined word "intensional" refers to words that point inward toward the speaker's views rather than outward toward the reality being discussed. They tend to be statements of judgment rather than statements of fact.

Fact-Inference Confusion—Inferences, opinions, and judgments, are types of communication which need to be used responsibly.

Allness—This communication is simplistic and absolute. "Allness" communication comes from the perspective of a person who does not see the world as very complex. The person speaking in allness terms uses absolute statements, which are often not accurate and are spoken only from a personal point of view.

Static Evaluation—In the English language, a reference to time is included in almost all sentences. Many sentences contain some reference to past, present, or future, making circumstances appear static over time. As a person learns the process of time-binding, the ability allows him or her to have a separate past, present, or future and to focus, at will, on each of these segmented times, allowing dynamic evaluations. Time-binding is not possible in all languages and causes much difficulty in reality-testing in the English language. Static Evaluation is found in the language of the mentally ill.

Indiscrimination—The English language contains common nouns such as teacher, student, and politician, focusing on similarity. Only looking at the similarity causes a prejudging or a prejudice toward classes or individual people. Using language in this way leads to stereotyping, which is a fixed mental picture of some group applied to each individual of the group without regard to his or her unique qualities.

Dead-Level Reckoning—A communication tendency that recycles to the same conclusion in response to all reasoning. In dead-level reckoning, there is an inability or an unwillingness to consider other information which might solve the problem. Flexibility in accessing different abstraction levels is needed to correctly reflect reality.

The knowledge of these general semantic errors is used to identify family speaking patterns which cause conflict in families. These patterns are linguistic legacies from the past which can be changed by understanding the cause and effect of their use in relationships.

Benjamin Whorf

Benjamin Whorf (1956) was a linguist who wrote, "Speech is the best show man puts on." He thought that much more went on behind language than what appeared on the surface. Whorf showed how the capacity for speech helped man in thinking but could also sometimes hinder thinking, working against man's best interests. Whorf discussed how individuals acquired language skills, how they differed in the facility in language, and how speech functions were dissociated in aphasia,[8] the psychoses, and other disorders.

Important to the *Uncapping Family Wisdom* program, Whorf's discussion on dissociation showed how speech and types of dissociation were important diagnostic tools for linguistic problems. According to Whorf, separation from the mainstream of consciousness or behavior was often a product of faulty linguistics in a family system. Whorf thought linguistic problems sometimes pointed to psychological problems caused by developmental issues. The *Uncapping Family Wisdom* program recognizes this connection and gives concrete ways to intervene in the developmental problems caused by linguistic and semantic problems.

Structural Violence in Society and Family

"Structural violence" is a misuse of language seen as a significant factor in creating political oppression and economic and social discrimination. The family speaking pattern can mirror these influences of structural violence. Evans (1996, p. 23) states,

> Verbal abuse is, in a sense, built into our culture. One-upmanship, defeating, putting down, topping, countering, manipulating, criticizing, hard selling, and intimidating are accepted as fair game by many. When these power plays are enacted in a relationship and denied by the perpetrator, confusion results.

According to Schaffner and Wenden (1995, pp. 1-75), the challenge for the twenty-first century is to use language to inspire

- inclusion rather than exclusion,
- conciliation rather than conflict, and
- peace rather than war.

They define *peace* as reality extending beyond the absence of war to include the absence of discriminatory and inegalitarian social structures and institutions. Schaffner and Wenden (1995, pp. 109-120) add that real peace is the absence of structural violence. Their studies emphasize

8 *Aphasia* is the loss or impairment of the power to use or to comprehend words.

that society affects families and families affect society. As the ways that social and cultural language impacts families are revealed, the levels of impact on an individual family can be seen. Clearly, the effect of societal language was observed in the four investigations in the case study research. The linguistics of the families demonstrated the power of words to trap individuals in static unprogressive states and to limit human potential.

As part of the treatment program, *Uncapping Family Wisdom* looks at structural violence and highlights the impact on families; moreover, the program introduces interventions into structural violence on the societal, community, and family levels. All interventions on societal, community and family levels are important contributing factors to the releasing of family wisdom. A family cannot be viewed as an isolated unit outside of societal and community influences. All levels are part of the whole of the influence on family systems.

Missing Affirmations in the Language of Family Speaking Patterns

There are also noticeably missing semantic affirmative elements in some family speaking patterns. Clarke and Dawson (1998, p. 290) discuss developmental affirmations. They state, "When we offer developmental affirmations to children, we offer powerful support that strengthens their ability to accomplish their developmental tasks successfully." Clarke and Dawson discovered unfinished business from any prior developmental period would demand to be addressed again until the child resolved the issue satisfactorily. The unfinished business would be resolved by receiving verbal or non-verbal permissions, making developmental progress possible for each individual. Clarke and Dawson offered specific affirmations for developmental stage progression and suggested that affirmations from preceding stages be offered in family linguistics, along with currently-needed, age-appropriate affirmations. They suggested a comprehensive model of linguistic intervention for parents who realize they were raised in dysfunctional homes and realized they lack the necessary skills for parenting their own children. In this manner, they are helped to avoid the mistakes of their own parents. Clarke and Dawson believed that as adults, we were continually recycling previous developmental stage permissions from day to day, so all the suggested affirmations were appropriate for adults. The authors emphasized the importance of reading the affirmations, saying the affirmations, and listening to the affirmations in order for the parents to have the affirmations, as well as the children. The affirmations that are needed for development gains for these parents are included in Chapter 8.

Case Study Research Semantic Evaluations

The emphasis in these studies is on self-evaluation and application of general semantics to find and address the errors that determine the conflict style of the family system. The individuals or family members in the four case studies included here used general semantics to diagnose the speech inaccuracies in their family language system. Korzybski (2000) stated that language must be looked at objectively and conceptual information corrected to better reflect reality. The case study research will reveal how that was done in the area of general semantics in the family systems that were studied. The semantic evaluations can be found on the developmental charting at the bottom of the tables. In Chapter 12, the tables will be expanded to follow the effects of the interventions in cognitive, social, psychosocial, and moral development.

Case Study Research #1—Amy

Unfortunately, this family was closed and declined to self-evaluate their speech communication patterns in an assessment. During the family therapy, observation of speech and interpersonal verbal and non-verbal action between the mother and the patient was a prime consideration. "Intensional" orientation, allness, and dead-level reckoning were the primary speech patterns observed in these meetings.

Examining the Family Speaking Errors

"Intensional" Orientation

Keeping her son-in-law out of jail and maintaining a positive relationship with her oldest daughter were more important to this mother than the truth her other daughter told. Her younger daughter would be sacrificed for a perceived greater good, since she insisted that an event occurred that would embarrass the people in the family system. The patient was lulled away from true reality testing and accepted reality according to the value of the name symbol, *mother*. In this case, the mother was not the nurturing figure the symbol would imply. In this case the rejection was confusing, and the rejection was more subtle than if actual words were directly being used. The mother was focused on defending herself and her family from the shame the truth might reveal. Instead of being able to face and admit the negative behavior of her son-in-law, she was fused with the shame of possible public exposure. She knew the truth was that the son-in-law was guilty, but the shame of people knowing that this happened and the possibility of the loss of her older daughter's love was more than the mother would face.

Allness

The mother saw things only from her perspective. She held firm to her views to protect herself from the possibility of being shamed. She thought she had said all there was to say about the situation. Amy saw things only from her own perspective and was unable to see or understand her mother's rejecting self-protective qualities. This meant that Amy's mother would choose to protect her reputation and the reputation of the family over Amy's well-being. The mother rationalized in therapy, "Amy has always been odd. Sometimes she sees things that are not there." Odd people, who were thought to see things that were not there, could not be believed. Instead of seeing the whole picture, which included the realities that her son-in-law would be enabled to continue to use drugs, and that Amy would be injured and perhaps become prey for other perpetrators, she limited her view of the consequences of her behavior. The mother would neither advance in moral development nor achieve a degree of freedom from being released from the pain of what others would think.

Dead-Level Reckoning

Both mother and daughter displayed the semantic error of dead-level reckoning. Because of her emotional age and the trauma she had endured, Amy looked for comfort from her mother. The end of all her reasoning recycled back to the same conclusion that she must go home with mother, thereby, displaying her lack of considering other possible solutions. The only option in her mind remained constant, "I can't go to a foster home, I want to go home with Mama."

The mother, paralyzed by her shame, and so morally undeveloped that she did not appear to have a stable code of ethics, refused to consider that her daughter had told the truth and remained in a state of strong denial. Even though the staff was in unison about believing the patient, the early denial defense mechanism of the mother could not be broken. Amy's mother was caught in the dead-level reckoning that Amy was "odd," so the event could not have happened.

The Effect of Linguistic Legacies upon Human Development

Table 7.1 has been created for analyzing the effect of the linguistic legacies upon Amy's development. At the bottom of the table are the semantic errors found in the interactions between Amy and her mother. In Amy's case, the semantic interventions included intensional orientation, allness, and dead-level reckoning. The period of treatment was six weeks.

Table 7.1 Case Study Research #1—Amy

Analysis of Linguistic Legacy on Human Development						
Stages of Development	Period of Treatment*					
	Beginning					End
	Weeks 1	*2*	*3*	*4*	*5*	*6*
Semantic Interventions	Intensional Orientation	Allness	Dead-Level Reckoning			

* The length of treatment for this patient was six weeks.

Note: At the bottom of Table 7.1 are the semantic interventions found in the Case Study Research #1—Amy. In future chapters, the left column of each table will contain information on cognitive, psychosocial, social, or moral development. As interventions are made by adjustments in semantics that cause conflict, the success will be measured in the main body of the table.

Case Study Research #2—Kay

The semantic evaluation yielded five areas of error. For a functioning family, a semantic evaluation usually yields less than three speaking errors of medium intensity, so it was safe to predict this family speaking system would have serious problems in the area of general semantics, which often indicate transgenerational dysfunction and mental illness.

Examining the Family Speaking Errors

Polarization

The patient came from a violent family of origin. The language depicted choices in terms of black or white statements, such as, "I'm messed up" and "It was all my fault." All statements were absolute. Kay did not know how to separate herself from her behavior, so all her statements about herself were judgmental. Kay was caught in an emotional bind of being very intelligent, and being given only two choices from her language legacy, neither of which felt right. The all-or-nothing reasoning generated a high level of frustration, which sometimes led to violence. Because Kay was so intelligent, the degree of frustration appeared to be in direct proportion to the degree of intelligence. Perhaps, if there were no innate ability to reason, the emotional pitch would have not been so high.

"Intensional" Orientation

Kay's husband had learned to use language to his advantage to manipulate his world. The patient believed the facade he had confidently presented originally. Kay became increasingly confused as she discovered that the words he used about her and the picture he presented with his words did not correspond to factual reality. She reasoned, "He is a minister. Everyone thinks he is very holy." Kay and her sons acted out the craziness of the disturbing contrasts. Unless she could break this facade for herself and learn to drop the judgment statements about her husband and express her emotions in a cause and effect manner, she and her sons would most likely stay trapped in the dynamic. She would have to learn to make only statements of fact regarding the behavior she saw, so her confusion would be abated and her mind cleared.

Static Evaluation

The source of the static evaluation found in Kay's speech pattern stemmed from the fact she was recovering from thinking she was to blame for everything happening around her. Also involved was the fact that she had not been able to observe any change in her family of origin or her own nuclear family. She could not use the skill of time-binding where certain events were bound in time frames, giving her a sense of the past, the present, and the future. Her speech mirrored her reality. Things never changed: Mother and Dad drank yesterday. Mother and Dad drank today. In her past, she had never had hope for the future; it seemed to her that the future would be the same as yesterday and today, with no reason to hope or to think that things would ever change. She did not understand what to change so that her future would be different. The problems she inherited were multigenerational with feeling content long disconnected from the original offense. Her belief system was that nothing seemed or would ever change.

Kay's language was the language of the powerless. "Everyone thinks I am crazy, they always have. I could never do well in school. The only thing I was good at was listening for my father's car and determining, by the sound of his footsteps, if he was drunk and I needed to hide." Regarding her husband, she described her worldview: "He always wins. He will find out how to break me."

Indiscrimination

The categories Kay had created to make sense of the world were disorganized and generalized in an atmosphere where chaos was the only sure thing. The evaluations she applied to these categories of persons were almost all fear based and represented the good/bad split of Kay's thinking: "Everyone knows more than me. The people in the congregation all think I am crazy. They are good people and could not be wrong. Ministers are all good. It's me."

Fact-Inference Confusion

The patient's processing of information was primitive. She did not know how to process through fact, inference, opinion, and judgment: the process was blurred. She was so depersonalized that she rarely had opinions or judgments without the accompanying emotions of anger and rage for having opinions or judgments. Kay's inferences were so painful that she was frequently lost in a cycle of rage, despair, incompatible optimism, and skepticism. From early childhood, she had injunctions placed on her by her parents that conditioned her to think it was wrong to have personal opinions or personal judgments. In her efforts to live out the "don't think, don't feel, don't be" message given to her by her parents, she found no sense of self-worth. "The clerk in the store looked mad at me. I don't know what I have done. I'll just go back tomorrow and maybe take her a flower or something."

The Effect of Linguistic Legacies upon Human Development

Table 7.2 has been created for analyzing the effect of the linguistic legacies upon Kay's development. At the bottom of the table are the semantic errors found by this client's self-evaluation. Notice the number of semantic errors included in Kay's generational legacy. The semantic interventions of this patient included polarization, intensional orientation, static evaluation, indiscrimination, and fact-inference confusion. The period of treatment was six years.

Table 7.2—Case Study Research #2—Kay

Analysis of Linguistic Legacy on Human Development						
	Period of Treatment*					
Stages of Development	Beginning					End
	Years 1	2	3	4	5	6
Semantic Interventions	Polarization Intensional Orientation Static Evaluation Indiscrimination Fact-Inference Confusion					

* The length of treatment for this patient was six years.

Note: At the bottom of Table 7.2 are the semantic interventions found in Case Study Research #2—Kay. In future chapters, the left column of each table will contain information on cognitive, moral, psychosocial, or social development. As interventions are made by adjustments in semantics that cause conflict, the success will be measured in the main body of the table.

Case Study Research #3—Charles

Charles and his wife, Susan, had evaluated their speech patterns in the first seminar meeting with a large group/small group format, with the family forming the small group. Susan, having the best social skills, had shared with the group at large. Susan had mild polarization and fact-inference confusion. Because of the serious nature of the speaking errors of Charles and his willingness to cooperate, he eventually became the subject of study.

Examining the Family Speaking Errors

Polarization

Charles had the same speech pattern as the guardian who had raised him: it was his way or no way. His employees described the same verbal pattern as his family described, "Get it out today. No excuses." Power and control were the ultimate goal. Charles had resented the pattern in his uncle and objectively really did not like the fact he was continuing the legacy. He did not know another way of handling the powerful emotions behind the need to control. The future was predictable, if the behavioral dynamic of polarization remained unchanged. Charles was capable of powerful rage attacks. In order to accommodate her behavior to offset the rage displays, Susan was forced into a hyper-vigilant behavior. Although no one would want to behave in inappropriate ways as Charles did many times, the children only saw two models from which to choose—the verbal abuser or the victim. Inevitably, at least one of the children would pick up the polarization speech pattern and victimize others, subconsciously deciding not to be the victim.

Fact-Inference Confusion

Charles did not follow a normal processing of facts through a fact, inference, opinion, and judgment cycle. He jumped from facts to judgments accompanied by direct hits of verbal abuse, aiming for character insults, rather than commenting on behavior. "You are the laziest kid I have ever seen!" He often accelerated into rage. Amnesia was a byproduct of his raging, and he often wondered why everyone seemed to distance themselves from him. This led to further judgment and toxic speech, leading to more feelings of abandonment on Charles' part. Fear of abandonment led to more controlling behavior which set up more abandonment dynamics with others.

Dead-Level Reckoning

The emotionally charged power of Charles' speech pattern left little room for true reasoning. Although he was cognitively well developed and made rational decisions at his place of employment, even the reasoning at his place of employment was contaminated by his need to control at all times: "My way is '*the* way.' You want to do things your way, see if you can take my job."

An undercurrent of dead-level reckoning reinforced Charles' egocentrism. Conversations with Charles were very circumstantial, as opposed to being concrete and focused on solving problems; others became exhausted and lost interest. He purposefully avoided responsibility by sidetracking the issues during conversations and then became "too busy" to cooperate until "later." Later, of course, never came. He did not encourage dialogue by using eye contact; he appeared uninterested which frustrated the other person, who would end up just doing the job himself or herself out of frustration.

The Effect of Linguistic Legacies upon Human Development

Table 7.3 has been created for analyzing the effect of the linguistic legacies upon Charles's development. At the bottom of the table are the semantic errors found in Charles's transgenerational legacy. The semantic interventions in this case included polarization, fact-inference confusion, and dead-level reckoning. The period of treatment was four months.

Table 7.3—Case Study Research #3—Charles

Analysis of Linguistic Legacy on Human Development				
Stages of Development	Period of Treatment*			
	Beginning			End
	Months 1	*2*	*3*	*4*
Semantic Interventions	Polarization	Dead-Level Reckoning		Fact-Inference Confusion

* The length of treatment for this patient was four months.

Note: At the bottom of Table 7.3 are the semantic interventions found in Case Study Research #3—Charles. In future chapters, the left column of each table will contain information on cognitive, social, psychosocial, or moral development. As interventions are made by adjustments in semantics that cause conflict, the success will be measured in the main body of the table.

Case Study Research #4—Paul

Paul was court appointed to counseling for sexual molestation of his 14-year-old daughter. Sexual abuse was a generational pattern in this family, and Paul's nuclear family and extended family participated in therapy. Paul and his wife completed the communication evaluation.

Examining the Family Speaking Errors

Polarization

Paul had a speech pattern inherited from past generations of male authoritarian figures and abusive figures. His choice of T-shirts and bumper stickers reflected his black-or-white thinking pattern. He really thought his global sense of entitlement was valid. He thought the satisfaction of meeting his needs should be the ultimate goal of those around him. His speech showed he rarely thought of others and he was very emphatic in his speaking style. "I told her I loved her once. That should be enough." Paul came from a family where sexual molestation occurred within the family system. Polarization was the standard communication Paul used in the home. The adult male figure was the abuser and determined the values of the home, a pattern begun generations before. The polarization was a signal to the victims not to have their own thoughts or feelings, but to monitor the language of the perpetrator and agree with the language of the perpetrator, regardless. Both Paul and two of his sisters had been molested as children. The lack of permissions to have individual thoughts and feelings had been passed down through the language.

Fact-Inference Confusion

Paul did not follow a normal processing of information through a fact, inference, opinion, and then judgment cycle. He jumped from facts to opinion, his being the most important, of course. Regarding his work as a truck driver, he commented, "I should be driving farther each week. I'll skip my rest periods." His ideas of how things should be done were impossible to live up to for himself or others, which often led to a desire for self-soothing, usually in the form of sexual encounter. Paul had antisocial traits and entitlement issues, but mostly exhibited symptoms of sexual addiction, with the accompanying compulsiveness. Preceding and during illicit sexual encounters, the visual memories and childhood feelings during his early molestation experience were replayed.

Allness

Paul only saw things from his view of life: "That is just the way things are." He failed to see the uniqueness of individuals in groups or in the family setting. His thinking and speaking style were toxic to those around him. For example, when beginning treatment, after the intake questionnaire was filled out, he returned the next week and asked the therapist why so many questions were asked about his sexual habits. He said he had told his wife he thought the questions were asked so the therapist could spice up her own sexual life. A pattern of allness overshadowed the family. The family members had barely tasted life, afraid to think or feel, or to enter into any new situation because the family shame might be activated.

Indiscrimination

Paul's speech was full of indiscrimination patterns: "Males are just alike, that is all there is to it." Life was divided into a few categories, which were mostly jumbled due to his severe immaturity. He thought the males were superior and females were put on earth to serve males. Therapists were in their occupation because they were crazy themselves. He thought teachers were always right. His idea that teachers were always right became an important clue in deciding how therapy could proceed. Paul was interested in new information and admired people with information, but he did not know how to obtain information. Paul's indiscrimination speech pattern revealed a mix of a recitation of positive and negative qualities chosen as reactions to lumping people or things into categories and not being able to see differences in the people. Teachers were smart; police were dumb. He was a hard worker, managed his finances well, and took good physical care of his daughter. Excelling in these areas allowed him to minimize other negative categories. He minimized his sexual behavior, thought everyone should see life through a sexual screen like he did, projecting his sexual tendencies into others. He was unaware that the sexual desire was in him and lacking in his victims.

Dead-Level Reckoning

Paul was very powerful in dead-level reckoning. His strongly stated opinions were encased in well-rehearsed themes and never included another's abstraction level in an attempt to connect with the other person. Predictably, he had married women who themselves had been victims as children and by marrying Paul had returned to the familiar. With his shortage of information, categories, and reasoning skill, Paul did not give up on his "beating-a-dead-horse" opinions easily. He stayed in one abstraction level while talking and could not relate to the feelings of others: "What do you mean you are not happy? You have everything anyone could ask for." As a result, he knew little about the activities of daily living in his family, which the family kept private in order to have some freedom. His occupation as a truck driver kept him away from home for long periods of time, which was fine with his family. Since no one wanted to argue with him, the distancing of his family reinforced his beliefs.

Returning from a state of estrangement, the extended family joined the immediate family in therapy to face the family system problems. After everyone learned to identify the language error, the family cued Paul when he tried the dead-level reasoning pattern and they did not use the pattern themselves. As a result, his dead-level reckoning pattern lost its power. In the analysis, Paul had five severe semantic errors, demonstrating the potential to have a serious personality disorder. The language patterns observed in Paul had likely been passed down through several generations. Without intervention, his "linguistic legacy" could have continued into future generations—and along with it the potential for sexual molestation.

The Effect of Linguistic Legacies upon Human Development

Table 7.4 has been created for analyzing the effect of the linguistic legacies upon Paul's development. At the bottom of the table are the semantic errors found in Paul's transgenerational legacy. These semantic errors were severe, and in order to stop the generational pattern of sexual abuse, the family and extended family became involved in therapy. The semantic interventions included polarization, fact-inference confusion, allness, indiscrimination, and dead-level reckoning. The length of treatment was four months.

Table 7.4—Case Study Research #4—Paul

Analysis of Linguistic Legacy on Human Development				
Stages of Development	Period of Treatment*			
	Beginning			End
	Months 1	*2*	*3*	*4*
Semantic Interventions	Polarization	Fact-Inference Confusion	Allness	
	Indiscrimination	Dead-Level Reckoning		

*The length of treatment for this patient was four months.

Note: At the bottom of Table 7.4 are the semantic interventions found in Case Study Research #4—Paul. In future chapters, the left column of each table will contain information on cognitive, social, psychosocial, or moral development. As interventions are made by adjustments in semantics that cause conflict, the success will be measured in the main body of the table.

Moving into the Meeting Environment

Objectives *(1 hour and 20 minutes)*

1. **Introduction of Communication Barriers and Evaluation of Family (35 minutes)**

   Exercise 7-A A Self-Evaluation of Strong Family Characteristics

   The participating individuals or family members will evaluate communication barriers of their own family system. An individual who is unmarried is considered a family.

2. **Break (10 minutes)**

3. **Introduction of Bridges to Communication by Facilitator (35 minutes)**

   Exercise 7-B "I Messages" (15 minutes)

   Exercise 7-C Reflective Listening (10 minutes)

   Exercise 7-D Feeling and Rational Messages (10 minutes)

   Exercise 7-E Take-home exercise

   All family members have an opportunity to practice simple communication exercises.

> ***Facilitator's Note:*** **The second meeting begins with the same process as the first meeting and sets the mode for working inside of the family boundaries. The facilitator can look to both Chapter 4 and this chapter to find more information on the subject of semantic errors. The discussion should begin while optional dinner is progressing.**

Communication Barriers

Interpersonal Communication

Albert Korzybski, who was a Polish count, wrote a book called *Science and Sanity* (2000). Based on his knowledge of eight different languages, he took a long look at the English language. He pointed out that if a person were born into an English-speaking society, he or she would automatically be exposed to seven different problem areas that cause conflict and communication problems. All of us can each find some of these in the language of our families.

Exercise 7-A

1. Polarization (Bumper Sticker Language)

"You are either for me or against me."

Polarization—A kind of communication that causes conflict because the communication implies that only two choices are available to the speakers. Most bumper stickers are designed to get a rise of emotion out of people. We usually agree with what we read, or we don't. Bumper sticker language—polarization—suggests that the statement is the only option available.

1. **Do you have this speech pattern?** ______________________________
2. **Can you give some examples of this speech pattern?** ____________________

____

____

____

3. **How could you change these statements to be more accurate?** ____________

____

____

____

2. "Intensional" Orientation

"Truman cannot be trusted!"

The coined word "**intensional**" refers to words that point inward toward the speaker's views rather than outward toward the reality being discussed. They tend to be statements of judgment rather than statements of fact. The use of "to be" verbs—is, was, are—signal a judgment statement. Judgments and beliefs are better received when used with responsible accompanying statements such as "It seems to me," "I think," and "I feel."

1. **Do you have this speech pattern?** ______________________________
2. **Can you give some examples of this speech pattern?** ____________________

____

____

____

3. How could you change these statements to be more accurate? ________________

____

____

____

3. Fact-Inference Confusion

Fact: "I have two children. The person I married made excellent grades in school. Even though I did not work up to my potential in school, I still made good grades."

Inference: "Therefore, if my children work up to their potential, they will make excellent grades in school."

Opinion: "We all need to work to see that these children reach their full potential so they will make excellent grades in school."

Judgment: "After all, grades are a measure of intelligence. Grades separate winners from losers."

Inferences, opinions, and judgments are types of communication which need to be used responsibly. Common habits in communication that cause conflict are

- stating a fact and moving to a opinion statement, or
- stating a fact and moving to a judgment statement.

In the conversation above, another person who is engaged in the conversation may want to restate the fact as the other person perceived the situation and add their inference, opinion, and judgment, saying "Since you married a person who made excellent grades in school and you made good grades, even though you did not work up to your potential, you believe that...I feel that..."

Fact: "I desire to be a good parent and do many nice things for my children. I spend much time and thought on how to do this. I think that I have very well-behaved children."

Inference: "Therefore, my children will notice what I do for them and want to help me around the house. They will naturally just assume some of the household responsibilities without even being told."

Opinion: "My children should want to help me."

Judgment: "It is not nice to skip household chores!"

In the examples above, we can see how two or more facts were taken (the first set of statements) and then an inference was made. The inference is a premise of logic, or a beginning way of thinking, that may or may not turn out to be accurate. Information continues to become less factual when a person gives an opinion. Opinions are how individuals personally feel things should be. Judgments have to do with personal moral imperatives, the way individuals believe things must be. Opinions and judgments are sometimes stated as facts, which they may not be to the listeners. Speech becomes more responsible when we add expressions such as "It seems to me," or "I feel," to nonfactual statements (inferences, opinions, and judgments).

Remember, an inference means that we make evaluations on the basis of what we observe plus our own conclusions. This is not wrong in itself. Inferential statements, opinions, and judgments are helpful if we talk about what is meaningful to us. These statements are not helpful if we state our own inference, opinion, or judgment as absolute reality to those around us.

1. **Do you have this speech pattern?** ______________________
2. **Can you give some examples of this speech pattern?** ______________________

____

____

____

3. **How could you change these statements to be more accurate?** ______________________

____

____

____

4. Allness

"I've seen the textbook; the course is going to be really dull."

The above statement is an example of "allness." It does not take into consideration that the instructor may not be planning to teach directly from the text, or that the instructor may use creative teaching methods. The story of the six blind men and the elephant is an excellent example of allness orientation and its problems. The first blind man touched the elephant's side and concluded that the elephant was like a wall. The second felt the tusks and said the elephant must be like a spear, etc. Allness happens when we jump to conclusions that are based on an inadequate review of all the facts concerning a situation.

The world is very complex, and because of this, we can never say all about anything. We may think we know all there is to know about individuals or about why they behave as they do, yet clearly we cannot know all.

1. **Do you have this speech pattern?** ______________________
2. **Can you give some examples of this speech pattern?** ______________________

____

____

____

3. How could you change the statement to be more accurate? ____________________

____

____

____

5. Static Evaluation

"I knew Bob when he was in high school. He was always in trouble. Let's not consider his application."

This statement does not take into consideration that Bob may have changed considerably since high school and may now be a responsible citizen. In the English language, a reference to time is included in almost all sentences. Many sentences contain some reference to past, present, or future. This is not true in all languages and our English language causes much difficulty in reality testing. When we form a word picture about a person or thing, that word picture has a tendency to remain unchanged, when in fact the object or person may have changed considerably.

1. Do you have this speech pattern?____
2. Can you give some examples of this speech pattern? ______________________

____

____

____

3. How could you change the statement to be more accurate? ____________________

____

____

____

6. Indiscrimination

"Teachers are smart. They don't like people like me."

Our language has categories or labels like teacher, student, politician, which lead us to focus on similarity. Sometimes these categories or labels cause individuals to think that all people affected by these labels are very similar. This type of thinking, in turn, causes a prejudging or prejudice toward classes or individual people. And this, in turn, causes stereotyping, which is a fixed mental picture of some group that is applied to each individual of the group without regard to his or her unique qualities.

We need to put people in categories to classify them to order our thinking. Problems arise, not from using classification alone, but rather by applying evaluation to a classification label. Using an evaluation label as a definition for everyone in a particular group is not accurate.

1. Do you have this speech pattern? ________________________________
2. Can you give some examples of this speech pattern? ____________________

____

____

____

3. How could you change the statement to be more accurate? ______________

____

____

____

7. Dead-Level Reckoning

"Because I said so. Because I said so. Because I said so."

In dead-level reckoning, a communication recycles to the same conclusion in response to all reasoning, and there is an inability or an unwillingness to see a different conclusion. Flexibility in accessing different abstraction levels is needed to correctly reflect reality. A person can get stuck in his or her thinking and speaking, staying at the same level. In the example above, the person speaking on the judgment level cannot sense the value and relationship that could be possible with others.

1. **Do you have this speech pattern?** ____________________
2. **Can you give some examples of this speech pattern?** ____________________

____

____

____

3. **How could you change the statement to be more accurate?** ____________________

____

____

____

Bridges to Communication

> ***Facilitator's Note:*** **In Exercise 7-B, go slowly in the explanation of the "I message."**
> **After the reading of the exercise is completed, select a family who has displayed interest in the program. Make an affirmative statement to the family as a whole using "I think," or "I feel," to introduce the dynamic that is in the exercise. Ask the family members to look at the list of feeling words in the right column to describe the feelings they felt, beginning with, "When you said that, I felt ________." Let the families work together on positive and negative responses to different statements to others in the family. The facilitator and assistants may want to walk around, listening and encouraging, if needed.**

Exercise 7-B

"I Messages"

We have taken a careful look at the barriers to communication. Now, let's talk about how we can build bridges to communication. John Stewart in his book, *Bridges, Not Walls* (1973), states that the quality of each person's life is directly linked to the quality of the communication he or she experiences with others. Here are some simple ways that communication can be improved in your family.

"I Messages"—One of the important things that children need to learn is how their behavior affects other people. They do this by hearing parents and other adults take responsibility for their feelings while advising others how their behavior is impacting these feelings. When a person is constructing an "I message," he or she needs a feeling vocabulary. Dinkmeyer and McKay in *Parenting Teenagers* (1990) list words that can be used to build an "I message":

> There are two parts to "I messages." The first is naming the behavior. This means that one person draws attention to a particular behavior that another is doing, both non-verbal and verbal. Comment on the non-verbal gestures of an oppositional child, rather than waiting for the behavior to accelerate and become verbal. Remember, much is said without speaking a word in terms of eye rolling, shoulder shrugs, hand gestures, and so forth.

Here is an example of how to build an "I message" for non-verbal behavior.
Example: "When you do not stay to listen, I feel discouraged."

Here is an example that can be used when addressing verbal behavior:
Example: "When you talk to me in that tone of voice, I feel put down."

You can use "I messages" to address other types of irresponsibly.
Example: "When I have to pick up your socks from the floor, I feel used."

"I messages" can also be used to express positive experiences.
Example: "When you came out to greet me, I felt important."
Example: "When you believe me, I feel trusted."

> ***Facilitator's Note:*** **Use this opportunity to practice reflective listening with a volunteer from the families attending before the attempt is made to learn this listening skill. Demonstrate the technique of repeating back what is said as a question. Try to end each listening conversation with a positive response. Tell the families what feelings you observed from the experience and what you learned. Then let the families practice listening. The facilitator and the assistants can walk around and assist if families have difficulty. Ask permission to come into the family circle and ask if anyone would let you practice listening.**

Exercise 7-C

Reflective Listening

Sometimes parents wonder what to do when children will not talk to them. One way to get a conversation started is by using a listening technique called "reflective listening." The way to listen reflectively is to take the last portion of the sentence that you just heard and repeat the portion back to the person who is talking.

Examples:

"The teacher didn't ask about my homework."

"She didn't ask about your homework?"

"No, I had it ready for the first time in a week, and she didn't even ask."

"And she didn't even ask?"

"No, she didn't even ask. I might as well not have done it."

"How did that make you feel?"

"I just felt irritated that she didn't even ask."

"I'm sorry your teacher didn't ask for your homework. I know you worked hard."

The listener used this conversation as an opportunity to provide encouragement for the child. Notice that the listener did not feel that it was necessary to give any advice or make any moral judgment. The listener was just letting the other person talk and was responding to what was said. The listener did not try to tell the other person what his feelings were, but gave the other person an opportunity to get in touch with their own feelings.

> ***Facilitator's Note:*** **Explain the Feeling and Rational Messages. This is another important step in building empathic thinking. This time, have the community share their messages with each other.**

Exercise 7-D

Feeling and Rational Messages

To understand how to answer messages that are meant to *convey feelings* and not necessarily just *give information* is very important. Look at these three examples of "Feeling and Rational Messages." There are unspoken feelings in the messages being given. See if you can guess the feelings:

Example—Feeling Message—Rational Response:

(Feeling Message) "Mom, when I go to visit Dad, I want to take my bear to sleep with."

(Rational Response) "I don't think there's room in the suitcase for your bear."

What do you think the child was feeling? Remember to ask questions when you think there might be a feeling message.

Example—Feeling Message—Feeling Response:

(Feeling Message) "Mom, I want to take my bear when I go to visit Dad."

(Feeling Response) "The suitcase is getting very crowded. Tell me why you want to take the bear." (Parent is requesting more information to check out feelings.)

Example—Rational Message—Feeling Response:

(Rational Message) "The suitcase is all full. Let's go to the car."

(Feeling Response) "I need my bear."

Just for fun, work together as a family to make each of the following:

1. **One feeling message with a rational response. Share the message with the group.**

   ____

   ____

   ____

2. **One feeling message with a feeling response. Share the message with the group.**

   ____

   ____

   ____

3. One rational message with a feeling response. Share the message with the group.

____

____

____

Facilitator's Note: **Upon leaving, compliment the families on the hard work they did during the meeting. Ask the families to try the following exercise at home to share in the opening next week. They are building community, learning the same things and coming back to share their experiences. Begin to direct affirmative statements to the community as well as to the individuals and families.**

Exercise 7-E

Take-Home Exercise

List three "I messages" that were used with your family this week.

____

____

____

Try the reflective listening exercise with one member of the family. Write down the feelings that you might have missed if you hadn't investigated.

____

____

____

Listen for the three types of feeling and rational responses that we discussed in this chapter. If you make a mistake and answer with a rational response to a feeling message, go back and correct the interchange with the family member.

References

Augustine, Saint. (1950). *The city of God* (M. Dods, D.D., trans.). New York: The Modern Library.

Clarke, J., and Dawson, C. (1998). *Growing up again: parenting ourselves, parenting our children.* Center City, MN: Hazelden.

Dinkmeyer, D., & McKay, G. (1990). *Parenting teenagers.* Circle Pines, MN: American Guidance Services.

d'Olivet, F. (2002). *Hebraic tongue restored (Vol. 1).* Whitefish, MT: Kessinger Publishing Co., LLC.

Evans, P. (1996). *The verbally abusive relationship: how to recognize it and how to respond.* Avon, MA: Adams Media.

Korzybski, A. (2000). *Science and sanity: an introduction to non-Aristotelian systems and general semantics* (5th ed.). New York: Institute of General Semantics (original work published in 1933).

Schaffner, C., & Wenden, A. (Eds.) (1995). *Language and Peace.* Dartmouth, UK: Aldershot.

Stewart, R. (Ed.) (1973). *Bridges not walls: a book about speech communications.* Reading, MA: Addison-Wesley Publishing Company.

Whorf, B. (1956). *Language, thought and reality.* Cambridge, MA: M.I.T. Wiley.

In Chapter 8...

Early developmental arrest is often the origin of mental health pathology. Unless intervention is available, early developmental arrests often remain in place throughout life. When arrest occurs, early defense mechanisms may remain arrested also, so that people who are physically mature may have defense mechanisms that would be more typical for someone much younger. Often the emotions are not balanced because of the absence of some developmental permission. Anger and rage appear in powerful displays, complicating communication dynamics.

Heinz Hartmann and Ernst Kris (1945, pp. 11-30) spoke about the "dynamic aspect" of being human. They saw a conflict of forces within and conflict in reaction to the external world as part of being human. When intervening in the "dynamic aspect" of the forces within and without, human developmental perspectives can be observed. In order to understand how missing affirmations, both verbal and non-verbal, can affect development, the importance of non-verbal and verbal interplay with parents is explained in this chapter. Affirmations are included which foster development over the life span.

Factors which affect developmental momentum also affect potential for reasoning ability and the control of emotions. For instance, trauma organization in family systems is recognized as being a factor that often interferes with optimal development in individuals. To receive developmental permissions from self and/or others, the questions (mentioned in past chapters), which require positive verbal and non-verbal affirmations, are expanded here:

- Will my cry be heard? Later, the question can become the cognitive thought: Can I learn to trust myself to speak up for my own needs?
- Can I be an autonomous person, or will I have to learn to stay safe by looking at faces to see if they are pleased with me? Later, the question can become the cognitive thought: Can I understand that I have the right to explore, make mistakes and take responsibility for mistakes, knowing that this is part of human maturity?
- Can I have my own personal initiative, or will I have to do what others want most or all of the time? Later, the question can become the cognitive thought: Can I draw appropriate boundaries with others that allow me to function in a healthy manner, so I won't have to second guess my motives or actions?
- Then, when the above permissions are in place, can I learn to get along with others and trust my skills to take care of myself? Later, the question becomes: Can I stay within the personhood boundaries that I have set, in order to keep my self-respect and interact with others in shaping the relationships that I desire?

After the semantic interventions measured in Chapter 7, the four case study research investigations now follow the developmental progress of the individuals in the areas of cognitive, social, psychosocial, and moral development. Observations of these individual case study research investigations aid in discovery of how linguistic legacies may have affected human development.

CHAPTER 8

DEVELOPMENTAL IMPACT AND MOMENTUM

Chapter 8 provides a path for a direct application of the information on developmental arrests (first presented in Chapter 4) to provide impact and momentum for development. The dynamic aspect of human development is discussed, and the static interference in the form of developmental arrests is illustrated. Defense mechanisms and developmental permissions that will increase the momentum for uncapping family wisdom are presented as resources for moving past any trauma organization in family dynamics.

Much mental health pathology has its origin in early developmental arrest(s). Hartmann and Kris (1945, pp. 11-30) refer to the "dynamic aspect." The dynamic aspect has two parts:

1. The interaction and the conflict of forces within the individual and their reaction to the external world at any given time.
2. Early developmental psychological factors, which come from one's personal past which may interfere with the incorporation of developmental permissions. Until intervention is available, these developmental psychological factors may extend through a person's entire lifespan.

The basic formula, introduced in Chapter 2, displays the difference between the natural orders of both function and dysfunction. The necessary components for transgenerational function must be present for normal human development to occur.

Transgenerational Function = (+) Human Development Permissions
(+) Conceptual Information

Transgenerational Dysfunction = (–) Human Development Permissions
(–) Conceptual Information

The knowledge of both human development permissions and conceptual language is needed. This program is designed to uncover the family wisdom that lies in the family system itself. The program unravels and filters by indirectly questioning the assumptions and implications found in the language by which individuals were trained. The program uncovers unconscious static rules, often unspoken, that keep individuals from achieving stages of basic human development.

In addition, the *Uncapping Family Wisdom* program supplies needed conceptual information, which can provide dynamic views of individual and family potential. The information and its application serve to energize development that creates the momentum to bypass shame and modify behavior.

Defense Mechanisms

The symptoms of mental health pathology often exhibit the manifestations of primitive defenses responding to protect an overwhelmed or assaulted self. From the *New World Encyclopedia* (2010):

> *Defense mechanisms* are psychological mechanisms aimed at reducing anxiety. Often unconscious, defense mechanisms involve protecting an individual from psychological pain or anxiety. While several may be helpful in the short term, alleviating suffering that might otherwise incapacitate the individual, they can easily become a substitute for addressing the underlying cause and so lead to additional problems. The solution, therefore, is to address the underlying causes of the pain these mechanisms are used to defray. The ideal, however, is that individuals grow and live in a healthy psychological environment, in a society that cares for and nurtures each person, so that the use of these defense mechanisms is no longer needed.

Defense mechanisms are directly related to developmental arrest. Different lists of defense mechanisms from various professionals may contain more that are listed in the Correlation of selected defense mechanisms with global assessment of mental health on page 54; however, this list is helpful because the chart includes the defense levels and the appropriate maturity level. The use of certain defenses could conform to a mental health diagnosis.

In order to develop properly, humans need permissions to feel, to think, to be, and to do, which foster the attainment of future mature defense mechanisms. Each individual needs to develop a personal conscience and a personal code of ethics, a process which normally begins during the early years of feeling formation but is subject to arrest due to missing developmental permission in one or more areas. Incomplete development limits the defense mechanism available to the individual.

Linguistic Legacy and Its Effect on Human Development

Accurately Describing Reality

In Chapter 7, testing one premise against another was explained in the fact-inference discussion. Here is how the process worked:

Facts—What really happened.

Inferences—What the facts meant to different people.

Opinion—What values were brought into the event.

Judgment—What judgment was made about the event.

Accepting the idea that different people see things differently and reasoning through the fact-inference process can determine if a person is stating an opinion or judgment as if it were the fact itself. This type of reasoning speech is regularly done in the language of those who speak the acrolect, who understand normal human development. The acrolect is filled with constructs capable of accurately describing reality, because the language use agrees with optimal human development. As reasoning constructs are applied in acrolect conversation, five processes result:

1. When a speaker gives an opinion of judgment that is stated as a fact, an emotional reaction from a listener signals something is wrong. The speaker and listener then revert back to establish what the facts are and to investigate the different inferences they made as they both heard the factual information.
2. The different inferences of those speaking with each other are allowed to be explained respectfully. The different inferences are accepted as equally valid observations and impressions of the facts.
3. Meaningful conversation is not blocked. Conflict is not given an opportunity to interrupt meaningful conversation, as each speaker is allowed to make his or her meaning understood.
4. Sometimes participants discover that they have brought another issue into the conversation or have misunderstood the fact.
5. All participants take personal responsibility for their opinions or judgments by adding "I feel" or "I think" to their statements.

Developmental impact and momentum is at its highest when people know how to communicate in this manner. Conversing in this way provides respect for the speakers. How different are the interactions seen in many family systems when the emotional reaction is not shared, the facts are not reexamined, and the different inference of the facts stated! Just changing this one interactive dynamic and following these five steps below will aid in achieving a higher level of quality interactions for the family. In the dynamics of the family, the greatest environment for optimal human development can be created when

1. developmental stages are understood;
2. reasoning ability is present;
3. problem-solving skills are used;
4. persuasive speech with consideration of the feelings of others is practiced; and
5. an understanding of how to scrutinize faulty reasoning is realized.

Supplying Developmental Permissions

In Chapter 2, in the case of Jim, the importance of understanding abstraction levels when trying to understand difficult cases was demonstrated. Probably due to a faulty general semantic speaking pattern in the family, the abstraction levels of behavior, neurology, feeling content, shame-perceived inadequacy, and irrational reactions to verbal stimuli may have begun with a missed developmental permission in psychosocial development. The total psychosocial developmental information contained the conceptual language. The language explained what was occurring in the various processes that were happening inside of Jim. The concept of psychosocial development helped explain what was happening that contributed to the erratic raging behavior of this young man. There was arrested development in the second stage of psychosocial development; it was not permissible for Jim to make a mistake. He also did not know how to take responsibility for a mistake and address the issue with dignity.

Again, let's look at the diagram first introduced in Chapter 2, which demonstrates the abstraction levels of potential causes of Jim's behavior:

***observed behavior*: shattering of objects**

***the cause*: acting out feelings of rage (adrenalin surge—anger turned out)**

***the cause of the cause*: emotion—mix of feelings (anger turned inward)**

***the cause of the cause of the cause*: shame-perceived inadequacy (depression)**

***the cause of the cause of the cause of the cause*: irrational response to verbal stimuli (helplessness)**

The cause of the cause of the cause of the cause of the cause:
arrested psychosocial development
Baseline Cause

Looking at the diagram that reasoned to the baseline cause, a person can see how the emotional content was considered, which added meaning to the cause of the behavior.[9] The reason for Jim's feeling of helplessness was that he had never received the psychosocial developmental permission and understanding that it was acceptable to make mistakes. Mistakes are common to humankind, but Jim did not know that or did not know how to take responsibility for his mistakes. The diagram displays how, due to a missing developmental permission to make a mistake, inadequacy and helplessness entered the picture. Jim had an uncritical acceptance of a false premise. The false premise was, "It is not acceptable to make a mistake." When this permission to make a mistake was granted, the helplessness was replaced by a choice of how to behave and knowledge of how to take responsibility for a mistake. Jim got control of himself by learning how to accept the responsibility for a mistake and learning how to self-soothe the part of him that was conditioned to the premise that making a mistake was not allowed. The emotional picture changed when there were no emotions to feed the adrenalin surge that produced the rage that resulted in the presenting behavior of the shattering of objects. Jim began to understand the dynamic aspects of the raging.

In addition to stopping the rage, Jim was indirectly taught cognitive responses to answer the beginning emotional signal of helplessness that would lead to a raging incident. Jim learned to engage the five-step method using his frustration as a signal to

1. Move to reinforce his permission to make mistakes.
2. Determine the facts regarding the event that was occurring.

9 Jim's development was arrested in Stage 2 of Erikson's psychosocial development rating.

3. Immediately get more information about his inferences of the event, and, if others were involved, seek to understand their inferences in order to begin a healthy discussion.
4. Begin with the agreed upon facts, compare the different inferences, opinions, and judgments.
5. Take responsibility for any mistakes that he would most certainly make at one time or another.

Cognitive Development

As individuals develop cognitively, the process of building a personal inventory of conceptual information is paramount. Persons who have experienced early developmental arrests were probably at a very early intuitive age when the development, in varying degrees, was interrupted. The normal way of learning conceptual information is to absorb the different concepts intuitively at a very young age. These concepts serve to train the emotions to submit to more rational thoughts as cognitive developmental permissions are acquired in the family. In addition, as the meaning of behavior is understood and discussed, the positive emotions in the family serve to reinforce normal behavior and further development.

Permissions to develop are mostly received by intuition through language, tone, or mood, during interactions with caregivers. The denied permissions for development can be very subtle in the interactions of the family, and many times these processes remain out of the awareness of the caregivers. In addition, due to trauma in the family or generational ignorance of the needed conceptual information, the concepts forming the basis of some rational thought may be unavailable.

If these developmental permissions are not granted in the interactions between the parents and the children, difficulties in advancement in one or more developmental stages begin. In order to reverse developmental arrest, the concepts that make up the store of conceptual information first have to be learned rationally, then emotionally and intuitively (Carroll, 1964, pp. 75-88). The process happens gradually, or sometimes, as in the case of Jim, dramatically, moving the locus of control inside and affecting behavior in natural way.

In past years, other studies in psychology have examined the results of developmental arrest and to a large extent have concentrated on behavioral interventions. Now, rather than exclusively treating the behavioral symptomology in the individuals, therapists may appreciate programs that look more toward cause and effect, getting to the root of the problem, and restoring missed developmental permissions. At this point, behavioral change should follow or can be facilitated by behavioral interventions, which will be discussed in Chapter 10. In such programs, many abstraction levels can be addressed simultaneously.

The individuals in the four case study research investigations exhibited behavioral patterns, defense mechanisms, and conflict patterns, which reflected that they had not received the developmental permissions needed to move beyond early stages. When developmental arrest occurs, unless conceptual information is forthcoming, the arrest often becomes part of a family legacy passed from generation to generation through the repeated patterns of verbal and non-verbal communication by the caregivers. In these families, the meaning and cause of behavior is poorly understood. When hypercharged emotions lead to feelings of helplessness or hopelessness, shame and blame become important intervening variables.

Trauma Organization in Families

The concept of trauma-organized families was discussed in Chapter 5, and the subject is now revisited to increase understanding of some of the developmental implications. When trauma occurs in early human development, especially during the first five years when feeling formation and conscience building are taking place, an arrest can occur in the areas of cognitive, social, psychosocial, and moral development. If a stage of development is missed, the person stumbles through other stages and may never know the joy of being fully human. If an intervention is not imminent, the interruption of development can affect human developmental potential. Since the individual who suffers developmental arrest does not understand normal development, the possibility of attracting a mate who does understand normal development is remote. Also, on becoming a parent, the individual may not understand behavior developmental patterns and may misinterpret the reasons for childhood behavior. For instance, if the parent was never allowed to individuate from his or her own parent, a quest for independence by a two year old can be misinterpreted by the parent as an attempt to disobey family norms or an emotional rejection of the parent. Without historical memories to guide correct reactions, the parent is stuck with these impressions. The parent may seek to stop this normal behavior in ways that cause shame in the child, who is really doing what comes naturally to a child at that particular age. To avoid these feelings of shame, the following dynamics may occur:

- There is an arrest in one or more developmental stages.
- The locus of control for the child does not internalize, but stays externalized. If intervention does not occur, possible further disorganization may manifest in future generations when an externalized locus of control becomes the standard for the family system.
- Without conceptual information regarding human development, a negative interdependence becomes the norm between the parent and the child. The negative interdependence reappears in future relationships and can be seen clearly in interactions with authority figures.

Many of these dynamics are generated through the language of the family system. Family system communication defines reality for the members of the family and can have positive or negative impact on future generations. If, because of the lack of conceptual language and experience, the language contains elements of dysfunction, the dynamics of family understanding is one of skewed reality. Families can then become organized toward trauma. They pass flawed information about family organization through their language to future generations, leading to individuals with perceptible degrees of arrested human development. Today in some communities, a complex cyclic pattern affecting individual, family, and community structure can be seen. The pattern leads to societal decay, as more and more children are affected by trauma and hindered development in their early childhood. These now troubled children can also affect their peers by invading the family boundaries of their peers, especially in adolescence, interjecting language, culture, and values not in conformity with the other family's rules for safety. As this process continues, large segments of society can lose information about what is normal and necessary for achieving optimal human development. Chapter 6 began to isolate characteristics of strong families, which conceptually can lead to generational healthy legacies and provide an ideal environment for optimal human development. In Chapter 7, general semantic variables were isolated by the self-evaluation of the families participating in the program. These variables let the family know how conflict is likely to enter the family. Here in Chapter 8, information is provided so family members can self-evaluate the developmental gains for the individuals in their family and also find out where developmental permissions might be needed and how to generate developmental potential. Information about cognitive, moral, social and psychosocial areas of development will provide valuable aid in applying constructs to improve the reasoning ability of the participating families and allow change to occur.

Case Study Research #1—Amy

Due to the mother's ambivalence concerning treatment, the therapist evaluated the patient.

Cognitive Developmental Analysis

Amy's chronological age was 14 when she was admitted to the hospital for safety reasons and to find out what really happened concerning her brother-in-law's alleged rape charge. Her cognitive development initially was 0-3½ years of age determined by Piaget's cognitive stage assessment. Her family wanted people to believe that she was "crazy." Pressures in her home were intense for her to retract her statement. As she entered the hospital, it was apparent that in addition to the trauma incurred, she also showed symptoms of extreme separation anxiety due to a developmental arrest in the area of object constancy. She appeared not to understand that when mother disappeared, mother was not gone forever. The strong feelings of abandonment were the true grief of permanent loss when mother was out of sight. However, over time her connection with hospital personnel enabled an attachment dynamic to take place with the staff, which started her up the developmental ladder and could lead to individuation from her mother. At first her speech was egocentric, although not narcissistic. She was interested in her room, her clothes, and her mother, but gradually she paid attention to what others were saying and added nonpersonal references to her speech.

Social Development Analysis

The patient was in the 3-6-year-old category of Selman's social development scale. If her brother-in law had given out any signals that he was seducing her, she probably would have missed the cues. She had not learned that others could feel differently in a given situation. She was too innocent to realize that others might have different motives. She was not able to reason using this conceptual information. Because Amy did not understand shame dynamics, her mother's behavior was especially painful to her. She began to learn much about the motives of others, when she had to confront the issues of shame, which had caused her mother to want to sacrifice Amy's well-being for the reputation of the family.

In a group situation, she did not understand much about how others viewed her actions and the view they had of her as a person. She had seldom interacted with others and had to learn that others needed her interaction to help them form a view of themselves. Without this developmental key, she was unable to understand the intentions of another person.

Psychosocial Development Analysis

The patient appeared to be advanced to the 6-12-year-old category in Erikson's psychosocial stage development scales; however, an important thing to remember was that development had been unusual. Perhaps her schizoid personality disorder traits allowed her to appear as if she had a strong sense of identity and to appear self-sufficient; but in fact, she was not relating to very many others in the world. She neither needed nor wanted but a very few friends and lived in a world cushioned against attachment to those outside her family. The patient was below average in intelligence, but she possessed a unique style and character, which made her endearing to her peers and the hospital staff. Like a small child before the age of attention-getting behavior, she did not seem to be aware of her charm and felt little need for compliments. She took pride in her small pick-up truck, dressed with a personal style, and kept her room neat, not for others, but because those activities were interesting to her and perhaps satisfied some obsessive-compulsive traits.

Amy had the same level of conscious development that a small innocent child would have before conflict came into her life. She had not chosen the "unsane"[10] rules of her family to form a warped value system based on defending from shame; but instead, she embraced the simple values of an innocent child now in an adolescent body with no understanding of the dynamics of shame.

Amy's psychosocial development was very interesting. Psychosocial development in the early feeling formation years is usually a measure of a person's degree of permission to develop trust in himself or herself to speak up for himself or herself, to be one's own person, to have one's own initiative, and to get along with others. But, in this case, Amy's choice of isolating herself from the world had caused her to rely on her own initiative. She was very responsible for herself. She either did not choose to or did not know how to interact. She appeared to have built thick cushions of defense between herself and the world.

Moral Development Analysis

The patient appeared to be exceptionally morally developed. Amy was in stage six of Kohlberg's moral development scale ratings. She was torn between preserving relationships and standing up for the truth. Standing up for the truth was her idea of what was right. Although under great pressure to change her story, the patient had not wavered in her stand for the truth to be spoken. Even though the code in her family was to lie to protect the reputation of the family, telling the truth was in the moral code of the patient. Because of an early developmental arrest, she remained very black and white in her moral processing; and in all probability, the patient had never learned to be untruthful. She still had much of the innocence of an eight-to-ten-month-old child where the schizoid character traits began to form. Individuation from her mother was denied, leaving her to display the degree of separation anxiety of a three year old. What the family expected and what she perceived as being right caused great conflict in this patient.

Again, the schizoid personality traits allowed Amy to develop away from a dysfunctional moral set of family rules. She probably never underwent the turmoil of a four year old that has to give up his or her self-determined idea of what is true for sometimes skewed adult family ideas. She still retained the forthrightness of a three-year-old child, who has not applied the family filters of what can be said in the family and what is restricted by covert or overt semantic rules. To observe the development of Amy, see Table 8.1.

10 Korzybski (2000, pp. 491-536) believed that insane vs. sane was a polarization of speech which did not reflect reality and was unfair to the persons who were labeled insane. He saw everyone behaving on a continuum between the extremes of sane and insane. He coined the word *unsane* for his work and used this word as a description of behavior appearing abnormal.

Table 8.1—Case Study Research #1—Amy

Age	Piaget's Cognitive Stages	Selman's Social Stages	Erikson's Psychosocial Stages	Kohlberg's Moral Stages
18		12- . Adolescents have ability to see things from national point of view, understand legal systems, moral ethics, and what is considered the conventional thing to do.	12-18. *Identity vs. Role Confusion.* Adolescence is a time of transition between childhood and adulthood. They test limits, break dependent ties, establish new identities. This is very important in becoming individuals in own right. Work hard to clarify own definition of self, to find life goals, discover meaning to life.	Stage 6. People think civil disobedience is acceptable in order to protest unjust laws that violate universal ethics. The principle of right and wrong takes precedence over obeying the unjust law.
17	12- . Adolescents begin to think in terms of possibilities. See reality, but know there may be more to life than meets the eye. They have ideas and try to prove them out.			
16		10-15. Can stand apart and understand what is going on between people. They can coordinate their own perspectives with those of others. Also, know others can do the same about them.		
14				Stage 5. Individuals have a commitment to the democratic process for making and changing laws, as well as to a social behavior contract and individual rights.
12	7-12. Learn to make inferences that go beyond information given. Can put two pieces of information together and draw inferences from information given. Can put information into categories and into order. Reasoning limited to what is familiar and known to child.		6-12. *Industry vs. Inferiority.* Need to expand understanding of world, continue to learn about sex-role identity. Learn skills needed to succeed in school. Need to learn to set and achieve personal goals.	
11		7-12. Can understand others' viewpoints of *them* and know that others can get information from *their* viewpoints as well. This makes it possible for children to understand another person's intentions.		Stage 4. Individuals obey because of duty and responsibility. They obey to keep social order of national system together.
10				
9			4-6. *Initiative vs. Guilt.* Children learn competence, initiative. Need to select activities they like so will develop positive view of selves and learn to follow through on projects. If not allowed to make decisions, will feel guilty when they take initiative; will learn to let others lead and choose for them.	Stage 3. Individuals obey out of loyalty to families and other groups such as church, teams, etc. They obey to preserve relationships. Behavior norms are important part of how people personally think individuals should be.
8		5-9. Learn what they think is not necessarily what others think. Realize others may feel differently about same situation. Understand behavior can be caused by different motives in different people.		
7	2-7. Think and speak according to what they pick up with senses.			
6				Stage 2. Individuals obey to get rewards. Rules for how to behave remain on outside—not internalized by individual.
5	2-$3\frac{1}{2}$. Do not understand systems yet. Center on own point of view; use large amount of egocentric speech. Cannot coordinate two points of view or take into account more than one dimension at a time.	3-6. Use physical remedies to handle personal problems. Confuse what they think with what others think. Easily frustrated, which leads to hitting, biting, etc.	1-3. *Autonomy vs. Shame and Doubt.* Main struggle is learning to rely on own judgment, finding out if "too much" independence will result in being shamed, or, if ok to explore, experiment.	
4				Stage 1. Individuals obey to avoid punishment. Rules for how to behave remain on outside and are not internalized by individual.
3			0-1. *Trust vs. Mistrust.* If basic needs are met, individual develops basic trust level. If physical, nurturance needs are not met, individual becomes mistrustful.	
2				
1	0-2. Learn to tell difference between physical bodies and world. Begin to understand when object goes out of sight, it still exists.			
0				

Note: The period of inpatient treatment for this patient was six weeks.

Case Study Research #2—Kay

Cognitive Development Analysis

Kay was in the 0-2-year-old stage of Piaget's cognitive stage assessment. She was unable to tell the difference between her physical body and the world, which was evidenced by the psychotic features in her borderline personality makeup. She was not individuated from her alcoholic mother. At one time during treatment her mother was hospitalized for alcoholism and began a 12-step program, which included drawing boundaries around herself and separating her problems from those of her troubled daughter. The process was extremely painful for Kay, who experienced the separation-anxiety feelings of the young part of herself, which had not yet achieved psychological individuation from her mother.

Kay still did not understand systems or her place in any system. She did not know how to coordinate two points of view or to take into consideration more than one dimension of an object at a time. She did not have enough social information to make proper inferences or to go beyond the information given. Kay described her beginning cognitive development:

> I was centered on black-and-white thinking. Any categories were all or nothing. I was nonanalytical and all information was current. I accepted labels. I saw me as looking into a beautiful ballroom, not knowing how to get in. The most important concept I learned about development in therapy was even if I missed a step, there was hope.

Social Development Analysis

Kay was at the lowest stage of social development. She had not moved past using physical remedies to handle personal problems. She had no boundaries between herself and her environment, causing her to confuse what others thought with what she thought. She was easily frustrated.

Psychosocial Development Analysis

Kay was in the 0-1-year-old stage of Erikson's psychosocial developmental category. People known to the patient had not provided for her basic physical and emotional needs. An infant gains a sense of power from having cries answered, thus having his or her needs met. I needs are not met, an attitude of mistrust is generalized to the world at large. Kay knew she could not trust, but thought it was her fault. She described this feeling:

> I thought lack of trust was my fault. I felt deformed—vacant. The message I gave to people was "see me deformed and fix me." I saw myself as deformed—no one would help me. If no one would help, I would drop them. I acted out deformity so they could see I was deformed, so then they would help me. Everyone else seemed O.K. I was not O.K. Now I know everyone is not O.K.
>
> My most common emotion at this time was anger. I wanted to destroy. I think I was fused with the world. I really did not have any boundaries between the world and me. Then one day—I had been in therapy for awhile—you (the therapist) had taken your time, then one night you held my hand and said, "I am sorry that happened to you." There was touch validation. Something had happened to "me." There was a "me" and something had happened to "me"...maybe everything was not my fault. You (the therapist) could abandon yourself and bring "me" in. That was the first time

> I knew I had a boundary. Now I can relate to the dentist I work for. He is amazed because I can say, "I believe this. I don't believe that." He is impressed. Yes, I do this to teach myself.

Moral Development Analysis

Kay was in Stage 1 of Kohlberg's scale of moral development. She obeyed only to avoid punishment. She lied, stole, and was involved in violent acts. The locus of control was externalized and she was controlled by the potential of shame. Kay told about being in the first stage of moral development as an adult:

> I was avoiding punishment. I lied—stole—was disobedient to the law of the land! I tried to avoid disgrace, to avoid non-love and the nonverbal turn of the face. That was punishment to me.

Kay's thinking demonstrated she was not bonded to anyone. Her main goal was to avoid the pain of rejecting verbal and nonverbal messages from others. Since she did not understand cause and effect, she often was not successful.

Table 8.2—Case Study Research #2—Kay

Age	Piaget's Cognitive Stages	Selman's Social Stages	Erikson's Psychosocial Stages	Kohlberg's Moral Stages
18		12- . Adolescents have ability to see things from national point of view, understand legal systems, moral ethics, and what is considered the conventional thing to do.	12-18. *Identity vs. Role Confusion.* Adolescence is a time of transition between childhood and adulthood. They test limits, break dependent ties, establish new identities. This is very important in becoming individuals in own right. Work hard to clarify own definition of self, to find life goals, discover meaning to life.	Stage 6. People think civil disobedience is acceptable in order to protest unjust laws that violate universal ethics. The principle of right and wrong takes precedence over obeying the unjust law.
17	12- . Adolescents begin to think in terms of possibilities. See reality, but know there may be more to life than meets the eye. They have ideas and try to prove them out.			
16				
14		10-15. Can stand apart and understand what is going on between people. They can coordinate their own perspectives with those of others. Also, know others can do the same about them.		Stage 5. Individuals have a commitment to the democratic process for making and changing laws, as well as to a social behavior contract and individual rights.
12	7-12. Learn to make inferences that go beyond information given. Can put two pieces of information together and draw inferences from information given. Can put information into categories and into order. Reasoning limited to what is familiar and known to child.		6-12. *Industry vs. Inferiority.* Need to expand understanding of world, continue to learn about sex-role identity. Learn skills needed to succeed in school. Need to learn to set and achieve personal goals.	
11		7-12. Can understand others' viewpoints of *them* and know that others can get information from *their* viewpoints as well. This makes it possible for children to understand another person's intentions.		Stage 4. Individuals obey because of duty and responsibility. They obey to keep social order of national system together.
10				
9			4-6. *Initiative vs. Guilt.* Children learn competence, initiative. Need to select activities they like so will develop positive view of selves and learn to follow through on projects. If not allowed to make decisions, will feel guilty when they take initiative; will learn to let others lead and choose for them.	Stage 3. Individuals obey out of loyalty to families and other groups such as church, teams, etc. They obey to preserve relationships. Behavior norms are important part of how people personally think individuals should be.
8		5-9. Learn what they think is not necessarily what others think. Realize others may feel differently about same situation. Understand behavior can be caused by different motives in different people.		
7	2-7. Think and speak according to what they pick up with senses.			
6				Stage 2. Individuals obey to get rewards. Rules for how to behave remain on outside—not internalized by individual.
5	2-3½. Do not understand systems yet. Center on own point of view; use large amount of egocentric speech. Cannot coordinate two points of view or take into account more than one dimension at a time.	3-6. Use physical remedies to handle personal problems. Confuse what they think with what others think. Easily frustrated, which leads to hitting, biting, etc.	1-3. *Autonomy vs. Shame and Doubt.* Main struggle is learning to rely on own judgment, finding out if "too much" independence will result in being shamed, or, if ok to explore, experiment.	
4				Stage 1. Individuals obey to avoid punishment. Rules for how to behave remain on outside and are not internalized by individual.
3				
2			0-1. *Trust vs. Mistrust.* If basic needs are met, individual develops basic trust level. If physical, nurturance needs are not met, individual becomes mistrustful.	
1	0-2. Learn to tell difference between physical bodies and world. Begin to understand when object goes out of sight, it still exists.			
0				

Note: The period of inpatient treatment for this patient was six years.

Case Study Research #3—Charles

Charles and Susan had evaluated the family members at the first seminar meeting. The couple already knew they were having difficulties, and the developmental evaluation gave them a piece of conceptual information needed to make changes in their family.

Cognitive Development Analysis

Charles was cognitively well developed, having achieved the highest accomplishments in Piaget's developmental scale. He also was obviously extremely intelligent. The high degree of advancement in cognitive development was contrasted by low development in one or more other areas, which is sometimes true of developmental arrest.

Social Development Analysis

Socially, Charles' development was in the 3-6-year-old range of Selman's social development scale. Although he did not hit others, he was so intimidating with his communication style that he had others in the family system trained to perfect obedience. All members feared him and feared loss of love from the strong male figure in the family.

Psychosocial Development Analysis

Charles really trusted no one and defended against shame and doubt by appearing super confident. Since he could not trust himself to be loved unless he was in total control at all times, he remained in the 0-1-year-old category of Erikson's psychosocial stage development. He also had several addictions indicative of this stage of development.

Moral Development Analysis

Charles only followed rules to avoid punishment, which put him in Stage 1 in Kohlberg's development scale. He did expect and work for rewards, but the main purpose of his achievement was to avoid punishment. He had not developed empathy; however, he was interested in being cooperative. His leadership style was authoritarian. To observe the development of Charles, see Table 8.3.

Table 8.3—Case Study Research #3—Charles

Age	Piaget's Cognitive Stages	Selman's Social Stages	Erikson's Psychosocial Stages	Kohlberg's Moral Stages
18		12- . Adolescents have ability to see things from national point of view, understand legal systems, moral ethics, and what is considered the conventional thing to do.	12-18. *Identity vs. Role Confusion.* Adolescence is a time of transition between childhood and adulthood. They test limits, break dependent ties, establish new identities. This is very important in becoming individuals in own right. Work hard to clarify own definition of self, to find life goals, discover meaning to life.	Stage 6. People think civil disobedience is acceptable in order to protest unjust laws that violate universal ethics. The principle of right and wrong takes precedence over obeying the unjust law.
17	12- . Adolescents begin to think in terms of possibilities. See reality, but know there may be more to life than meets the eye. They have ideas and try to prove them out.			
16		10-15. Can stand apart and understand what is going on between people. They can coordinate their own perspectives with those of others. Also, know others can do the same about them.		
14				Stage 5. Individuals have a commitment to the democratic process for making and changing laws, as well as to a social behavior contract and individual rights.
12	7-12. Learn to make inferences that go beyond information given. Can put two pieces of information together and draw inferences from information given. Can put information into categories and into order. Reasoning limited to what is familiar and known to child.		6-12. *Industry vs. Inferiority.* Need to expand understanding of world, continue to learn about sex-role identity. Learn skills needed to succeed in school. Need to learn to set and achieve personal goals.	
11		7-12. Can understand others' viewpoints of *them* and know that others can get information from *their* viewpoints as well. This makes it possible for children to understand another person's intentions.		Stage 4. Individuals obey because of duty and responsibility. They obey to keep social order of national system together.
10				
9			4-6. *Initiative vs. Guilt.* Children learn competence, initiative. Need to select activities they like so will develop positive view of selves and learn to follow through on projects. If not allowed to make decisions, will feel guilty when they take initiative; will learn to let others lead and choose for them.	Stage 3. Individuals obey out of loyalty to families and other groups such as church, teams, etc. They obey to preserve relationships. Behavior norms are important part of how people personally think individuals should be.
8		5-9. Learn what they think is not necessarily what others think. Realize others may feel differently about same situation. Understand behavior can be caused by different motives in different people.		
7	2-7. Think and speak according to what they pick up with senses.			
6				Stage 2. Individuals obey to get rewards. Rules for how to behave remain on outside—not internalized by individual.
5	2-3½. Do not understand systems yet. Center on own point of view; use large amount of egocentric speech. Cannot coordinate two points of view or take into account more than one dimension at a time.	3-6. Use physical remedies to handle personal problems. Confuse what they think with what others think. Easily frustrated, which leads to hitting, biting, etc.	1-3. *Autonomy vs. Shame and Doubt.* Main struggle is learning to rely on own judgment, finding out if "too much" independence will result in being shamed, or, if ok to explore, experiment.	
4				Stage 1. Individuals obey to avoid punishment. Rules for how to behave remain on outside and are not internalized by individual.
3			0-1. *Trust vs. Mistrust.* If basic needs are met, individual develops basic trust level. If physical, nurturance needs are not met, individual becomes mistrustful.	
2				
1	0-2. Learn to tell difference between physical bodies and world. Begin to understand when object goes out of sight, it still exists.			
0				

Note: The period of inpatient treatment for this patient was four months.

Case Study Research #4—Paul

The developmental evaluation was completed by Paul and his wife Carly.

Cognitive Development Analysis

Paul was seriously arrested in the 7-12-year-old stage of Piaget's cognitive stage assessment. His only reality was what he had known around his family of origin. He could not see any other possibilities in a household of females with no real male model to guide him, and in his extended family, the males were authoritarian. Reasoning was limited to what was familiar and known to him. "At this time, I believed there was no wrong, and I was just doing what my cousin did to me and what other people did to me." Paul had never had the cognitive skills needed to be successful in a learning environment and had not graduated from high school.

Social Development Analysis

The patient was in the 10-15-year-old category of Selman's social development scale. He was raised in an authoritarian extended family system where the male figure was in total authority and made all the decisions. He was given that role as a child. Others were expected to monitor his moods and to obey without question. He knew little about legal systems, moral ethics, and what was considered the conventional thing to do. In addition, he really knew little about the activities of those in his family. Because he was so hard to deal with, the family did not try to communicate. In order to hold on to any personhood at all, the other individuals in the family lived most of their lives in secret. The self-protective behavior of his family kept him from learning to stand apart to understand what was going on between people to coordinate the perspectives of others with his own. Paul commented on his views of the situation: "At that time [before treatment], my mind was at a 10-15-year-old stage, and I didn't know how to have a social life with my own age group." The developmental arrest corresponded to the time when his sexual abuse began. His daughter was more of a peer. Even though sometimes he would attempt to parent, he was not sure of the role. All the roles in his family were confused. He adulterated[11] his child, leaning on her emotionally.

Psychosocial Development Analysis

Paul was in the 6-12-year-old stage of Erikson's psychosocial development. He needed to expand his understanding of the world and continue to learn about sex-role identity. Paul needed to learn to set and achieve personal goals. He never got to test limits, because there had been no limits or boundaries. He never thought about who he was or thought about the meaning of life. His failure to find a sense of personal identity resulted in role confusion. Due to his lack of conceptual knowledge and his lack of feeling vocabulary, Paul found it difficult to express himself. He remembered, "Since I didn't talk good, I did better if I could show them to teach them, by hands on. I can do things with my hands, but not by telling." (He meant he used the motioning of his hands and head to express himself when he ran out of words.)

11 *Adulteration* refers to conditioning a child to be an adult in the family, instead of having generational boundaries between adults and children.

Moral Development Analysis

Paul was in Stage 1 of moral development. He obeyed to avoid punishment. Rules for how to behave remained on the outside and were not internalized. Trying to understand rules on the outside confused him and seemed to put others in control. Paul explained how his development looked to him, "I always wanted to obey because it was the right thing to do. At times what I thought was right was wrong. I must learn more about what is right."

He was dependent on others for knowledge about right or wrong, because what was really right or wrong was confused in his family. Paul described his emotional state during this time: "I was feeling sad and depressed and lonely, not knowing what to do. I did not know boundaries or how they worked. My parents never taught me that or never disciplined me when I did sexual things with my sisters." To observe the development of Paul, see Table 8.4.

Table 8.4—Case Study Research #4—Paul

Age	Piaget's Cognitive Stages	Selman's Social Stages	Erikson's Psychosocial Stages	Kohlberg's Moral Stages
18		12- . Adolescents have ability to see things from national point of view, understand legal systems, moral ethics, and what is considered the conventional thing to do.	12-18. *Identity vs. Role Confusion.* Adolescence is a time of transition between childhood and adulthood. They test limits, break dependent ties, establish new identities. This is very important in becoming individuals in own right. Work hard to clarify own definition of self, to find life goals, discover meaning to life.	Stage 6. People think civil disobedience is acceptable in order to protest unjust laws that violate universal ethics. The principle of right and wrong takes precedence over obeying the unjust law.
17 16 14	12- . Adolescents begin to think in terms of possibilities. See reality, but know there may be more to life than meets the eye. They have ideas and try to prove them out.	10-15. Can stand apart and understand what is going on between people. They can coordinate their own perspectives with those of others. Also, know others can do the same about them.		Stage 5. Individuals have a commitment to the democratic process for making and changing laws, as well as to a social behavior contract and individual rights.
12 11 10 9	7-12. Learn to make inferences that go beyond information given. Can put two pieces of information together and draw inferences from information given. Can put information into categories and into order. Reasoning limited to what is familiar and known to child.	7-12. Can understand others' viewpoints of *them* and know that others can get information from *their* viewpoints as well. This makes it possible for children to understand another person's intentions.	6-12. *Industry vs. Inferiority.* Need to expand understanding of world, continue to learn about sex-role identity. Learn skills needed to succeed in school. Need to learn to set and achieve personal goals.	Stage 4. Individuals obey because of duty and responsibility. They obey to keep social order of national system together.
8 7 6	2-7. Think and speak according to what they pick up with senses.	5-9. Learn what they think is not necessarily what others think. Realize others may feel differently about same situation. Understand behavior can be caused by different motives in different people.	4-6. *Initiative vs. Guilt.* Children learn competence, initiative. Need to select activities they like so will develop positive view of selves and learn to follow through on projects. If not allowed to make decisions, will feel guilty when they take initiative; will learn to let others lead and choose for them.	Stage 3. Individuals obey out of loyalty to families and other groups such as church, teams, etc. They obey to preserve relationships. Behavior norms are important part of how people personally think individuals should be.
5 4 3	2-3½. Do not understand systems yet. Center on own point of view; use large amount of egocentric speech. Cannot coordinate two points of view or take into account more than one dimension at a time.	3-6. Use physical remedies to handle personal problems. Confuse what they think with what others think. Easily frustrated, which leads to hitting, biting, etc.	1-3. *Autonomy vs. Shame and Doubt.* Main struggle is learning to rely on own judgment, finding out if "too much" independence will result in being shamed, or, if ok to explore, experiment.	Stage 2. Individuals obey to get rewards. Rules for how to behave remain on outside—not internalized by individual. Stage 1. Individuals obey to avoid punishment. Rules for how to behave remain on outside and are not internalized by individual.
2 1 0	0-2. Learn to tell difference between physical bodies and world. Begin to understand when object goes out of sight, it still exists.		0-1. *Trust vs. Mistrust.* If basic needs are met, individual develops basic trust level. If physical, nurturance needs are not met, individual becomes mistrustful.	

Note: The period of inpatient treatment for this patient was four months.

Note to Facilitator: After a brief lecture, allow a break of 10 minutes for mothers to exit to another table to complete Exercise 8-A—Developmental Evaluation of the Family and learn how to use Exercise 8-B—Affirmation Ovals. These exercises need to be placed on the table the mothers will be using. Materials needed for the positive feedback time with the fathers are index-card-size post-it notes, pencils, and letter-sized envelopes for all the families and all the aides.

The mothers will then return to the table to interact with the children and the fathers will leave for the other location to see the assessments and Affirmation Ovals. They will also have an opportunity to ask questions and to voice their opinions.

Facilitator's Note: The second meeting begins with the same process as the first meeting and sets the mode for working inside of the family boundaries. This unit is a direct application of

1. Piaget's cognitive development stages,
2. Selman's social development stages,
3. Erikson's psychosocial developmental stages, and
4. Kohlberg's moral development stages.

Only the seminal models of these writers were used because of the concepts they contain. Later, debate about these concepts may have caused regulation of some of the models; but, for our purposes, we are not interested in what came first or what could have been be stated in a more fine-tuned manner. We are looking for the basic conceptual information that these writers were attempting to present, not to find the perfectly stated principle. We are just looking for simple constructs, which may be new to those who need to receive conceptual information in order to understand the significant underworkings that impact family dynamics and personhood of the individuals in the family.

This meeting is very important. You and the assistants must take care that the process of the meeting is understood. The facilitator can remind the families that the assistants are there to help and reintroduce them before the exercise is begun. Tell the families that you or the assistants may not come into the family boundaries unless asked. Tell them to raise their hand if they want assistance. Now is the time for the facilitator to assist the families in a more direct way, still always asking permission to come into the family boundaries. Now pass out Exercise 8-A.

Application of Developmental Models to the Family System

These developmental models are used in three ways:

1. To allow the parents to gather conceptual information regarding the way that human development progresses from birth. The parents will acquire

information on human development from reading the developmental descriptions in the evaluation assessments, in addition to the explanation in class presentations.

2. To assist the participants in internalizing the locus of control. The parents are already learning how to look inside and see what they think. An adult parent is in charge of thinking and evaluating the children, enlarging their cognitive scope. In the early moral and psychosocial development definitions, they will see the need for all the family members to receive the developmental permissions as a precursor to responsible living.

3. To identify areas of transgenerational dysfunction. The parents evaluate their children and then evaluate themselves. The female parents are usually able to grasp the material and quickly complete the evaluations of the family members first. Any male parent can sit next to the female parent, if both are present. Emphasis is put on the strength of the family to build what society and family history may have denied.

It is important for adults to learn about the various developmental stages of children. If the developmental stages are understood, parents will not make mistakes in judging the reasons behind some of the behaviors of their children. A child may behave in a certain way that would have a different meaning if the child were older. For instance, a child who is learning to be independent may seem to be "trying to take over"; but, in actuality, the child may be acting appropriately for that particular stage of development.

Another reason it is important to understand developmental stages is that one stage normally builds upon the previous stages. If the first stage is not successfully completed, the child will not have the skills to successfully complete the following stages. Many adults, especially in cases of substance abuse that has extended over generations, have not passed through some, or parts of some, of the developmental stages. Failure to complete development can become the source of a dysfunctional behavioral pattern that feels normal in that particular family, setting up a pattern of addiction for a child at a very early age. In older children and adults, the developmental conceptual information can be introduced cognitively. Then the stages can often be passed through by understanding the conceptual information regarding development.

To begin the exercise with the families, look in more detail at the cognitive, social, psychosocial, and moral developmental stages. Explain to the parents that everyone will go through each developmental stage description together.

Moving into the Meeting Environment

Objectives *(1 hour and 20 minutes)*

1. **Introduction of Background Information for Developmental Evaluation of the Family by the Facilitator (35 minutes)**

   Exercise 8-A Developmental Evaluation of the Family

   An adult (usually the female) will evaluate the family members.

2. **Break (10 minutes)**

3. **Introduction of Affirmation Ovals by Facilitator (35 minutes)**

   Exercise 8-B Affirmation Ovals

Exercise 8-A

Developmental Evaluation of the Family

Here is your opportunity to see where everyone is according to development. This is an opportunity to find developmental arrests that may be traveling through the family line, being helped by some of the communication that was discovered in the Communications study in Chapter 7. Remember that we are not just the age we say right now, but are really 1, 2, 3, 4, and so forth. (These stages may be summarized versions of the actual information from the authors of origin.)

Cognitive Stages—Piaget

0-2 years. Gradually, infants can tell the difference between their physical bodies and the world. They begin to understand that when mother disappears, it does not mean that she is gone forever; that is, when an object goes out of sight, it still exists.

2-7 years. Children think and speak according to what they pick up with their senses. They do not understand systems yet. They center on their own point of view and use a large amount of egocentric speech. They cannot coordinate two points of view or take into account more than one dimension of an object at a time.

7-12 years. Children now can make inferences that go beyond the information given. They can put two different pieces of information together and make an inference from the blended information. They can put information into categories and put information into order. Reasoning is limited to what is familiar and known to the child.

12 years and above. Adolescents begin to think in terms of possibilities. They see reality, but know there may be more to life than meets the eye. They have ideas and try to prove them.

It is important to understand the cognitive stages, so behavior appropriate to a child's age can be recognized. Sometimes a child's motives are questioned, even when the child is not able to be consciously manipulative due to the immaturity of his or her cognitive development.

Social Stages—Selman

3-6 years. Children use physical remedies to handle personal problems. They confuse what they think with what others think. Easy frustration leads to hitting, etc.

5-9 years. Children learn that what they think is not necessarily what others think. They realize that other people may feel differently in a given situation. They also understand that behavior can be caused by different motives in different people.

7-12 years. Children can understand others' viewpoints of them and know that others can get information about themselves through their viewpoints, also. This makes it possible for children to understand another person's intentions.

10-15 years. Children can stand apart and understand what is going on between people. They can coordinate their own perspectives with those of others. Also, they can realize that others can do the same about them.

12 years and above. Adolescents have the ability to see things from a national point of view. They can understand legal systems, moral ethics, and what is considered the conventional thing to do.

Psychosocial Stages—Erikson

0-1 years—trust versus mistrust. If people who are known to the infant consistently provide for the basic physical and emotional needs, the infant will develop a sense of trust. If these needs are not met, the result is an attitude of mistrust toward the world, especially toward interpersonal relationships.

1-3 years—autonomy versus shame and doubt. The main struggle at this age is, "Is it all right for me to rely on my judgment and find out that I can do lots of different things? Will I be shamed and always doubt if I am doing the 'right' thing if I become 'too' independent?" The child needs to explore and experiment, to make mistakes, and to test limits. If parents do not let the child think, act independently, and misinterpret the quest for independence as willful disobedience, the child cannot learn to deal with the world.

4-6 years—initiative versus guilt. Children need to learn competence and initiative. Through selecting activities that they like, they will develop a positive view of themselves and learn to follow through on their projects. If they are not allowed to make decisions, they feel guilty whenever they take the initiative. They learn not to lead and allow others to choose for them.

6-12 years—industry versus inferiority. Children need to expand their understanding of the world, continue to learn about sex-role identity, and learn the skills that it takes to succeed in school. Children need to learn to set and achieve personal goals.

12-18 years—identity versus role confusion. Adolescence is a time of transition between childhood and adulthood. Adolescents test limits, break dependent ties, and establish new identities. This is very important because it allows adolescents to become individual personalities in their own right. They work hard to clarify their own definition of themselves, to find life goals, and to discover meaning in life. Failure to achieve a sense of personal identity results in role confusion.

It is also important to know the developmental stages that Erikson observed which adults may go through as they pass through the life cycle. Below are listed some of their stages and the developmental tasks that are undertaken at each step. It is important for the health of a family that the adults continue to advance through the developmental stages so that all needs in the family can be considered.

18-35 years—intimacy versus isolation. Adults learn at this time to form intimate relationships. Failure to achieve intimacy can lead to alienation and isolation.

35-60 years—generativity versus stagnation. To go beyond self and family and to get involved in helping the next generation is an important developmental task at this time. People begin to adjust to any discrepancies between former dreams and the present actual accomplishments. If there is a failure to achieve a sense of productivity, people become psychologically stagnant and cease to grow.

60+ years—integrity versus despair. At this time in later life, people do a life review. If they can look back on life with few regrets and feel personally worthwhile, they will have a sense of achievement and feel that they have accomplished something in this life. Looking back and having a sense of failure about who they are and what they have accomplished can lead to feelings of despair, hopelessness, guilt, resentment, and self-rejection.

Moral Stages—Kohlberg

Stage 1. Individuals obey to avoid punishment. Rules for how to behave remain on the outside and are not internalized by individuals.

Stage 2. Individuals obey to get rewards. Rules for how to behave remain on the outside—not internalized by individuals.

Stage 3. Individuals obey out of loyalty to their families and other groups such as church groups. They obey to preserve relationships. Behavior norms are an important part of how people personally think they should be.

Stage 4. Individuals obey because of duty and responsibility. They obey to keep the social order of the national system together.

Stage 5. Individuals have a commitment to the democratic process for making and changing laws, as well as to a social behavior contract and individual rights.

Stage 6. People think civil disobedience is acceptable in order to protest unjust laws that violate universal ethics. The principle of right and wrong takes precedence over obeying the unjust law.

Begin to introduce these developmental concepts to your children, verbally and by modeling them. For instance, begin to reward your child in very concrete ways like using a star chart (stage 2) instead of punishing (stage 1). By building a sense of family pride and finding the child an accepting peer group, the child can understand what it means to obey to preserve relationships (stage 3). By advancing through the moral stages, children are moving the locus of control from outside to inside. The rules become part of the individual and a conscience is formed. By understanding the developmental stages and learning the skills involved at each level, we can give ourselves "permission" to grow into fully functioning adults.

Look at the Developmental Stages Chart. Under each of the following headings, determine where you think each one of your children belongs, and then evaluate the adults in the family. If information is needed on the stages, a quick review can be found on the page that follows the Developmental Stages Chart.

Developmental Stages Chart

Age	Cognitive Stage	Social Stage	Psychosocial Stage	Moral Stage
0	0-2. Learn to tell difference between physical bodies and world. Begin to understand when object goes out of sight, it still exists.		0-1. *Trust vs. Mistrust.* If basic needs are met, individual develops basic trust level. If physical, nurturance needs are not met, individual becomes mistrustful.	*Stage 1.* Individuals obey to avoid punishment. Rules for how to behave remain on outside and are not internalized by individual.
1				
2	2-7. Think and speak according to what they pick up with senses. Do not understand systems yet. Center on own point of view; use large amount of egocentric speech. Cannot coordinate two points of view or take into account more than one dimension at a time.		1-3. *Autonomy vs. Shame and Doubt.* Main struggle is learning to rely on own judgment, finding out if "too much" independence will result in being shamed, or, if ok to explore, experiment.	
3		3-6. Use physical remedies to handle personal problems. Confuse what they think with what others think. Easily frustrated, which leads to hitting, biting, etc.		
4				*Stage 2.* Individuals obey to get rewards. Rules for how to behave remain on outside—not internalized by individual.
5			4-6. *Initiative vs. Guilt.* Children learn competence, initiative. Need to select activities they like so will develop positive view of selves and learn to follow through on projects. If not allowed to make decisions, will feel guilty when they take initiative; will learn to let others lead and choose for them.	
6		5-9. Learn what they think is not necessarily what others think. Realize others may feel differently about same situation. Understand behavior can be caused by different motives in different people.		
7	7-12. Learn to make inferences that go beyond information given. Can put two pieces of information together and draw inferences from information given. Can put information into categories and into order. Reasoning limited to what is familiar and known to child.			
8		7-12. Can understand others' viewpoints of them and know that others can get information from their viewpoints as well. This makes it possible for children to understand another person's intentions.		*Stage 3.* Individuals obey out of loyalty to families and other groups such as church, teams, etc. They obey to preserve relationships. Behavior norms are important part of how people personally think individuals should be.
9				
10			6-12. *Industry vs. Inferiority.* Need to expand understanding of world, continue to learn about sex-role identity. Learn skills needed to succeed in school. Need to learn to set and achieve personal goals.	
11		10-15. Can stand apart and understand what is going on between people. They can coordinate their own perspectives with those of others. Also, know others can do the same about them.		
12	12- . Adolescents begin to think in terms of possibilities. See reality, but know there may be more to life than meets the eye. They have ideas and try to prove them out.			
13			12-18. *Identity vs. Role Confusion.* Adolescence is a time of transition between childhood and adulthood. They test limits, break dependent ties, establish new identities. This is very important in becoming individuals in own right. Work hard to clarify own definition of self, to find life goals, discover meaning to life.	
14		12- . Adolescents have ability to see things from national point of view, understand legal systems, moral ethics, and what is considered the conventional thing to do.		*Stage 4.* Individuals obey because of duty and responsibility. They obey to keep social order of national system together.
15				
16				
17				
18				

Note: The period of inpatient treatment for this patient was six years.

1. **As a parent, what new ideas can you use for your own personal growth?**

___

___

___

2. **Now that you have a picture of stage development, what are some new ideas of understanding that you can use in raising your child?**

___

___

___

Facilitator's Note: **Exercise 8-B—The Affirmation Ovals**

Have the parents choose the first child sitting on the left of the male parent. Designate this as the "affirmation chair" and pull the chair out some from the table. Have one adult in the family in charge of the developmental pages for each child. Find the child's developmental evaluation. Look at the developmental category that shows the youngest level. Find the affirmations that relate to each age of development from the cognitive, social, psychosocial, and moral development sheets for each child and adult as they take their place in the affirmation chair. Pass the affirmation page around the table and let every person at the table affirm the person who has been chosen. Go on to the next person seated to the left. They must get up and sit in the "affirmation chair." (If someone refuses, don't let it become an issue. Let them stay in their chair.) The adults can take turns finding the youngest developmental level and select the affirmations for the person now sitting in the "affirmation chair." They continue selecting the affirmations for each person until everyone, including the parents, in the family has been affirmed by the family.

Ask the parents to continue this throughout the week and ask other members if they would take the leadership on one day to make sure the process gets started. The developmental information needs to remain with the adults and not be shared. Ask the adults to over time not only match the affirmations to the individual needs of the family but also get in touch with the affirmations in general in order to begin sharing a few affirmations equally in the family. Remind the adults present that saying the affirmations to themselves is strongly recommended. Ask the families to bring back to the next meeting creative ways their families used the Affirmation Ovals.

Affirmation Ovals

The following pages contain the Affirmation Ovals for Clarke and Dawson's *Growing Up Again* (1998, pp. 218-242). These exercises are recommended for everyone attending the *Uncapping Family Wisdom* program. Since most families have some transgenerational dysfunction, a good place to begin is to say the affirmations to your child; then, say the affirmations to yourself.

Exercise 8-B The Affirmation Ovals

Today we are going to do an exercise to learn how to affirm each person and make sure that they have all the developmental permissions they need to develop fully as a person. Later, the parents may want to study the Ovals more carefully. Be sure to give the permissions—and also *say* them—to yourself, if you feel that this may be an area where you need the same affirmation.

Prenatal Stage—Becoming Affirmations From Conception to Birth

I celebrate that you are alive.

Your needs and safety are important to me.

We are connected and you are whole.

You can make healthy decisions about your experiences.

You can be born when you are ready.

Your life is your own.

I love you just as you are.

Prenatal One—Being Affirmations From Birth to 6 Months

I am glad that you are alive.

You belong here.

What you need is important to me.

I am glad you are you.

You can grow at your own pace.

You can feel all of your feelings.

I love you and I care for you willingly.

Stage Two—Doing Affirmations From 6 to 18 Months

You can explore and experiment and I will support and protect you.

You can use all of your senses when you explore.

You can do things as many times as you need to.

You can know what you know.

You can be interested in everything.

I like to watch you initiate and grow and learn.

I love you when you are active and when you are quiet.

Stage Three—Thinking Affirmations From 18 Months to 3 Years

I'm glad you are starting to think for yourself.

It's okay for you to be angry, and I won't let you hurt yourself or others.

You can say no and push and test limits as much as you need to.

You can learn to think for yourself and I will think for myself.

You can think and feel at the same time.

You can know what you need and ask for help.

You can become separate from me and I will continue to love you.

Fourth Stage—Identity and Power Affirmations From 3 to 6 Years

- You can explore who you are and find out who other people are.
- You can be powerful and ask for help at the same time.
- You can try out different roles and ways of being powerful.
- You can learn the results of your behavior.
- All of your feelings are okay with me.
- You can learn what is pretend and what is real.
- I love who you are.

Fifth Stage—Structure Affirmations From 6 to 12 Years

You can think before you say yes or no and learn from your mistakes.

You can trust your intuition to help you decide what to do.

You can find a way of doing things that works for you.

You can learn the rules that help you live with others.

You can learn when and how to disagree.

You can think for yourself and get help instead of staying in distress.

I love you even when we differ; I love growing with you.

Sixth Stage—Identity, Sexuality, and Separation Affirmations—From 12 to 19 Years

You can know who you are and practice skills for independence.

You can learn the difference between sex and nurturing and be responsible for your needs, feelings, and behaviors.

You can develop your own interests, relationships, and causes.

You can learn to use old skills in new ways.

You can grow in your maleness or femaleness and still be dependent at times.

I look forward to knowing you as an adult.

My love is always with you. I trust you to ask for my support.

Seventh Stage— Interdependence Affirmations—Adults

Your needs are important.

You can be uniquely yourself and honor the uniqueness of others.

You can be independent and interdependent.

You can expand your commitments to your own growth, to your family, your friends, your community, and to all humankind.

You can build and examine your commitments to your values and causes, your roles, and your tasks.

You can be responsible for your contributions to each of your commitments.

You can be creative, competent, productive, and joyful.

You can trust your inner wisdom.

You can say your hellos and goodbyes to people, roles, dreams, and decisions.

You can finish each part of your journey and look forward to the next.

Your love matures and expands.

You are lovable at every age.

Eighth Stage—Integration Toward Death

You can grow your whole life through.

You can look upon the process of dying as a natural transition.

You can make your preparations for leaving and die when you are ready.

You can celebrate the gifts you have received and the gifts you have given.

You deserve the support that you need.

You can share your wisdom in your way.

You are lovable just the way you are.

References

Carroll, J. (1964). *Language and thought.* London, UK: Prentice-Hall.

Clarke, J., & Dawson, C. (1998). *Growing up again.* New York: Hazelden Press, Inc.

Defense mechanism. (2008, August 29). *New World Encyclopedia.* Retrieved 18:09, June 22, 2010 from http://www.newworldencyclopedia.org/entry/Defense_mechanism?oldid =794483.

Erikson, E. (1982). *The life cycle completed.* New York: Norton.

Hartmann, H., & Kris, E. (1945). The Genetic Approach in Psychoanalysis, *Psychoanal. Study Child* 1:11-30.

Kohlberg, L. (1981). *Essays on moral development: Vol. 1.* The philosophy of moral development. New York: Harper & Row.

Kohlberg, L. (1984). *Essays on moral development: Vol. 2.* The philosophy of moral development. New York: Harper & Row.

Korzybski, A. (2000). *Science and sanity: an introduction to non-Aristotelian systems and general semantics,* 5th edition. Brooklyn, NY: Institute of General Semantics.

Piaget, J. (1971). *The construction of reality in the child* (M. Cook, trans.). New York: Ballantine (original work published 1936).

Selman, R. (1971). Taking another's perspective: role-taking development in early childhood. *Child Development, 42,* 1721-1734.

Selman R. (1976). A developmental approach to interpersonal and moral awareness in young children: some educational implications of levels of social perspective-taking. In T. C. Hennessy (Ed.), *Value and moral development.* New York: Holt, Rinehart & Winston.

In Chapter 9...

In Chapter 9, the family members will have the opportunity to enter a testing ground where the adventures in application bring together what they have learned in previous meetings. This chapter indirectly furnishes a review of Chapters 6, 7, and 8 and introduces management theory, especially as the theory allows for productivity which depends upon the motivational level of the family. Business management theory is applied to the home environment, and the facilitators lead the first management meeting, which is conducted in a supportive environment. The families will have an opportunity to evaluate and understand their own work environment, their family-of-origin leadership styles, and their feelings about management in general. Praise and criticism are investigated as to their usefulness, and encouragement is introduced as a productive alternative. Ranging from externalizing responsibility to an exaggerated internalizing of responsibility, the styles of the individuals in the family can be carefully observed and explained to the individuals involved. In this way, home management can serve as a normalization process for children who have formed extreme habits or extreme views of responsibility.

CHAPTER 9

THE TESTING GROUND—ADVENTURES IN APPLICATION

Facilitator's Note: **The information and the exercises in Chapter 9 will take two meetings to cover. Using these exercises, the families apply what the program has prepared them to do. They enter the adventure of application, using what they have learned about their family language and development to advance into the testing ground of home management. This chapter follows a slightly different format than the other chapters in *Uncapping Family Wisdom*. For best time management, the facilitator takes more leeway in how to direct the exercises. Combined with motivational assessment, the affirmations for developmental permissions at the end of Chapter 8 empower the leaders of the home to manage and to subdue the environment of the home.**

Chapter 9 provides hands-on instruction on how to manage a family residence, demonstrating a very practical application of management theory used in professional settings. In order to succeed with a practical application of management theory in the home setting, the emphasis is on combining the features of the family identified so far—the characteristics of a strong family, the family-semantic patterns, and the developmental information of the family members.

Chapter 9 introduces the idea of productivity and its relationship to motivation (Exercise 9-A). Also, encouragement and its correlation to criticism will be discussed. The aspect of encouragement, replacing praise, will yield a perspective on building self-confidence rather than depending upon approval by others (Exercises 9-B and 9-C). Problem solving (Exercise 9-D) will be the final skill learned in the first week of trying to apply the management principles. Then the family will begin to actually make a plan for household management using Exercise 9-D, Exercise 9-E, and Exercise 9-F.

The process of attempting successful home management will very likely highlight some negative behavior, which will be the focus of the next chapter, The Art of Modifying Behavior.

Leadership Styles

In this chapter, the families investigate leadership styles to see how different styles have impacted the family life. The families take what they have learned from the first three units, using these skills to determine the leadership style found in the family system. Taking a bird's eye view of the situation, they determine which style of management to adopt that will help them learn to work together in the home environment.

When the twelve characteristics of a strong family are examined, new conceptual information is introduced to the family. At first, the characteristics are just new ideas that, when tried out, become a new part of family interactions. Little by little, members of the family unit begin to learn what respect for human personhood actually means. The members learn that some families know how to treat one another with dignity and that they can learn to show respect to one another also. The members learn not to feel ashamed for not knowing this new information before now, understanding that no one can be held responsible for knowing information or behaviors to which they have never exposed.

Then, general semantics information allows the family to look at the interactions in their family communication. Some are able to identify their conflict style, which perhaps for a few generations, has been passed down through the family speaking pattern. The family learns that a pattern of the use of certain words can lead to conflict. If the pattern is not corrected, and family members allow insult to occur in the family communication, the dignity of personhood is threatened. As these patterns of conflict are cued by having the family members name the pattern, mutual respect among family members grows.

When the family looks at the human developmental stages and evaluates the family system, they find how the linguistic legacy has affected development in the family members. They begin to see that because the legacies are identified, the legacies can be changed. As the family begins to interject developmental permissions into the family speaking pattern, they learn to say what they mean, taking the time to use a fact, inference, opinion, and judgment sequence of communication. Affirmations that are appropriate for every stage of development have been included at the end of Chapter 8, so that parents will know what affirmations children needed to receive at each age. At the same time, the parents are urged to also give the affirmations to themselves to provide any parts of missing developmental permissions that did not come their way as children.

At this point in the program, as the family continues to receive support, the program now goes to a testing ground. This will show that when the family attempts to work together, they can use the changes they have made in the program to see and experience how the problems they laid aside will try to come back. As the family begins to practice a different style of leadership in their household management, they will also be attempting to use what they have learned to enter into a full-fledged adventure of application. Probably, when the actual work process begins, there will be some negative behavior exposed. The parents have many skills that can be used to intervene in the negative patterns: dealing with communication errors, noticing developmental arrests, giving statements of affirmation, or using the Plan of Action Worksheet. Now, leadership training will be added, including a problem-solving exercise.

The second week, the family will have an opportunity to do executive planning. They will have a real management meeting complete with attitudes for successful management. They will create a household management plan with which to experiment. The cognitive training on how to complete goals will be reiterated. Perfection is not expected; but for now, the individuals in the families have access to people and written guides on how to proceed.

Plan of Action Worksheet

Plan of Action	Goals	Steps to Goal	First Step: When will you take it?	Barriers to Goal	How will you overcome barriers?	How will you check progress?
Zone 1	Responsibilities					
Zone 2						
Zone 3						
Zone 4						

The attempt at working together may have revealed the need for behavior modification, as some behavior might pose a hindrance to the process required to meet the goal of effective household management. If the interventions in this chapter are not successful, the next chapter, The Art of Modifying Behavior, will directly address resistant behavior.

Moving into the Meeting Environment

Objectives *(3 hours)*

First Meeting—Management Preparation Meeting (1 hour and 30 minutes)

Review of what has been learned so far in the *Uncapping Family Wisdom* program (15 minutes)

1. **Introduction and Facilitation of Leadership Styles**

   Exercise 9-A Leadership Styles (20 minutes)

   The family will discover what leadership style is used in the workplace of family members. Productivity and its relation to motivation will be explored.

   Exercise 9-B Leadership Styles and the Characteristics of a Strong Family (20 minutes)

   The family will discover that some leadership styles, due to their compatibility with natural human development are more likely to succeed.

2. **Break** ***(10 minutes)***

3. **Transitioning to Empowerment through Encouragement and Problem Solving**

   Exercise 9-C Encouragement vs. Criticism in Leadership Styles (15 minutes)

   The family will understand that encouragement develops independent cooperation without the negative effects of being controlled by another.

   Exercise 9-D Problem Solving for the Family (10 minutes)

   Learning problem-solving skills will allow the family to participate in solving the problems that surface in the management of the home.

Second Meeting—Home Management Meeting (1 hour and 30 minutes)

1. **Working the Plan**

   Exercise 9-E Creating a Household Management Plan (25 minutes)

   The family will create a household management plan, where the home is owned by all and everyone has an opportunity to practice good management techniques.

Exercise 9-F Attitudes for Successful Management (20 minutes)

The family learns that if everyone pitches in, creating a positive work climate, daily tasks will not be so overwhelming.

2. **Break (10 minutes)**

3. **The Family Management Meeting**

Exercise 9-G Having a Family Management Meeting (35 minutes)

The first family meeting is held within a community setting and consists of a mental planning time. The exercise is to be done in class and repeated at home to ensure the plan matches the reality of the home environment.

Facilitator's Note: **Get ready for action! Much hard work has been done learning all the skills that will be needed for the action which takes place here in Chapter 9. Hopefully, the goal sheet introduced in Chapter 6 and included in this chapter has been used in the home setting by now, and the process of dynamic cognitive reasoning is becoming a part of the family dynamics.**

Encourage the families to go online and find chore sheets and other helps they may need to organize their own home. As a facilitator, your responsibility is to expose the family to high-level practical management techniques, which will offer the nuts and bolts of organizing a home and teach basic management skills, which will enhance the future prospects of the members of the family.

During the exercises in this chapter, we will have an opportunity to see what problems begin to occur in trying to achieve a goal of working as a team toward home management. Using what has already been learned in Chapters 6, 7, and 8, the family will try to identify the source of the problem. For instance, can the source of the problem be found in the information contained in the list of the characteristics of a strong family? Can a reversion to an old semantic style of the family be the problem? Perhaps a lack of a developmental permission or an arrested area of development in a family member may be the source of the difficulties in trying to work together. Perhaps someone in the family system needs an affirmation.

Until the members of the family understand how to apply what they have learned in the earlier units to these action-oriented applications, the facilitator and the assistants should become more available during the family exercises. Orienting a family to information in a particular unit may be all that is necessary. The important thing is to let the family discover as much as they can for themselves, avoiding giving them a bottom-line answer that may void the necessary process of discovery and integration.

First Meeting—Management Preparation

Facilitator's Note: To begin, hand out Exercise 9-A. Read the Leadership Styles page, and then let the family work together on the exercise. Allow the adults to share their stories regarding their experiences in the workplace and the experiences from their family of origin. This gives the adults a chance to share their life with their children and put things in perspective for themselves. Let the families work on the exercise alone; but be sure you and the assistants are available to help, in case difficulties arise.

The problem-solving exercise presents a criteria section and allows the families to consider the feelings of others, to take into account the timing and wisdom of a decision, and to understand how the decision may affect others.

The last exercise can be started in class. If the families have not finished the exercise, collect it and hand it out the next week to work on and discuss in class.

Exercise 9-A

Leadership Styles

Productivity is about the process of bringing something into view. When we are productive, we see that something is being made and we are able to see how it is being made. We see that the attitudes of those who supervise workers affect productivity.

The Importance of Motivation

People work more efficiently when they are motivated to work. Industrial psychologists have taken a close look at the motivations behind productivity. The psychologists developed three theories, Theory X, Theory Y, and Theory Z, that describe what type of supervision is thought to aid managers in increasing productivity. Robert Baron (1983) describes the three views in this way:

Theory X—The supervisors who adopt Theory X believe that most persons are lazy and irresponsible. Baron suggests that the supervisors believe that managers have to watch over these people carefully and provide them with direction and discipline. They believe that the reason that the workers need so much supervision is that they don't care about the organization's needs. The managers believe that the workers lack ambition and are selfish individuals. They believe that, in general, people are mostly unmotivated to work and do not care if they do a good job or not. Often, under Theory X, because of the attitude of management, unions form and workers go on strike.

Theory Y—The supervisors who adopt Theory Y have a more optimistic approach in that it suggests that under appropriate circumstances, employees are capable of working productively and even assuming responsibility. Theory Y is what is called the human-relations approach. It is believed that the employees do want to develop their skills in accord with the organization's needs. The workers usually are not expected to think creatively to increase their level of input in the company. The supervisors believe that it is up to the management to create the policies and motivational systems that will allow workers to develop their own potential. In return, the theory looks to the workers themselves to bring a positive attitude toward work and doing their jobs.

We find Theory Y in many sales positions, where the management sets the quota and provides rewards to those who make their quota. The management stays in control by setting the quotas and giving praise or withholding praise from the workers.

Theory Z—Theory Z is used in many large Japanese companies. The companies guarantee long-term employment, sometimes for life. They have concern for employees that extends beyond the work days, with outstanding benefits which give the employees a sense of belonging. In these companies, most decision-making is by consensus; that is, everyone participates in the decisions, not just the managers or the executives, but everyone. In return for the devotion and concern that the companies show to their employees, the Japanese workers give outstanding levels of commitment, motivation, and productivity. The Japanese workers understand how the organization works and know how to do many jobs within the organization. If someone becomes ill, another person on the team can temporarily be moved into the position. The manager is usually on the floor with the employees, not in a private room away from the workers.

Leadership Questions for Family Discussion

1. **For those who are employed: What leadership style operates in your workplace?**

____

____

____

2. **For those who are employed: What leadership style would you like to be in operation in your workplace? What would be the benefits?**

____

____

____

3. **For the adults: Looking back now, what leadership style was used in your family of origin?**

____

____

____

> ***Facilitator's Note:*** **Welcome the families. Introduce the exercise and explain to the families that they are to circle the management style that best suits the characteristic. This is a strong review of previous material that can reinforce the characteristics of a strong family. Let the families work alone, but remain available. You might do this together as a community and have the families vote and have some tell why they thought a strong family might choose a particular leadership style.**

Exercise 9-B

Leadership Styles and the Characteristics of a Strong Family

Characteristics of a strong family and efficient management styles are sometimes compatible; that is, they seem to fit together. Review the management styles of Theory X, Theory Y, and Theory Z. Circle the management style that best suits each characteristic of a strong family.

X Y Z 1. Strong families know how to work as a team. The family members are committed to one another. The family as a whole is committed to seeing that each member reaches his or her potential. The family as a whole is committed to see that no individuals in the family suffer, so that other members of the family can have exclusive entitlement to reach their full potential.

X Y Z 2. Strong families know how to set clear goals and are committed to the goals. Many people may know how to set individual goals, but goal setting will be more difficult within the family. A strong family looks for things that may be getting in the way of family unity.

X Y Z 3. Strong families tend to have communications that are clear. There is no message discrepancy between verbal and non-verbal messages. The family members have developed listening skills, and each family member can express what he or she wants and expect to be understood.

X Y Z 4. Strong families can respect differences. Differences are not regarded as an insult to a person's self-esteem. In contrast, each individual is able to freely comment and report on what he or she sees, feels, and hears.

X Y Z 5. Strong families operate under constructive forms of leadership and share most decision-making responsibilities. Each member of the family is free to express an opinion and therefore share in the decision-making process.

X Y Z 6. Strong families know how to show appreciation. This involves being able to recognize the positive aspects of others and to let them know that these qualities are valued. It also means that individuals in the family feel comfortable about receiving compliments themselves.

X Y Z 7. A strong family feels safe. They have developed a reasonable set of rules to offset problems involving power and control. Discipline is built into the family organization, and when something upsets the balance of the family, the control goes into operation. The family uses the rules as boundaries and becomes creative within these boundaries.

X Y Z 8. Strong families own their own problems and do not blame them on others. Individuals in the family know how to take responsibility for their own problems and how to enable the family to solve them.

X Y Z 9. Strong families use change as an opportunity for learning. They see the world as constantly changing and view problems as an opportunity for individuals to stretch and grow.

X Y Z 10. Strong families can demonstrate openness and trust because they know and use problem-solving techniques to handle conflict in the family. The family knows how to use a specialized techniques, "I messages" and "Reverse I-messages" that take into consideration how reality is viewed by each family member. How the emotional factors of the decision affect different family members is also considered.

X Y Z 11. Strong families have strong external boundaries. They understand the pressures that society places upon these boundaries and maintain the boundaries through family loyalties. They can identify external cultural problems that impinge upon the family boundaries and face them openly. The family moves the power of control into their family when the society is not providing firm boundaries of safety and well being.

X Y Z 12. Strong families understand the importance of having a positive family climate. When respect is lessening and hostility seems to be expanding, these families seek outside help in the form of counseling and/or support groups.

The characteristics of a strong family and good management skills fit together. This is because individuals have learned to assume responsibility for their jobs and can think for themselves without needing others to coax them into positive cooperative action. Positive cooperative action brings respect from others.

Facilitator's Note: **Discuss Exercise 9-B. Allow the families to share their results and ask for comments. Make the connection between the characteristics that reflect strong family traits and good management characteristics.**

Transition to empowerment through encouragement by presenting the following material on Encouragement versus Criticism in Leadership. Use personal examples to prompt interaction with the audience.

Exercise 9-C

Encouragement versus Criticism in Leadership

According to Nelson, there is no such thing as constructive criticism. She believes, "...it is a contradiction in terms. Constructive means to *build up*. Criticism means to *tear down*" (2006, p. 159). A person can separate his or her behavior from who he or she is. A person can know that one is not one's behavior. A person can learn to objectify one's behavior and can learn to control the behavior.

This does not mean that one shouldn't let others know there is room for improvement; however, criticism can only become constructive when a person has the mature skills to not internalize the criticism but rather to construct a change process from the information about what is wrong. Children *do not* have this ability and *neither do* some adults. Using criticism in a positive way *is a learned behavior developed from self-dependence*, which means that a person *can hear the information and separate out the fact, opinion, and judgment.*

We do not have to make others feel worse in order to enable them to do better. A better way is to use encouragement as a process. Theory X and Theory Y use the method of using power to make others feel worse or to wield the power to punish or reward them. Using power to make others feel worse or using power to reward others is not encouraging. Encouragement takes more time initially, but gets more lasting results. Encouragement grows as self-evaluation is supported with adequate training on what actually need to be given and received in communication in order to foster development. For instance, in order to know how to properly encourage others, a person has to know the difference between encouragement and praise.

Encouragement versus Praise

There's been much talk regarding the importance of building self-esteem in children. Praise does inspire some to improve their behavior; however, Nelson points out the dangers of praise:

> The problem is that they become *pleasers* and *approval "junkies."* These children (and later these adults) may develop self-concepts that are totally dependent on the opinions of others. Other children resent and rebel against praise, sometimes because they fear they can't compete with those who seem to get praise so easily. Even though initially the praise may seem to work, we must consider the long-range effects (2006, p. 157).

A Better Choice

A better long-range effect is encouragement, which leads to self-confidence, rather than dependence upon the approval of others. Encouragement requires mutual respect and interest in the child's point of view, and focuses on skill building toward self-confident independence. Remember, the rules of behavior can be inside the child (internalized), so that he or she can develop self-control and not always have to be controlled from the outside. The rules can be internalized. Encouragement does not have any elements of personal evaluation. Nelson (2006, p. 157) suggests asking yourself, "Would I make this comment to a friend?" Friends are usually considered equal, and we do not make patronizing praise statements to them. Here are some examples of encouragement versus praise:

Encouragement	Praise
"What do you think?"	"I like it."
"Talk to me about what I said."	"Good boy! You listened to me!"
"Thank you for helping."	"You are such a good boy."
"Who can show me the proper way to sit?"	"I like the way Sue is sitting."
"How do you feel that you did?"	"You did it right."
"I can see you enjoyed that!"	"I'm so proud of you."
"I appreciate your help!"	"I like the way you do that."

Which management style is more likely to contain the most statements of encouragement: Theory X, Theory Y, or Theory Z? ________________________________

Why? ________________________________

____

____

____

Exercise 9-D

Problem Solving for the Family

What movie should we go to? What game should we buy? Who is going to give up their room when Aunt Ida comes to visit? What dog should we get? These types of decisions have to do with change. Two of the characteristics of a strong family are

- Strong families use change as an opportunity for learning.
- Strong families can demonstrate openness and trust because they know and use problem-solving techniques to handle conflict in the family.

From time to time, all families have problems concerning change and must make some practical decisions. Problem solving helps the family learn to work as a team. It is also a great opportunity to send messages to the family regarding the importance of their input. Here are the five steps for problem solving in the family:

Define the problem. Make sure everyone understands and agrees on exactly what the problem is. You'd be surprised how many arguments begin because people are arguing about two different things. It is very important for people to understand clearly what the problem is. *The relational message is, What you think is important to me; you are important to me! You are important enough to have your needs expressed and heard. We can really learn to understand one another.*

Review all options. This is the time to write down all possible solutions to a problem in order to review them. Do not discount any option at this point, because sometimes the best solutions come from a combination of listed options. *The relational message is, I value your creative thinking and mind, and believe that together we can be even more creative in dealing with our common problem.*

Determine the criteria for selecting the best options. Determining criteria means that the option must fit in with the family belief system and values. The option must not be put into effect without thinking about the responsibility that will go with the option. *The relational message is, Are any of these options going to make anybody feel uncomfortable because of their beliefs, or values, or a shaky self-esteem? Does anyone have any hidden agendas (that we need to talk about first) that might make any of these options impractical?*

Select the best option. The selection is made based on the review of the options with the criteria. *The relational message is, I want you to have your needs satisfied. I want my needs satisfied. We don't have to deny our uniqueness. I think we all can "win." Let's think of how to do that.*

Implement the plan. During this stage of decision-making, a goal may be set to solve the problem, using your goal sheet from Characteristics of a Strong Family. *The relationship message: You and I are willing to make joint decisions and coordinate plans to help each other in getting our needs met.*

Problem Solving Worksheet

State the problem: ______________________________

____

____

____

List the options: ______________________________

____

____

____

What are the criteria for choosing the option?______________________________

____

____

____

Using the criteria above, what is the best option? ______________________________

____

____

____

How will the option be implemented, and when?______________________________

____

____

____

Review of option after trial period: Is the option working? If yes, proceed. If no, repeat the steps again. ______________________________

Second Meeting—Home Management Meeting

Facilitator's Note: **Directions for Exercise 9-E—Facilitator leads this introduction commenting and stopping for questions or comments. The facilitator goes through the Parent's Guide, stopping to comment either on the section about human nature or the responses from children or other adults that are designed to exhaust authority figures. The facilitator models methods of handling inappropriate behavior which may come up in this meeting, staying positive, enthusiastic, firm, and friendly.**

Exercise 9-E

Creating a Household Management Plan

Daily responsibilities are necessary for successful home management. They are a part of every person's life. If everyone pitches in, daily tasks need not be overwhelming or extremely time consuming. Some of the reasons that make home management difficult are

- The family members have not owned the home. The members believe they live there, but the home really belongs to someone else who has the responsibilities for home management and for doing household tasks.
- The family does not have an overall plan of action for household management.
- Responsibilities are not allocated fairly among the family members.
- The managers in the family are uncomfortable about the other members assuming responsibility, perhaps because their family of origin did not have a plan of action and organization is a new idea that doesn't "feel" right.
- A standard is not in place for responsibilities, and the steps for each responsibility are not clearly defined.
- Either the standards for the responsibility task are too high, or the responsibilities are not age appropriate for certain members of the family.
- Passive and aggressive diversionary tactics are used by family members who do not understand the benefits of family cooperation in the Theory Z management style. The members resort to slowdowns, strikes, sidetracking, and verbal negativity found in the workers who are represented under Theory X. They do not own the responsibilities.
- The members feel that their schedules supersede the general community needs of the family.

Some reasons that keep homes from being organized successfully are listed above.

1. Which apply to your home management experience? ______________________

____

____

____

2. Can you think of any other reasons that make management of your home difficult?

____

____

____

> ***Facilitator's Note:*** **We have learned about leadership styles, the characteristics of a strong family, the difference between encouragement and criticism in leadership, and problem solving for the family. In this meeting, we are going to have the opportunity to put those topics to use. We will be creating a household management plan.**
>
> **Review the entire Parents' Guide with the families. They will need to look at the information again at home and keep the sheet as a reference in the future.**

Parents' Guide

When all family members do not cooperate in doing household tasks, parents often become resentful. They may feel that children should be "naturally" thoughtful and want to help with the workload. Unfortunately, this is very rare, but learning to cooperate and to share responsibilities are important skills for children to learn. Here are six ways to use encouragement in teaching household responsibilities (Dinkmeyer, 1997):

- Let everyone take turns being manager and trainer for the responsibilities they have mastered. Everyone needs to learn management skills. Some family members may need to partner with an older or more experienced person to learn management practices.
- Take time for training. Be very specific about expectations and use a written card for assignments. Let each family member make a list of what materials will be necessary for each task. Have carriers to hold the materials ready for each member.
- Instead of repeating an expectation, ask for information. "What is your understanding of what needs to be done?"
- Keep the atmosphere pleasant. Build on strengths, not weaknesses. Remember the management style needed for prime efficiency. When something is pointed out that was done well, family members will be more likely to want to do better. Remember to ask, "How do you think you did?"

- Let the family members think for themselves. Ask questions like "What do you think needs to be done before the kitchen is clean?" and "What about the glasses on the table?"
- Give yourself and family members the courage to be imperfect. Teach yourself and your child to be accepting of mistakes as opportunities to learn. Without problems, there would be no solutions. Think of the training as a process, understanding that habits need approximately 21 days to stabilize. Comment on successes and enjoy progress together.

Having a Family Meeting to Create a Positive Work Climate

Let each person determine the attitudes that may keep him or her from participating fully. A parent can take the lead by owning a personal "negative" emotion and telling how he or she plans to change the negative emotion. Affirm the positive responses and ignore the negative responses.

Handle resistance throughout the meeting by discussing human nature and the various methods people use to resist. Urge the members to learn to identify and own these methods in themselves. Discuss the terms "slowdowns," "strikes," and "side tracking." These are negative passive-aggressive behavior characteristics that are designed to exhaust authority figures. The family members must understand that they cannot resort to slowdowns, strikes, or side tracking to avoid responsibility or verbal negativity.

Ground rules are that the family must agree to own the fairly-defined responsibilities assigned to them, and family members cannot assume their schedules take precedence over family responsibilities. In case of disagreements, go back to Chapter 7, Communication of the Family System, to determine the cause of the conflict and to see if this is part of the family speaking pattern interfering with family progress.

***Facilitator's Note:* Look at Exercise 9-F—Attitudes for Successful Management. Urge the family members to think about their plan of action step. Something needs to be done before having a management meeting. Negative attitudes may come from past experiences, so emphasize the positive attitudes as the family groups share. If time does not allow completion in class, send Exercise 9-F home. Try to work through naming the goal and then work through the first goal with the families, if possible.**

Exercise 9-F
Attitudes for Successful Management

Negative Attitude	Positive Attitude

Facilitator's Note: The first family meeting is held within the community meeting. All families will be working quietly at the same time. Please encourage the assistants to watch for difficulty in a group. If the group cannot solve the problem and the assistant cannot solve the problem, open it up to the wisdom of the community.

Encourage the parents to get the children engaged in forethought about what the family will be doing later at home. Now is the mental planning time. Let them determine zones and think out the chores and cleaning supplies that will be needed for each zone.

Supplies needed for this meeting: Four sets of different-colored index-sized post-it notes for each family and pencils for all. Use smaller sized post-it notes for ADD or ADHD family members. Hand out 11" × 14" Plan of Action Worksheets to each family.

This exercise is to be done in class and repeated at home to assure the plan matches the reality at home. The facilitator and the aides need to walk around in class and encourage the families, waiting to help until they are asked.

Exercise 9-G

Having a Family Management Meeting

Organizing the Meeting

Think of what usually happens when the family tries to work together. Determine the attitudes that will need to be replaced by a positive attitude in order to develop a positive family climate and cooperation in household tasks. Use the Plan of Action worksheet to lead the family members into a discussion as to how the home can be run more efficiently.

Discuss what you have learned about the XYZ management theories and stress that everyone is going to have a turn at learning management techniques. Discuss the reasons that keep your home from being managed successfully. Be sure that all of the reasons that the family listed are included in the discussion. Knowing that behavior will be "cued" is very important to creating a peaceful setting in the home. Behavior is cued by naming the behavior, such as staging slowdowns, detouring from the work, becoming busy with activities not on the agenda, not working up to par, and picking arguments. Work all the way across the Plan of Action Sheet to determine the steps for each goal. The zones represent a group of rooms assigned, which will require independent goals.

How to Proceed

- Walk through the home mentally, using the Plan of Action Sheet; divide the home into four different cleaning zones, and put someone in charge of supervising each zone as the zone leader. Then, a parent will take the leaders on a mental tour of all of the zones. (The personal cleaning of individual bedrooms is included with the duties in cleaning zones.) Go over the leadership styles to make sure the "middle management" zone leaders understand the style that is appropriate to use when they begin their leadership at home.

- For the first management experience at home, the family goes on a tour together to all the zones, one at a time. A parent will walk around with everyone in the family and let the zone members discover the duties in each room of their zones with others observing. The parent will explain the steps for fulfilling each responsibility. The zone leader will write the responsibilities on a colored index card. (Provide a separate index card color to each zone leader.)
- Then go on to the next zone and repeat the process until all zones have been covered. Then have the zones separate and go to their own zones. Let the members of the team try out different room responsibilities to find out how long they actually take. The zone leader then writes the times on the back of the card and the total time for each room. To end, let the teams set time schedules for formal work sessions based on the total time it will take to clean their zone. The parent keeps the cards for the zone leaders the first time.
- Let the zone leaders assign pairs for working. Pair off younger children with a parent or an older child.
- Have the zone leaders make a list of supplies that will be needed for each zone. Let the groups in the four zones try out their own plans the first week. Encourage everyone to use some of the skills they have learned and try to let them work out the problems themselves.

Small children or children with attention deficit disorder (ADD) or attention deficit hyperactivity disorder (ADHD) sometimes work better if the children can write the directions for the steps of the chore themselves on a slip of paper with an adhesive backing. When they complete the task they can remove the paper, putting the direction slips in a storage place for later use.

As the groups try out their plans, let them report back any changes in their assessments. Openly discuss all difficulties in a positive atmosphere. Affirm anything that you can, remembering to comment on process over result. After one month, exchange areas by having each team move up one number with the top number taking the lowest number. Each team who had one zone then trains the next team on how to do the chores in that zone.

Don't underestimate how practical experience with the Plan of Action Sheet can extend into leadership knowledge in employment settings of the future. Consider

- having a *plan of action* for an overall definition,
- setting *goals* for the plan of action,
- finding out the *first step,*
- determining *when you will take the first step* to get the action started,
- giving some forethought to the *barriers to the goal,*
- planning *how you will overcome the barriers*, and then
- taking responsibility for being accountable by planning *how you will check your progress.*

The ordering of household responsibilities results in the integration of time-management techniques. Finally, when the children leave home, they will have self-confidence because they have learned to manage their physical lives and have learned how to live in a community with others. As the parents learn to share responsibility and not feel guilty about doing so, they are modeling appropriate roles and gifting their children with management skills that can become a very positive legacy.

> ***Facilitator's Note:*** **Use your judgment regarding the next meeting. Hand out a note that will advise the parents that the next meeting will be mostly a lecture time with only one exercise. The parents can use their judgment about what children will attend.**

References

Baron, R. (1983). *Behavior in organizations.* Newton, MA: Allyn and Bacon, Inc.

Beavers, W. (1977). *Psychotherapy and growth: family systems perspective.* New York: Brunner/Mazel.

Dinkmeyer, D., McKay, G. & Dinkmeyer, D., Jr. (1997). *The parent's handbook* (from the STEP program). Bowling Green, KY: STEP Publishers.

Nelson, J. (2006). *Positive discipline.* New York: Ballantine Books.

In Chapter 10...

The problems the families found in home management are often the same problems managers find in office and industrial environments. Communication, developmental arrests, and unsatisfactory management styles often show the types of training that managers and workers had in their early home environment. Helping children internalize their locus of control and gain the confidence in knowing how to take responsibility will enhance their chances of success in the future.

Isolating the behaviors that helped or hindered progress is important. Resistance to progress, failure to accept responsibility, taking too much responsibility, and problems with becoming an uninvited assistant to the parents (a behavior that first-born children often display) can lead to feelings of frustration when trying to organize the household. The authority figures feel forced to take control, goals are sabotaged, and some even give up, feeling drained by the negative dynamics. By learning to use self-reflexiveness and stepping outside the situation, parents can anticipate reactionary behavior and continue to use their ability to state their feelings about the behavior they see. They can point out family dynamics that need to change, revealing the power that comes with having words that describe situations.

The Stern Model of Discipline, introduced in this chapter, uses three essential components: modeling, separation, and communication. These components allow a child to learn physical, emotional, and verbal self-control. Regarding any misbehavior, the child has six points to discuss:

- the behavior and why was it a problem,
- the "being the boss" issue,
- the need the child was trying to meet,
- the nature of the appropriate behavior,
- the feelings that got out of control, and
- how the child should manage the next time the dynamic occurs.

The discussion regarding misbehavior ends with positive feedback and a hug. With the application of the Stern Model of Discipline, it's important to remember that anger and rage may have been a part of the parents' childhood and may be ready to surface again when similar family dynamics occur. This model allows the child and the parent to stay in control.

An appropriate model of discipline creates a *conscious will*, which is described as the "self-portrait" of the mind. The experiences of conscious will, which is an authorship of *emotion* that anchors self-perception, will serve as a personal guide to authorship of *action*. The direction of the emotions, which leads to actions of relevant behavior, becomes a "self-portrait" in the mind, regarding who a person is and how a person behaves (Wegner, 2008, pp. 222-223).

CHAPTER 10

THE ART OF MODIFYING BEHAVIOR

The Meeting: Determining Who Will Attend

Facilitator's Note: **Depending on the population, this meeting might be for parents only, to discuss the problems they found in the home management exercise. On the other hand, sometimes it is very helpful for all family members to hear the same thing at the same time. The community setting can help set the standard for behavioral norms. In some cases, such as problems with adult/child role reversal, the attendance of the entire family might be in order. The session with all the family members present should provide an atmosphere where a therapist is lending energy to the parents and labeling certain behavior as inappropriate. If all the family has attended scheduled therapy sessions together to regain control in the home, or if the family is moving away from trauma organization, the family may want to attend together to hear the process of reasoning (plainly stated), concerning how unacceptable behavior will be handled.**

This chapter on The Art of Modifying Behavior follows the leadership and management information in the last chapter. The family has had an opportunity to work together at home and probably has gotten a close look at which behaviors are going to have to be modified in order for the family to be able to successfully work together. This is exactly what is needed, because now the families can understand how to actually apply parts of the program to what they have experienced as a result of trying to work together. It is now time for patience and perseverance in applying knowledge to real-life experience. The attempt at working together may have revealed the need for behavior modification, as some behavior might pose a hindrance to the process required to meet the goal of effective household management.

Isolating the Behaviors that Helped or Hindered Progress in Home Management

The home arena is chosen to provide insight into what behavior needs changing. The family now can see and address any behavior that will hinder progress or prevent successful management of the home. The management principles are being applied in the home at present, but the same skills will be useful in the future for leadership in educational pursuits or in work settings.

Before behavior can be modified, a person has to see the behavior. What better place than in a home, where family members have to work together to manage the home! Change occurs when

- a person is exposed to new information,
- a person internalizes the information,
- cognitive process filters subjective reasoning, or
- a person puts the information that has been received into action.

A good example of using subjective reasoning in the completion of responsibilities is cleaning one's room only when one feels like it versus cleaning a room in an organized routine method that considers the needs of other family members. The family must recognize that all diversionary techniques that are used in the family must end. The results are judged by the completion of a plan.

Moving into the Meeting Environment

Objectives *(1 hour and 30 minutes)*

1. **Introduction to The Art of Modifying Behavior by the facilitator (20 minutes)**
   a. *Defining the goal of behavior modification in the program.*
   b. *Addressing old habits.*
   c. *Moving away from old patterns.*
   d. *Building trust during behavior modification.*

2. **Family Problems Found in Home Management (15 minutes)**
   Exercise 10-A Problems Found in Home Management

3. **Beginning Behavior Modification (5 minutes)**
   a. *Getting the developmental permission for initiative during behavior modification.*
   b. *Building the will and self-esteem during behavior modification.*

   Break (10 minutes)

4. **The Stern Model of Discipline (30 minutes)**
   a. *Modeling, separation, and communication.*
   b. *The "being the boss" issue.*

c. *Options for responding to feelings.*
d. *Giving positive feedback.*

5. **Family-Systems Application of the Stern Model of Discipline (5 minutes)**
   a. *Curbing inherited reactive traits.*

6. **Conscious Will—the Self-Portrait of the Mind (5 minutes)**
   a. *The conscious premeditation.*
   b. *Authorship of action—the authorship of emotion.*

Introduction: The Art of Modifying Behavior

Defining the Goal of Behavior Modification in the Program

Remember the stages of moral development? The punishment-and-reward stages were at an age where learning took place on a subjective level before more mature cognitive processes were in place. Now, the goal is to engage cognitive and personhood qualities in the behavior modification process, internalizing the locus of control to build self-discipline. When that happens, appropriate behavior is not simply chosen, but also the "why" behind the need for appropriate behavior is understood. Outside reinforcement of rewards or punishment may then become unnecessary, because not only is the conceptual information from the program integrated, but also reward-and-punishment reinforcements are integrated into the child in the form of responsible self-discipline. The locus of control can usually begin to be internalized early in development, perhaps around three to five years old. Internalizing the locus of control has advantages. To understand the process of the internalization of locus of control is desirable because as long as the parents contribute to the reward-or-punishment responsibility, the locus of control will remain externalized on the outside in the parents, causing

- a dynamic that forces them into a role of permanent reinforcers with children putting pressure on the parents to stretch the limits, and
- a dynamic that blocks the formation of self-discipline.

Before formally thinking about how to modify particular behavior patterns, what has been learned in the program is important to consider, because the integration and use of the information is the objective. When people come into the program, almost everyone is doing what has been known in the past. Most people did not come from family systems with knowledge of how to guide children so that they would pass through all the normal developmental stages. (Many people in most communities would not have such knowledge.) The expectation is that by understanding development, families can move confidently forward, enabled to influence the next generation who can receive, as a way of life, all of the developmental permissions.

If we had begun the program with a discussion of behavior modification, the danger would have been that attempts at modification of behavior might

- continue the power and control dynamics in a family;
- propagate an external locus of control rather than an internal locus of control, thus failing to build in personal responsibility and self-discipline;

- further inhibit normal human development through a reward-or-punishment mindset; or
- continue generational legacies, because behavior would be modified according to what was familiar.

Now the informational base of the family has been significantly enlarged. Responsibility, as a valued character trait, has become a desirable factor in family dynamics. Individuals have been taught to take personal responsibility for their own behavior. The locus of control is understood and is being internalized. At this point, the ideal behavioral modification for successful family dynamics need not be reward, manipulation or punishment. Combined with what has been learned in this program, changes in family behavior can now be understandable, methodical, planned, open, and fair to the family unit as a whole.

Addressing Old Habits

In Chapter 9, the information learned in the earlier chapters began to have a practical application in the area of household management. When trying to develop an efficient application of household management principles, some remaining behavior problems were probably noticed which could be attributed to habits from old family patterns. For instance,

- resistance may be observed in one or more family members.
- a failure to accept responsibility may still be encountered in the family.
- a family member may be seen taking on too much responsibility.
- someone may be taking on the role of "assistant parent," bossing others around.

Intervening in these old habits is more important than just assuring that home management runs smoothly, as old habits can have deep and harmful psychological ramifications. For example, taking too much responsibility is called internalizing, becoming too self-focused. Taking too little responsibility is called externalizing, becoming too focused upon what others "should" be doing. Studies in children have shown that children who internalize problems, or become too self-focused, have more negative thoughts about themselves, the world, and the future. They distort reality in their thinking processes, accept more blame when things go wrong, and have depressive and anxious thought content (Epkins, 2000, pp. 199-208).

Ranging from externalizing responsibility to an exaggerated internalizing of responsibility, the styles of the individuals in the family can be carefully observed and explained to the individuals involved. In this way, home management can serve as a normalization process for children who have formed extreme habits or extreme views of responsibility.

During behavior modification, a different kind of issue, involving fairness and self-esteem, may surface. What is being sought is a fair division of responsibility, finding the model in the family that is fair for the whole family system, not just for those who have strong personalities with feelings of entitlement, who avoid responsibilities, dictating to others what needs to be done.

All these traits and stressors often lead to feelings of frustration and anger by the people in authority who are trying to get things done. Frustration, then anger, is a natural reaction to resistive dynamics, which are almost always encountered when trying to organize the household.

Because self-discipline may not be present in all the family members, and as some of the family members may disown responsibility, the authority figure leading the team might feel forced to take back all control. Often, at this point, all forward action toward management goals is sabotaged, and the family members, even the parents, just give up. If so, the negative, draining dynamics have prevailed and old habits and patterns will continue unchanged. To assure that members of the family understand and are using the information that they have been given, further intervention may be necessary. Some things learned from past chapters can be put to use to move further past old habits. For example, in Chapter 7, family members learned to listen to their own speech patterns and to isolate patterns that were not productive in building relationships. They also learned to correct speaking patterns which did not correctly mirror reality. Now everyone probably understands that mistakes will be made. The important thing is to take responsibility for any mistakes and understand that people can correct their own semantic errors at any time without guilt or shame.

Moving Away from Old Patterns

How can we move away from old patterns and select a better path? Problems can be looked at objectively; and the familiar behavior which no longer serves a purpose can be identified and addressed. It can be done. The members of the family really can learn and expand into new behavior. The process seems difficult at first, but there is satisfaction in living in an orderly place with appropriate behavior. When they see the results, the family members can gain satisfaction from the perspective of an internalized, balanced sense of responsibility.

At this point, using all the information that was learned in earlier chapters, the subject of direct specific behavior modification is very appropriate to "fine tune" family dynamics. At this point, there is a practical way to intervene in behavior while learning to work together. To signal that they have integrated the developmental permissions needed to live in dignity and good mental health, each family member will demonstrate growth in their ability to

- trust themselves to speak up for themselves,
- have permission to be their own person,
- have permission to have their own initiative, and
- be involved in the process of learning how to get along with one another.

Building Trust during Behavior Modification

Before behavior modification begins in earnest, by anticipating some reactionary behaviors, the family can develop a growing awareness of their feelings by using self-reflexiveness to slow down any reactions. Stepping outside of any frustration situation, a person can give an "I message" about his or her feelings. This will allow others to know what is happening and prevent the acting out of feelings which would accelerate reactions in others and lead to disagreements. For a time, stopping to talk about feelings might need to become an automatic planned part of behavior modification. For example, Stern (1992, pp. 65-73) states that even understanding feelings of anger can actually bring people closer together in a relationship:

> The reason that anger can bring people closer together is that the qualities that are necessary to have a close relationship become evident if people resolve anger in a healthy way. These qualities include listening, empathizing, negotiating, communicating, identifying feelings, talking about feelings, and working out a solution to the anger together....Since anger may point to the source of a problem in a relationship, resolving the issue often makes the relationship stronger.

In behavior modification, it is helpful to remember that anger is rarely a first emotion but often is a reaction to other feelings. Anger gets a person's attention because the adrenalin has begun to pump through the body. If, at this time, the person can stop to find out what the original preceding feelings were and report the emotions in the order that they occurred, then he or she can slow the action down, take a second step toward finding an answer to a relationship problem, and increase understanding in the family. Helping others learn cause and effect is very important. The following is a method one can use to delay or even prevent an anger reaction:

> Tune in to the beginning physical sensations of anger. Notice the change in body chemistry. Immediately sit down and stop the blood from rushing through the broad muscle mass in the legs, arms, and upper back. Fill the capacities of the lungs, hold for a count of ten, and blow air out of the mouth slowly. Repeat the deep breathing until you feel your shoulders relax and you are in control.

Even when the anger reaction comes too quickly and is overly explosive, the person can later revisit the episode. What was happening when the feelings started? What happened next? What were the feelings and memories that came later? What were the feelings that led to anger? How could the process have been stopped sooner? Understanding what other feelings were occurring is extremely helpful to know, and learning to speak up at the first sign of a feeling is also helpful.

A good time to test feelings against the reality of the situation is after the cool-down period after experiencing anger feelings. The matter can often be clarified and resolved at this time. Some good questions to ask are *What was my inference of a fact?*, *What was my opinion?*, *What was my judgment?*, and *What were the feelings I was having that led to anger?*

Facilitator's Note: **Now is the time to discuss what happened during the application period for the household management. Let the individual representatives from the families answer the questions and share the problems and answers to the exercises with the group as a whole. Stress the commonality of home management difficulties and adopt a "we are all in this together" attitude. Ask those who share to not mention any children by name in their discussion and help them with this, if needed.**

Don't be surprised if a family did not do the homework. Have no expectations but ask if they would share next time. All is not lost, because listening to the others will be helpful. Be very supportive because the practicing of new skills may be uncomfortable but must be attempted before an appropriate behavior modification can be determined.

Exercise 10-A

Problems Found in Home Management

1. **Describe one problem that came up during the application period for the household management exercise.** ________________

2. **How many family members were involved (mother, father, girls, boys, ages)?** ________________

3. **What was the behavior that precipitated the change in the level of feelings? What were the feelings that came up as a result of the initial behavior? (Look back to Chapter 7 for a list of feelings.)** ________________

4. **What were the facts about the problem?** ________________

5. **What were the different inferences that people had about the facts?** ________________

6. **Did anyone state his or her opinion as if it were fact? What was said?** ________________

7. **Did anyone state his or her judgment as if it were fact? What was said?** ________________

Beginning Behavior Modification

Getting Permission to Have Initiative during Behavior Modification

Learning to have one's own initiative is an important building block of development. Unless children see adults modeling how to have one's own initiative, they will implicitly and unconditionally absorb only the rules and information which are familiar to them. If you ask a group of school children what rules are needed, they will often repeat what a teacher has said or other rules they have heard. They tend not to question the factual basis of information, the logic of assumptions, or the reasonableness of conclusions, nor do they have the acquired grammatical framework to do so (LeDoux, 2002, p. 231). At certain ages, when children are very concrete thinkers, the tendency to not question the factual basis of information, the logic of assumptions, or the reasonableness of conclusions is normal. But if this continues throughout a lifetime, the children will be blind to other possibilities or think that they have to remain shackled with a particular standard. In World War II, in the Nazi movement, we saw the sad results of a whole culture being brought up in an authoritarian atmosphere. The children never learned to think for themselves or to form their own impressions or to ask questions as a result of those formed impressions.

How can an atmosphere be created which will ensure that all individuals in the family can learn initiative and be free to have initiative? Many future problems can be prevented by correcting the general semantics in the family speaking system (Korzybski, 1940). The adult leaders can listen to their interaction with the family and seek to speak person to person with others in the family. The hierarchical parent-to-child conversation, where one has to be the boss, can really backfire and become the basis of communication throughout the family, trapping the family in "should," "ought," "must," "need," or "have to" interactions, which prevent creative thinking and initiative and invoke shame. Remembering to use responsible grammar such as, "It seems to me," "I think," or "I feel," can allow openings for others to express their thoughts and feelings. Also, the family members can commit to own the standards they have set for their family. Then after standards and responsibilities are learned, taking initiative can be creative and inspiring to others, taking care that individual initiative not infringe upon the rights of others.

Using Behavior Modification to Build the Will and Self-Esteem

Part of moral development is accomplishing things without the need for punishment or rewards (Kohlberg, 1981). The locus of control moves inside, not remaining outside, with someone else having to watch to make sure things get done and get done properly. The person learns how to work as a team member. Turk et al. (2003, pp. 65-78) define the self as a "representation of what we know about ourselves." To have a representation of ourselves as someone who knows how to take responsibility is important. To know how to take responsibility and to know that others have seen you take responsibility is an important factor in building self-esteem.

Naomi Quinn, a cultural anthropologist, reports (2003): "Researchers have been searching for recurrent, vital, complex, widespread tasks that require cultural solutions to the universal task of socializing children." These tasks are critical to human survival and community well-being. All the models studied specified

- practices that maximize the constancy of the child's experiences around the learning of important lessons;
- practices that make the child's experience of learning emotionally arousing; and
- the attachment of these lessons to more global evaluations of the child's behavior—and to the child himself or herself—as good or bad.

Across cultural boundaries, these practices and global evaluations are considered necessary to complete the tasks of raising children. Human development and socialization needs in cultural settings seem to be stable across societies.

What is needed now is to know what to do when things go wrong and discipline is necessary. On the following pages, you will find a model of discipline developed by psychiatrist Patrick Stern (1992, pp. 63-73), who specializes in developmental behavioral pediatrics. His model may meet the specifications found in the cultural models studied by Naomi Quinn. The Stern Model of Discipline and his discipline protocol are used here by permission.

> ***Facilitator's Note:*** **The model of discipline suggested by Stern will be new to many. You may have to watch for developmental permissions that are missing in some parents. Use as many visual aids as possible and use a fun-loving adult or large older child to act in a child's role, while you carry out the specified behavioral modification. Encourage the parents to try the home management homework again—this time intervening in the behavior that prevented successful completion of their home management project.**

The Stern Model of Discipline

Modeling, Separation, and Communication

There are three essential components, which must occur for a parents to effectively discipline his or her child:

1. Modeling
2. Separation
3. Communication

The first and most important component to discipline, modeling, is what the parent conveys through his or her own behavior to the child. Most parents forget that we imitate what people do more than what they say "should" be done. Children are much more affected by watching what their parents do than by being told what the parents want them to do. When parents say their child should do one thing but they themselves do another, the child will copy the behavior of the parent every time. All parents must examine their own behavior, which they model for their children, and make changes if they are doing things they do not want their child to learn. This is the most difficult part of discipline for a parent. Inappropriate modeling by a parent is one of the most common reasons for failure of a child's misbehavior to change. Younger children are more affected by modeling than older children, so a parent must be particularly sensitive to modeling with an infant or toddler.

In order to successfully discipline their children, the parents must become the persons they want their children to be. A parent who truly disciplines his or her child grows more than the child does. This is likely part of the grand spiritual design for humans.

The second key component to effective discipline is separation and isolation of the child when he or she misbehaves. Separation requires the child to practice getting himself or herself back under control. Separation also protects a parent from being pushed beyond his or her limits, thus, modeling inappropriate behavior to the child. A child must be separated from the parent and should not be with anyone else. A bedroom or any other room is acceptable. A child should be required to stay there until he or she accomplishes five things:

1. The child must get himself or herself back in control physically.
2. The child must get himself or herself back in control emotionally.
3. The child must get himself or herself back in control verbally.
4. The child must make a verbal commitment to change his or her behavior.
5. The child must state that he or she is willing to talk with and listen to the parent.

A child should not be required simply to stay for a set length of time, because a lack of expectation to change his or her behavior makes the separation a pure punishment. It is true, there is always a small element of punishment in separating and isolating a child, but the purpose of "untimed" separation is to allow the child to change his or her behavior. The child, not the parent, is in control of determining the length of separation. During the separation, a child is learning to regain emotional, physical, and verbal control, thinking about what led to his or her misbehavior, and how misbehaving can be avoided in the future.

Separating a child, especially during the preschool years, is the most powerful influence parents possess to mold the child's behavior. This is true, because all normal children are born with a relationship drive, which is the need to relate to other people. A parent is the one who primarily fulfills this inborn need; and even if not at a conscious level, a child is very aware of this. The use of separation in discipline is the parent's statement to a child that either the child will have to conduct his or her behavior the way the parent wishes, or the parent will not permit the child to be with the parent to fulfill the relationship drive.

Separation also requires a child to change his or her own behavior instead of the parent trying to control it. This causes the control to become internalized within the child. The separation also keeps parents from being pushed beyond their own limits, losing control of their own behavior, and then modeling behavior they do not want their child to learn. A disciplinary encounter is one of the most critical instances for a parent to model how to deal with his or her own feelings and control issues appropriately. Quickly separating a child who misbehaves is the best way parents can keep themselves from losing control of their own behavior....

...Staying out of the room when a child escalates is very hard for many parents, but it is a must for successful discipline. A child should be required to let the parent know when he or she has accomplished the five tasks of separation, by telling the parent, "I'll be good and I'm ready to talk." Before a child can talk, he or she needs to show that he or she is back in control physically, emotionally, and verbally. The final component of effective discipline is communication between the parent and child about the misbehavior. This cannot occur until both the parent and child are in control, and both are willing to talk. No one can be forced to communicate at a specific time, and the child should not be forced; however, a child can be required to communicate in order to be permitted to come out of the room.

1. A parent should begin the discussion by telling the child that he or she loves them, and how the parent feels about the misbehavior. When the child misbehaves, a parent will usually be angry and disappointed, embarrassed, or scared. Telling a child how the parent feels models for a child one appropriate way to deal with feelings.
2. A parent should then tell their child that he or she will keep them safe. This is particularly important when a parent and child have been angry at each other. A child expects to be hurt physically and/or emotionally when the parent becomes angry.

3. The final thing a parent should tell the child is that the parent knows the child can and will change his or her behavior. Positive thinking by a parent is very powerful. For a child to learn self-control, the parent must believe the child can act appropriately.
4. To start the communication component of discipline, each of the above three statements should be made by a parent to their child each time. There are six things, which should then be discussed with the child every time:
5. What was the misbehavior, and why it was a problem?
   a. What "being the boss" issue was involved?
   b. What need was the child trying to meet?
   c. What the appropriate behavior should have been, and why that would have been better?
   d. What feelings got out of control?
   e. How should a child manage his or her feelings the next time it occurs? Notice that a child is not asked why she or he misbehaved. (A child does not know why he or she misbehaved. Discussion of these questions will teach the child.)

Being the Boss

"Being the boss" is a natural desire that every person has throughout their lives. The desire is stronger in some children than others, but it is present in all normal children. The need to be the boss occurs because each person is trying to fulfill his or her drives. Drives create needs and wants; however, we know that no one can ever be the boss all the time. Probably the most frequent cause of anger in a child is not being able to be the boss and tell the parent what to do. This frustration leads to normal anger in a child, which then triggers the misbehavior.

During the communication part of discipline, each time the child misbehaves a parent should discuss the desire of their child to "be the boss." This occurs because one part of essentially every misbehavior is that a child breaks a rule, does not do something he or she was told to do, or does something he or she was told not to do. A parent should acknowledge that it is normal to want to "be the boss" all the time, but no one can. Every child must learn to accept when someone else will make the decision, rather than giving the child the option to choose. A parent should express the fact that it is normal for the child to feel angry when the child wants to "be the boss" but cannot. A child has to learn to respond to that normal anger in socially acceptable ways. Since a child continues to seek more responsibilities throughout childhood, the parent will be disciplining the child about "being the boss" issues until the child no longer lives at home.

The desire for the child to "be the boss" exists as an attempt to fulfill a need or a want. Children must be taught to understand which longings are needs, and which are wants, and the difference between them. A child must also be taught to express his or her needs and wants to others. This must occur in order for the other person to know the need or want exists, so he or she can choose whether or not to respond. An inability for a person to understand his or her own needs or wants, or more frequently to express them, is a very common problem. Identifying and clarifying wants or needs appear to be more difficult for young girls than young boys. This part of the discipline will teach a child a very crucial interpersonal skill. A child who can understand and express his or her wants and needs will have them met more frequently; and, therefore, that child will be less likely to misbehave.

Children believe that when they become adults, they can do whatever they want to do—only a child must do what an authority requires. The truth is that even the President of the United States, probably the most powerful person in the world, cannot always do what he or she wants. This should be discussed repeatedly when a parent addresses the "being the boss" topic. A child must learn this fact to accept that he or she cannot always be in control. To manage feelings and "boss issues" in socially appropriate ways, the natural desire to be in control should be directed internally, not toward things in the external world over which the child has little or no control.

All misbehavior ultimately results from a feeling getting out of control. The feeling can be emotional, such as anger, sadness, fear or excitement; or physical, such as pain, hunger, fatigue or feeling ill. A child, and most adults, does not understand that feelings are the final trigger for misbehavior. Conscience monitors feelings and makes socially appropriate choices about how to respond when a feeling occurs. The feeling, which causes the misbehavior, should be identified; and a child should be told how to deal with it in appropriate ways in the future....

Giving Positive Feedback

After a child successfully completes the separation and communication components of discipline is an ideal time for a parent to give their child positive feedback. When the communication part of discipline is completed, a parent should give the child a hug and verbal praise.

Many children are never taught how to recognize their feelings or how to deal with them in appropriate ways. This is the key fact a child must learn to maintain good behavior. A young child will need for their parent to clarify the six issues in communication, and then have the child repeat them. By six-to-eight years old, a child should be required to discuss these issues with the parent.... Many parents wonder if modeling, separation, and communication are appropriate with young children, such as toddlers. Twelve-to-fifteen months old is actually the most important age during which to begin discipline. A child is far more responsive to modeling, separation/isolation, and communication at that age. From a practical standpoint, a young child can be safely carried to his or her room when needed and required to stay by securing the door. This cannot be done with an adolescent, which is why a psychiatric hospital may be needed at that age. Critical foundations are formed which allow a child to deal more appropriately with his or her behavior throughout the rest of their childhood. Though a young child may not understand everything the parent says, a toddler is able to comprehend far more than that for which he or she is given credit, and the child is learning the process of dealing with problems. The child is taught that problems, which are inevitable in everyone's life, are solved by each person assuming responsibility for his or her own actions and then communicating together in a thoughtful, problem-solving discussion.

Teaching a child to develop conscience and self-control is like teaching a child math. A child begins to learn math in kindergarten and continues to take more advanced courses through high school and college. A math curriculum, not positive feedback and punishment alone, must be used for a child to learn math. Discipline, likewise, requires a curriculum, which must be taught throughout child rearing. A parent will deal with misbehavior related to a tricycle with a toddler, a bicycle with a ten-year-old child, and a car with an adolescent. At each age, the child is struggling with a "boss issue" and not responding to a feeling in a socially appropriate way. The details of the curriculum change, but the basic fundamentals never do. The discipline outlined in this chapter provides the curriculum for a parent. A child cannot learn math without being taught. Without discipline, children cannot learn to deal appropriately with their desires to always "be the boss," understand and clarify their feelings to others, or monitor their feelings and make socially appropriate choices in response to their feelings. A child who is not taught conscience will fail the most important course he or she ever takes—life itself.

Family-Systems Application of the Stern Model of Discipline

In a family system, misbehavior in children sometimes mirrors the undeveloped part of the adults in the family. Old anger and rage patterns can lurk and cause extreme reactionary behavior in the discipline interventions that are necessary. Parents who suffered abuse as a child may feel that it is unfair for their children to have what might appear to be special privileges, which are really not special privileges at all, but normal, age-appropriate, right-of-passage entitlements. The parents may need coaching on long-term consequences and information on what is considered normal and what is considered appropriate. They may need information on learning how to control their reactions. Knowing that abuse has affected reactions and development and allowing the adults and children to have opportunities to pass through developmental stages together is very important. Care must be taken that punitive reactions to childhood misbehavior not be extreme. At times, when extreme reactions may be likely to occur, the parent may want to wait until calmness has returned to go forward with the behavior modification, using physical signs as signals to wait or proceed with the process. Allowing a heartbeat to return to normal, learning to breathe slowly to stabilize, and acquiring a mature defense mechanism such as a good sense of humor may aid in mediating strong reactions which can go far in changing old anger or rage patterns.

Conscious Will: The Self-Portrait of the Mind

In his article, "The Mind's Self-Portrait," Wegner (2003, pp. 1-14) discusses the importance of conscious will. He believes that previews of action create feeling of conscious will, when we find ourselves doing the action we premeditated. The feelings, perhaps with the energy that feelings provide, will seem unlikely to arise if we do not experience preview of action.

> The experience of conscious will is valuable as a marker, a quasi-emotional experience that highlights the actions that feel as though they are our own, and this marker function is sufficiently important for human social life that it could well motivate the processes that produce previews.

The Stern Model of Discipline exhibits a conscious preview of action that will create feelings of conscious will, when the child finds himself or herself doing the actions he or she has been asked to premeditate.

The conscious preview and the emotional experience of owning the preview as something we will do give us a feeling of authorship of action. We experience a will for an action, which can lead to responsibility for that action, and so, depending upon the effects of the action, we will be susceptible to moral emotions such as pride or guilt. As Wegner (2003, pp. 11-12) states:

> All that is needed is the occurrence of previews, and the subsequent self-attribution of authorship that results when the person perceives them as causes of action. The mind's self-portrait leads the person to think of the self as an author of action—a certain *kind* of author, one who does good or bad things. This, in turn creates opportunities for subsequent behavior. Thoughts and feelings about the self derive from memories of what one has done, and the determination of authorship is the basis for these memories....We become selves by experiencing what we do, and this experience then informs the processes that determine what we will do next. The self, in this view, is not an agent, an origin of action—but instead is an accumulated structure of knowledge about *what this particular mind can do.*

References

Epkins, C. (2000). Cognitive specificity in internalizing and externalizing problems in community and clinic-referred children. *Journal of Clinical Child Psychology, 29*, pp. 199-208.

Kohlberg, L. (1981). Essays on moral development: Vol. 1. *The philosophy of moral development.* New York: Harper & Row.

Kohlberg, L. (1984). Essays on moral development: Vol. 2. *The philosophy of moral development.* New York: Harper & Row.

Korzybski, A. (1940). General semantics, psychiatry, psychotherapy, and prevention. In C. & C. S. Read (Eds.), *General semantics in psychotherapy: selected writings on methods aiding therapy* (pp. 19-39). Brooklyn, NY: Institute of General Semantics.

LeDoux, J. (2002). *Synaptic self: how our brains become who we are.* New York: Russell Sage Foundation.

Quinn, N. (2003). Cultural selves. *Annals of the New York Academy of Sciences, Vol. 1001, Issue 1, pp. 145-176.*

Stern, P. (1992). *A Wellness Prescription: How to Raise a Happy, Healthy Child.* H. Patrick Stern, M.D., Telford, Tennessee.

Turk, D., Heatherton, T., Macrea, C., Kelley, W., & Gazzaniga, M. (2003). Out of contact, out of mind: the distributed nature of the self. *Annals of the New York Academy of Sciences, Vol. 1001*, pp. 65-78.

Wegner, D. (2008). The mind's self-portrait. *Annals of the New York Academy of Sciences, Vol. 1001*, 222-223.

In Chapter 11...

The elements that enabled the families to uncap and utilize their own family wisdom are reviewed in this chapter. This will be the last meeting of the program for the families, so the chapter contains an important discussion of how best to affirm the program participants and to assure the participants that they are now qualified to be involved in building a healthy community. Healthy community building will be discussed.

The families will be able to see themselves as emerging powerful influences in their communities with the potential to impact their communities in positive ways. Along with the discussion, steps for bringing closure to the program will be included.

CHAPTER 11

SHAME DIFFUSION AND COMMUNITY BUILDING

Facilitator's Note: The purpose of this chapter is to close out the program. No new material will be introduced for exercises. The material that has been covered is reinforced and the emphasis moves to the families and what they think. Use every opportunity to highlight the participants. Another important emphasis is the recognition of the ability for these families to impact their communities as positive "building blocks." The content and process of the program has been formulated to protect the families from shame. Now an attempt will be made to "shame proof" the families by giving the families information on the multigenerational nature of shame, information on how they may have been affected, and information on how to prevent the cycle from continuing in their own families.

A 20-minute lecture and discussion needs to be prepared for the following sections: Breaking the Cycle of Shame in Family Systems, Shame Diffusion, Nonverbal and Verbal Abuse, and Emerging Families. The lecture and discussion will orient the families into space and time. Chapter 5 can be also reviewed regarding the section on shame and how the program has tried to highlight this normally silent partner in family and community dynamics.

Moving into the Meeting Environment

Objectives *(1 hour and 30 minutes)*

1. **Overview for closing out the program (20 minutes)**

   The purpose of this chapter is to close out the program. No new material will be introduced for exercises. The material that has been covered is reinforced and the emphasis moves to the families and what they think.

   a. Breaking the cycle of shame in family systems

   b. Shame diffusion

c. Injunctions
d. Nonverbal and verbal abuse
e. Emerging families

2. Community building—past and present (5 minutes)

a. Qualifications for community building
b. The wisdom of the people in the community

3. Characteristics of a Strong Family (30 minutes)

Exercise 11-A Characteristics of a Strong Family

Each facilitator can decide how to use this section. The questions can be asked to the group as a whole, or some questions can be assigned to a family to answer.

4. Awards and exit interview (35 minutes)

Breaking the Cycle of Shame in Family Systems

Hays (1998, p. 194) observes that there are four necessary steps to be taken to break the cycle of multi-generational shame:

1. Making available, to all those intending to be parents, courses embracing communications, family systems, parenting skills, power-struggle issues, forms of abuse of children, conflict resolution, and developmental dependency needs.
2. Strengthening marriages and relationships through the adoption of similar courses.
3. Offering programs aimed at negotiating changes in parenting styles within family systems—that is, programs which challenge the delusion, denial, toxic rules, and multi-generational parenting practices that inhibit the personal growth and development of children.
4. Providing parents with outcome of research into family and child issues. The material should be in easily-digested formats—including books, video, internet, and cassette/CDs—and include the addictions and compulsive behaviors used to mask the emotional pain of shame.

The families have been exposed to many of these recommendations, furnishing new information to actually change the linguistic legacy and general semantics of the family. The families have self-evaluated the general semantics of their own family and have seen the speaking patterns leading to conflict and where the long-term consequences of the speaking patterns have led. The families have been introduced to four different types of developmental stages, and the children and parents have been evaluated, touching the "inner children" of the adults. The roots of shame have been revealed and the information lost to the misbegotten has, to some degree, been restored. The structure and self-evaluations have kept the participants on task and have protected them from shame as they gained more information.

Shame Diffusion

Shame is uncovered as a silent partner to many individuals, families, and communities. Uncovering shame is very necessary, because shame attaches family systems to dynamics that prevent optimal development in the family. In other words, because of the risk of shaming statements from others, three things can happen:

1. The individuals in the family may spend an inordinate amount of time and energy defending against imagined or real shame.
2. The individuals in the family may avoid spontaneous interactions of any kind and may stop advancing in developmental stages, having to carefully plan conversations to avoid shaming reactions, instead of being free and spontaneous.
3. An individual in the family may tire of saying only what is acceptable and will "buck the system" and face the consequences of rejection for not following the injunctions found in family rules. Rejection may be used to bring the individual back in line.

Shame has been alluded to in Chapter 5, especially in discussing childhood behavior. Shame was also discussed in Chapter 8 in the context of its propensity to interfere with developmental impact and momentum. Now shame will be spotlighted and shown to be the cause of many troubling and puzzling interactions that lie at the root of much family discord. In this chapter, shame will be openly discussed and diffused, by reviewing the information and the processes learned in earlier chapters and by understanding the lasting effects of shame.

The most powerful weapon that shame has is secrecy. Frustration and shame are veiled in family relationships where one does not

- know what to say in response to insult,
- have an understanding how the systems work, or
- know how to maintain dignity as a human being.

Injunctions

In Chapter 8, early developmental permissions were discussed so that the concepts of developmental stages could be understood, along with the permissions necessary for furthering developmental growth. If one or more developmental permissions are missed, the absence of the permission(s) can cause individuals within a family unit to go through the world in a wounded condition with injunctions "to not do" or "to not say" things about what is going on in the family. In other families where developmental permissions were naturally received, family members without these injunctions would not even have second thoughts about speaking up.

For instance, what if family members could not trust themselves to speak up for themselves because speaking up for one's self was not safe in their family of origin? Speaking up for one's self would be considered "talking back." Then in interactions with future authority figures, when something was said that was inaccurate, there might be a huge internal debate about whether to speak up or not. After all, the veiled injunction was "don't talk back" to authority figures.

Mary and Robert Goulding (1997) isolated internalized injunctions in their work in redecision therapy. The focus of *Uncapping Family Wisdom* is to attract and begin a process for troubled family systems; the interventions the Gouldings mentioned in their writings would be a logical next step for therapeutic intervention. After the program, the participants will be ready to enter a normal therapy milieu.

Injunctions, which were based on false ideas contrary to human development, were learned by individuals in their family system. These injunctions created an interpersonal monitoring of one's personal behavior and fostered the development of painful emotions. Having this type of intrapersonal monitoring going on keeps these individuals from living a full life. With such chronic emotional wounds, individuals lack the ability to call up the integrity of confident self-evaluation. Some individuals do not know the power and satisfaction of taking responsibility for mistakes, because they do not understand that everyone makes mistakes. With each mistake, or negative self-judgment, comes the potential to collapse into shame, because it is not all right to make a mistake. In addition, these individuals, shouldering a load of shame and blame, may not have developed knowledge of cause and effect, which could define reality more clearly and provide boundaries from the shame and blame; moreover, making mistakes is one of the best ways to learn cause and effect.

Where did it all begin? Wilson (1990, p. 79) describes a phenomenon, something called "binding shame":

> An unbroken chain of brokenness spans the centuries as each succeeding generation of children lives with the falsehoods of their parents and their parents' parents before them....The cause of binding shame is an interaction of these falsehoods, the magical thinking of children, and the need of a protective illusion of control.

Wilson (1990, p. 76) describes parents as doing the best they knew—not the best they could, but the best they knew—because even if they cared to do better, knowing how was the crucial factor.

> ***Facilitator's Note:*** **Have a beginning discussion to see how the Stern Model of Discipline worked for the families. Keep the conversation lighthearted and optimistic. Display confidence in the families, asking them how they felt about what they accomplished. Use the problem solving model from Chapter 9, if there are any disagreements or tension in the meeting. Then proceed into a short lecture on verbal and nonverbal abuse.**

Nonverbal and Verbal Abuse

John and Linda Friel (1990, pp. 129-130) warn about nonverbal and verbal abuse, which is important to identify. They state that at least 80% of the emotional communication between two people is done nonverbally. When a nonverbal message is delivered along with a verbal message, which is more likely to be believed? The nonverbal! The Friels maintain that learning to notice nonverbal gestures and cues keeps the nonverbal message from hiding in the unconscious and causing confusion. Eyebrows, eyes and eyelids, mouth, tone of voice, and body posture have a language of their own.

Chapter 7 showed us how to identify communication errors in families. The information is useful not only for one's own family, but can also be used to learn how to cope with the shaming practices of others who have not examined their own communication patterns. Individuals are taught to watch for the shaming messages found in the sentences which contain verbs like "is" or "was" that are used to make absolute statements. For example, "You are crazy" is someone's judgment stated as fact. Some questions are disguised or indirect insults, such as, "Why did you get this 'B' grade?" Still other questions have an emphasis on one word, such as, "Why do you feel *that* way?" This type of statement is designed to imply something is wrong by questioning an individual's right to have his or her own feelings. Another example, "You are going to do *what*?", causes people to doubt their initiative and double back to investigate their actions. All of these are examples of shaming devices and can be understood as such. Was someone born knowing how to do things like that? No, the language came from individuals, families, and cultural influences. Shaming communication styles are learned behavior.

The Friels suggest direct ways to deal with shaming messages:

- keep good eye contact, remaining calm, matter of fact, and firm when answering;
- respond rationally to emotional statements; and
- practice future responses (to use when one has been caught off guard) by referring to the speaking errors found in Chapter 7 (1990, pp. 129-130).

Evans (1996, p. 85) lists categories of verbal abuse as withholding, countering, discounting, hurtful "joking," blocking and diverting, accusation and blame, judging and criticizing, trivializing, undermining, threatening, name calling, forgetting, ordering, denial, and abusive anger. *The Verbally Abusive Relationship: How to Recognize It and How to Respond* is a good resource for learning how to undermine possible responses to specific categories of verbal abuse that may be found in the home or in the community setting. Abuse is learned behavior and with the proper interventions, sometimes the person is able to change.

Emerging Families

After learning to understand their family system through the program, individuals are qualified to be involved in building healthy communities. They are more qualified than many other individuals who have not ever considered studying their family system. Many have opened their minds to experiment with new ideas and have seen family wisdom emerging. Having learned the importance of setting strong external boundaries and keeping themselves away from the negative forces of society, they can now move forward within their boundaries to change that society.

Recognizing the Strength of Emerging Families

As a result of the information and skills learned and practiced, these families can see themselves as emerging, powerful influences in their communities and know that they can impact their communities in positive ways. Combining with other emerging families, they can make a difference in their communities. Since families are an important building block of communities, and communities are an important building block of society, many communities can benefit from emerging families who are confident in using their proficiency to change their community environment. In this chapter, the characteristics of a strong family are reviewed, with the special purpose of empowering the families to enter into community building to influence the future in positive ways for themselves and others.

Community Building

In searching for a way to build in hope for the families and to alert them to possibilities, the families may enjoy hearing about how some novel grassroots efforts that received national attention were researched. Only a few programs were really family centered and self-governed, seeking their leadership from the grass roots. In these programs, the families combined with other families to improve neighborhoods or financial potential; however, these programs did not focus on changing a community by uncapping the wisdom in individual families. In the long run, the goal of community building is, therefore, not only to improve neighborhoods and financial potential, but also to move the community into a functioning society, where any dysfunction handed down from past generations is identified as such, and information is provided to stimulate a process of growth and development for all members of the community.

Bottom-Up Initiatives

In 1990, Pulitzer Prize winning news reporter Robin Garr left daily journalism to seek out America's most-innovative grassroots organizations. He did what few policy experts do. He actually went to the places where solutions were being crafted; and based on what he discovered, he wrote *Reinvesting in America.* David Osborne, author and vice-presidential adviser stated at that time, "If we can figure out how government can empower the grassroots, bottom-up initiatives captured here, we can make a dent in poverty" (Garr, 1995).

Garr thought that, unlike the forces who legislate far away from the problems, the masses of people have wisdom of their own. The *Uncapping Family Wisdom* program can further increase the cooperation and deepen the thinking about current problems. These emerging families who have come through the program are especially equipped to return back into their communities and neighborhoods and take leadership roles. With strong families as building blocks, communities can normalize their communities and diffuse the shame of "not knowing":

- not knowing what is correct,
- not knowing a way to success, and/or
- not knowing how to break the pattern of problems that have plagued the family, perhaps for generations.

The Wisdom of the People

Who is better able to influence society than those families who participated in the *Uncapping Family Wisdom* program? What do they have to offer? First, they now know much about how healthy families interact. While no family is perfectly healthy, there is value in thinking about how to be healthy in a relational way. Second, the people who have gone through this program have been committed to studying their own family unit. They learned the different concepts in the developmental information and applied them to their own families and, hopefully, began to see a different way the family could go. They felt the good feelings that come with appropriate family interaction. They identified the developmental barriers, silent killers of personhood, which had been traveling down their family line. The participants learned that humankind needs certain developmental permissions:

- The permission to speak up for one's self and to know how to do that in an appropriate way. When self-trust could be utilized to answer, then others could be trusted. One could listen to others and decide if what others say was harmful or true, and know that they had the freedom to answer and the assurance that the other person would be forthrightly addressed.
- The permission to be an authentic person (not the scapegoat, the hero, or any other role in the family) with the freedom to own their own personhood. The members of the family found out what could be done, and many had the courage to act upon what they learned. Possibly this generation will begin on a path to freedom from the restraints they uncovered in the program.
- The permission to have their own initiative—to not look at someone else for validation. The participants who went through this program located the communication snares in their family language. They stood back during or after an argument, determined what was happening in their family and used tools they had learned to gain closure to unhealthy communication. The families learned how to move away from authoritarianism.
- The permission to learn to get along with one another. Program participants learned to respect their families by finding ways to modify behavior in order to allow each other to preserve a sense of self-esteem. They learned positive ways to teach discipline, so that their children could learn how to internalize the locus of control so they could practice self-discipline. These families learned to recognize the long-term consequences of inappropriate behavior. Most importantly, they learned about the cause and effect and how the emotions were affected by the behaviors found in their family system.

The participants in the program were exposed to management principles that could be implemented at home in their own family systems. Going beyond controlling others by rewards or punishment, they learned how to move further up the moral development ladder to form family teams. A review of the principles of the *Uncapping Family Wisdom* program will allow us to understand how prepared individuals and families achieved, in varying degrees, the twelve points of the program reviewed in the following exercise.

***Facilitator's Note:* Some of the characteristics of a strong family work as an exercise for all families. Divide the time-consuming ones among different families to answer by handing out assignments beforehand. Have families read their questions and have an appointed member of the family lead the family group in answering the question, summarizing as necessary.**

Exercise 11-A

The Characteristics of a Strong Family

1. **Strong families know how to work as a team.**

   The family members are committed to one another. The family as a whole is committed to seeing that each member reaches his or her potential. The family as a whole is committed to seeing that no individuals in the family are required to suffer, so that other members of the family can have exclusive entitlement to reach their full potential. This principle is the first step in learning how to work as a team.

   How has your family learned to support one another?

   ___

   ___

   ___

   How has your family learned to apply useful management skills in household management?

   ___

   ___

   ___

2. **Strong families know how to set clear goals and are committed to the goals.**

   Many individuals may know how to set goals, but goal setting may be more difficult within the family and may interfere with family unity.

Uncapping Family Wisdom
Exercise 6-D

Your Plan of Action	Goal	Steps to Goal	First Step: When will you take it?	Barriers to Goal	How will you overcome Barriers?	How will you progress?

3. **Strong families tend to have communications that are clear.**

   There is no message discrepancy between non-verbal and verbal messages. The family members have developed listening skills, and each family member can express what it is he or she wants and expect to be understood. Who in the family has learned to listen? Who could teach listening skills with an "I message" sheet and a list of feelings? Please demonstrate.

   ___

   ___

   ___

4. **Strong families can respect differences.**

   Differences are not regarded as an insult to a person's self-esteem. In contrast, each individual is able to freely comment and report on what is seen, felt, and heard. List some original problem areas, and then let the different family members decide what important changes have occurred.

   ____

   ____

   ____

   How has your family used this goal-setting technique and what did you accomplish as your result?

   ____

   ____

   ____

   How could the goal-setting technique be useful in a community setting?

   ____

   ____

   ____

   Do you think that you could identify similar problem areas in a community meeting and understand what was happening?

   ____

   ____

   ____

5. **Strong families operate under constructive forms of leadership and share most decision-making responsibilities.**

   Each member of the family is free to express an opinion and, therefore, share in the decision-making process. Could you explain the three types of theories concerning leadership styles? What constructive form of leadership do you think would work best in a community setting?

   ____

   ____

   ____

6. **Strong families know how to show appreciation.**

   This involves being able to recognize the positive aspects of others and to let them know that these qualities are valued. It also means that within the family, individuals themselves feel comfortable about receiving compliments. Have each family member state a positive aspect of each of the other family members. Hand out a sheet that lists each person's name. Have each family member write a positive comment about every person on the sheets that come by. What are some ways to show appreciation of individuals in a community meeting? How would this improve the environment of the meeting?

___

___

___

7. **Strong families feel safe.**

These families have developed a reasonable set of rules to offset problems involving power and control. Discipline is built into the family organization, and when something upsets the balance of the family, the control goes into operation. The family uses the rules as boundaries and becomes creative within these boundaries. Look at this section from Chapter 10:

> How can an atmosphere be created which will ensure that all individuals in the family can learn self-initiative and be free to exhibit this initiative? The adult leaders can listen to their interactions with the family and seek to speak person to person with others in the family. Maintaining the hierarchal parent-to-child conversation style, where one has to be the boss, can really backfire and become the basic style of communication throughout the family. This traps the family in "should," "ought to," "must," "need to," "have to" interactions, which prevent creative thinking and initiative and invoke shame. Remembering to use self-responsible phrases such as, "It seems to me," "I think," "I feel," can allow openings for others to express their thoughts and feelings. The family members can choose to commit to owning the standards they have set for their family. Then individuals who take initiative can be creative and inspiring to others. Care must be taken, however, that such individual initiative does not infringe upon the rights of others.

What would be some good standards to set for community meetings using some of the above ideas?

___

___

___

Remember to have the people present at the community meeting adopt the standards as their own; then they will be responsible for obeying their own rules!

8. **Strong families own their own problems and do not blame them on others.**

Individuals in the family know how to take responsibility for their own problems, and how to enable the family to solve them.

Name one problem that you have solved during the time we have been meeting together.

___

___

___

Now take this to the community. The problems in a community meeting belong to an individual, a group, or the whole community. In order to determine how the problem solving is to proceed, it is important to establish to whom the problem belongs. It is also important to determine whether the problem is about something regarding the content (what people are saying) of the meeting or the process (how things are being done) at the meeting. Why do you think it might be a good idea for a community to own their own problems and not blame them on others?

____

____

____

9. **Strong families use change as an opportunity for learning.**

Strong families see the world as constantly changing and view problems as an opportunity for individuals to stretch and grow. Because of the uncertainty of what might happen, the fact that the world is always changing can be overwhelming; however, when someone is constantly trying to build their skills, changes can become challenges to grow and the individual becomes more and more confident that he or she will be able to handle problems as they arise. We know that all problems must be addressed in the here and now, to prevent anxiety (an emotion about the future) or remorse (an emotion about the past). How could this information be helpful for community problem solving? How would you try to talk to someone who has a different idea about what the community needs? Use the problem-solving model from Exercise 9-D.

____

____

____

10. **Strong families can demonstrate openness and trust because they know and use problem-solving techniques to handle conflict in the family.**

During a conflict, the family knows how to take into consideration how each family member views reality. The emotional factors, no longer ignored, are now considered important criteria in the decision-making process. Who would like to demonstrate how to problem solve? (Assign this question to a family privately at the first of the meeting for them to demonstrate later.)

____

____

____

11. **Strong families have strong external boundaries.**

Strong families understand the pressures that society places upon these boundaries, and they maintain the boundaries through family loyalties. They can identify and face openly external cultural problems that impinge upon their family boundaries. When the society is not providing firm boundaries that ensure safety for all, the family moves the power of control into their family.

What cultural problems in your community might infringe on your family, and how would you handle these problems? Have individual families discuss this question and then ask the community, "Who would like to share?"

____

____

____

12. **Strong families understand the importance of having a positive family climate.**

    When respect is lessening and hostility seems to be expanding, these families seek outside help in the form of counseling and/or support groups.

Facilitator's Note: **Each individual or family who goes through the program will now receive a Certificate of Completion, attendance awards, and other affirmative awards. Each participant will have fulfilled the last characteristic of a strong family, introduced at the beginning of the program, because they sought outside help in the form of counseling and/or support groups.**

That is what all the families involved in this program have done. The time of sharing and giving out awards to the participants in the program will lead toward an exit interview with the facilitator or an assistant. During the sharing time, congratulations and recommendations for each family will be made, and names of local counselors, interested trained pastors, and support groups will be distributed.

References

Evans, P. (1996). *The verbally abusive relationship: how to recognize it and how to respond.* Avon, MA: Adams Media.

Friel, J., & Friel, L. (1990). *An adult child's guide to what is "normal."* Deerfield Beach, FL: Health Communications, Inc.

Garr, R. (1995). *Reinvested in America: the grassroots movements that are feeding the hungry, housing the homeless, and putting America back to work.* Reading, MA: Addison-Wesley Publishing Company.

Goulding, M., and Goulding, R. (1997). *Changing lives through redecision therapy.* New York: Grove Press.

Hays, D. (1998). *Nobody told me: the impact of shame in multi-generational family systems and parenting practice.* Cowes, Victoria, Australia: Pacific-Downunder.

Pate, S. (1990). *Mindsets and monkeyshines: the Rivendell parents enrichment manual.* Benton, AR: Rivendell.

Wilson, S. (1990). *Released from shame: recovery for adult children of dysfunctional families.* Downers Grove, IL: InterVarsity Press.

Uncapping Family Wisdom

Part III

PART III

UNCAPPING FAMILY WISDOM: SUMMARY OF LINGUISTIC INTERVENTIONS DEVELOPMENTAL PROGRESS FOR CASE STUDIES

Chapter 12 contains the summaries of the linguistic interventions and the developmental progress for each study. The comparative study for developmental gain for the four case study research investigations are charted. The summary shows an overall comparative review of the four case study researches and includes the diagnosis, age, gender, inpatient, outpatient, length of treatment, semantic intervention, and the beginning and ending developmental gains for social, cognitive, psychosocial, and moral development.

In Chapter 12...

The case studies that began in Chapter 7 and continued in Chapter 8 are finalized in this chapter. These four case studies are detailed studies of the semantic evaluations and the developmental level of the individuals in family systems which exhibited transgenerational dysfunction.

These case studies represent different pathologies and different combinations of semantic error and describe how intervention was accomplished through the use of interventions into the family speaking pattern. In these research studies, the errors of the family speaking patterns were uncovered, revealing how the family systems were likely to engage in conflict. The developmental arrests which were uncovered were often the underlying baseline cause of inappropriate behavior by the individuals or other family members.

These case studies demonstrate a method to address serious cases involving transgenerational dysfunction. These cases all involved families caught in systems where developmental arrest(s) had occurred three or more generations ago. The use of structured general semantics and standardized developmental screens helped evaluate what needed changing. Important practical education was also part of the therapy. The amazing fact is that most evaluations are extremely accurate and interesting to the participants, and little assistance is needed from the observing professional. The information opens new horizons of thinking. The style of intervention and methods used are client friendly. The process appears to be calming to the client and gives the client a working vocabulary at the first meeting, which will expand and be used throughout the continuing process.

For Further Study

Additional charts that compare the cases can be found at the end of Chapter 12. Further studies may investigate whether patterns of development can be associated with diagnoses of one kind or another. It appears that some extreme semantic labels would fit certain diagnoses. For example, persons with antisocial traits would seem to prefer dead-level reckoning. Persons with borderline or narcissistic personality disorders may find themselves with fact-inference difficulties.

A summary of components for this chapter is listed below:

I. Case Studies

a. Case Study Research #1—Amy

b. Case Study Research #2—Kay

c. Case Study Research #3—Charles

d. Case Study Research #4—Paul

II. Multi-Case Study Research Summary Chart

CHAPTER 12

GAINING CLOSURE ON TRANSGENERATIONAL DYSFUNCTION

Four case studies were followed in order that certain linguistic, communication, and developmental aspects of the people in these studies could be manipulated in the hopes of breaking the dysfunctional family legacies they had carried into their lives. Moving away from those stagnant aspects took trust and courage. Now, it is time to see how these people were able to progress in this time-binding study, which can act as a foundation upon which others can build.

Case Study Research #1—Amy

Amy was seen over a six-week period. She was admitted to an adolescent treatment center after allegedly being raped by her brother-in-law at the home of her parents while they slept in another room. The parents reported that Amy was "odd" and made up the allegation. Due to the fact that the brother-in-law was suspected of drug trafficking, officials of the county where the patient lived were interested in the case, and they believed Amy's story.

Interventions for Case Study Research #1—Amy

In this case, the nurses and staff who came in contact with the patient agreed to be trained in general semantic principles and learned especially how to identify and respond to the speaking errors specific to the family interactions.

As the patient had some traits of schizoid personality disorder, she did not connect with the other patients but was content to be in the same room with them, perhaps staying calm in her boundary of privacy. She almost always chose solitary activities and demonstrated separation anxiety being away from her mother. The family dynamics had contributed to her arrested development. A specialized environment was set up surrounding the patient with positive, healthy semantics, which served to electrify her development. On the unit, by hearing the errors made and then corrected by a staff member, the specialized environment indirectly lent itself to instructing her to respond to the semantic errors in her family. The atmosphere served as a stable environment where object relationship dynamics toward individuation could occur. General semantics provided the stability for her individuation from mother figures. The nurses consistently asked Amy's opinion and affirmed her independence. Her moral stance to tell the truth brought despair as she received the message from her family that truthfulness would lead to the family's abandoning of her. The patient was unskilled in the social ability needed to determine the motive of others; so a plan for therapy was begun with a specialized use of "I messages." First, the patient learned to use "I messages" to convey her information about herself and to make her actions and feelings understandable to others. For instance, an "I message" was

"When you (*name a behavior*), I feel _______________."

An "I message" gave information to Amy and to others about how the behavior of others was affecting her feelings:

"When Tim gets angry, I feel confused."

"When Mother does not come to see me, I feel punished."

When she saw that her reporting of the behavior of others affected their response to her, she began to lower her protective defenses and interact with others in a more appropriate way. However, due to the strength of her long-held protective boundaries, the process was very slow. The boundaries had protected her but had also caused rigidity in her interactions with others.

In order to get some idea of the motives of others, Amy also learned to question others on her unit with reverse "I messages." Since this patient had little information on how her own behavior affected the feelings of others, as the "I message" was reversed, she could learn directly the effect of her behavior on others. As a second step, she checked out the feelings she had assumed others were having. She then verbalized her understanding in the following way and also asked for qualification from others:

"When I (*name a behavior*), you feel ____________."

"When I (*name a behavior*), I thought you would feel _____________."

She was able to compare her evaluations with the reality of how others understood their feelings. The investigation of cause and effect regarding the behavior of others toward her and she toward them was entirely new to Amy. First, she learned how the behavior of others affected her. Second, she learned how her behavior affected others. She learned to objectify the interactions and found it was safe to lower her boundaries around others who were open to relating in this new way.

Family Semantic Evaluation

The family continued to be closed and declined to self-evaluate their speech communication patterns. During the family therapy, observation of speech and interpersonal verbal and nonverbal action between the mother and the patient was a prime consideration of the therapist. "Intensional" orientation, allness, and dead-level reckoning (Ward, 1987) were the primary speech patterns in these meetings.

"Intensional" Orientation

To review, the coined work "intensional" refers to words that point inward toward the speaker rather than outward toward the reality being discussed. They tend to be statements of judgment rather than statements of fact (Ward, 1987, p. 19). The patient exhibited "intensional" orientation in that she could not comprehend the actions of her mother who was presently "not on her side." She wanted her mother to behave like the mother who had cared for her since childhood. She did not know how to test reality before she entered the treatment center and had accepted much of what the family said as being true. The patient saw things from one perspective and displayed innocence in interfacing with her mother's self-protective qualities. Though she continued to receive the message that mother did not believe her, she still thought that mother would believe her. Amy had to examine her ideas about what her mother was capable of now and give up the idea of the good mother parent, which did not reflect reality at this time.

Allness

Allness means that if a person names an object or person within a group or category, the person may mistakenly feel that he or she understands and has said all there is to say about the subject. Amy's mother had put Amy in a category, missing the uniqueness of Amy within the group and the ability of Amy to develop. When asked about the alleged rape that Amy had reported to her, the mother replied, "Amy has always been odd. Sometimes she sees things that are not there." Under careful scrutiny in the hospital setting, the patient exhibited none of this behavior, and no psychotic features were observed.

The mother continued to exhibit the semantic error of allness in two ways:

1. She saw things only from her perspective and spoke about Amy in a static manner, blaming Amy's "oddness" for the problems. Amy was put in a category of being "odd and different." Her premise was that Amy's "oddness," or mild schizoid personality traits, discounted any possibility of Amy's truthfulness in this accusation.
2. She held firm to her views that served to protect her from the possibility of being shamed by "those people out there," the people who lived in her hometown. She did not consider that some of them would not blame her for an incident that happened in her family, but might have compassionate feelings for her. Her denial of the potential of Amy's truthfulness left Amy in the scapegoat position in the family.

The mother saw only the immediate consequences of her self-protective behavior, not the long-term picture. With her unchanging perspective, her son-in-law would be enabled to continue to use drugs, and Amy would be injured and perhaps become prey for other men. The mother herself would not advance in moral development by moving to a level where truth would be more important than what others would think.

Dead-Level Reckoning

Dead-level reckoning means that an individual can get stuck in thinking or speaking, staying on the same abstraction level without understanding that one can draw an inference, form an opinion, or reach a judgment. The individual does not take into account the inferences, opinions, or judgments of others.

At the end of all her reasoning, Amy recycled back to the same conclusion that she wanted to go home with her mother. She had not gone to another abstraction level of thinking with her family and was still exhibiting dead-level reckoning when discussing her family. Dead-level reckoning was a part of the family's overall speaking pattern. On the unit, with her peers and staff, when she was discussing her family, she was not able to use the exercises with which she had learned to fact find. When discharged, she remained firm in her decision to refuse to go to a foster home placement; instead, she chose to go home with her mother.

The mother also continued the dead-level reckoning speech pattern. Because there was no evidence to the contrary, the staff remained in unison about believing the patient's story concerning the rape. The family retained their perspective that nothing had happened. They had not participated in any meaningful manner in family therapy. Even though the mother was confronted with the facts of Amy's non-psychotic behavior on the unit, her defense mechanism of denial still could not be broken and she refused to consider any other level of thinking regarding the rape allegations.

Analysis of Developmental Progress

Cognitive Development Analysis

Cognitively speaking, due to her apparent separation anxiety, Amy's development initially was 0-2 years of age when she was admitted to the hospital. She had strong boundaries from the external world and detached herself from much interaction with others. Amy did not understand that when mother disappeared, she was not gone forever. When mother was out of sight, the strong feelings of abandonment were the true grief of permanent loss.

The separation anxiety demonstrated lack of individuation from her mother. Later behavior showed that the connection she made with hospital personnel had enabled an attachment dynamic to take place. This connection allowed her to individuate from her mother to some extent, which did indicate the beginning of developmental progress. The crying for mother ceased, but the treatment staff could not predict whether or not the changes were permanent. When first admitted, her speech was egocentric, although not narcissistic. During this time, she was interested in her room, her clothes, and her mother, but gradually, as she used the "I messages" and the reverse "I messages," she learned to pay attention to what others were saying and added non-personal references to her speech patterns. In the groups, as she objectified the interactions and lowered her boundaries around others who were open to relating in the "I message" and reverse "I message" styles, she began to develop cognitively and control her emotions without the need to withdraw from others.

At first, she was very detached. Amy got along with everyone; but the desirable relationships, so easy for some her age, did not form. She gradually received valuable affirming information from the nursing staff and began going to the staff for advice. They found she was able to reason by putting two different pieces of information together, which was a sign of a new developmental skill. They could see that she was beginning to think in terms of possibilities, another sign of growing development, but they did not know for sure whether or not, when she returned home, she could individuate enough to stick with her own good decisions. The treatment team was aware that when Amy left the hospital center, though she had been recognizing reality in the hospital, she would return to an environment of denial and distortion. Amazingly, during her inpatient experience, she had achieved the traits of a 12-year-old level in Piaget's Cognitive Developmental stage. Amy's progress during treatment for all stages is shown on the following tables. (See Amy's cognitive development in Table 12.1.)

Table 12.1—Case Study Research #1—Amy

Analysis of Cognitive Development						
	Period of Treatment*					
Stages of Development	**Beginning**					**End**
	Weeks 1	*2*	*3*	*4*	*5*	*6*
12+ years Adolescents begin to think in terms of possibilities. See reality but know there may be more to life than meets the eye. They have ideas and try to prove them out.						
7–12 years Learn to make inferences that go beyond information given. Can put two pieces of information together and draw inferences from information given. Can put information into categories and into order. Reasoning limited to what is familiar and known to child.						
2–7 years Think and speak according to what they pick up with senses. Do not understand systems yet. Center on own point of view; use large amount of egocentric speech. Cannot coordinate two points of view or take into account more than one dimension at a time.						
0–2 years Learn to tell difference between physical bodies and world. Begin to understand when an object goes out of sight it still exists.						
Semantic Interventions	**Allness**	**Intensional Orientation**		**Dead-Level Reckoning**		

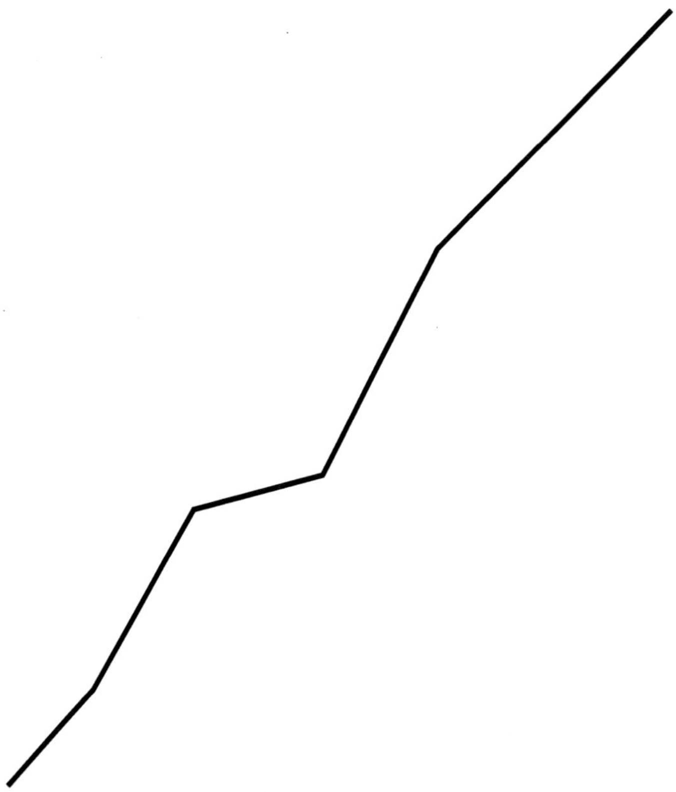

*The period of inpatient treatment for this patient was 6 weeks.

Social Development Analysis

When hospitalized, Amy showed symptoms of arrested social development, which placed her in the category of 3-6 years of age in Selman's Social Development Scale. During inpatient treatment, she processed through several social developmental criteria. She could at last objectively observe others and understand what was going on between people, putting her in the 10-15 year category.

As the nursing staff on the unit began to use appropriate general semantics during their interactions with Amy, she began to show some attachment to the some members of the nursing staff. The crying stopped, and she became more able to pay attention to her environment. The nurses began to ask her what she thought and how she would go about doing different things. On the unit, the "I messages" and reverse "I messages," that were listed in her therapeutic goals, forced interaction. Her primary therapist helped her understand the cause and effect of her behavior and the cause and effect of the behavior of others. She was a part of a team that helped her talk through hard times, with others on the floor "lending her their egos," explaining their inner reasoning dynamics used when dealing with problems, until she could learn to respond appropriately. On the social developmental chart, notice that as Amy prepared to leave the treatment program, there was a slight regression. Although, she was preparing to return to her home environment, she was still attached to the treatment center routine and staff. In her post-treatment setting with her family, Amy experienced a two-week "honeymoon" period at home, but ultimately she was unable to readjust to the home environment. (See Amy's social development advancement in Table 12.2.)

Table 12.2——Case Study Research #1—Amy

Analysis of Social Development						
Stages of Development	Period of Treatment					
	Beginning					End
	Weeks 1	*2*	*3*	*4*	*5*	*6*
12+ years Adolescents have the ability to see things from a national point of view, understand legal systems, moral ethics, and what is considered the traditional thing to do.						
10–15 years Knows others can do the same. Can stand apart and understand what is going on between people.						
7–12 years Understand intentions of others. Can understand others' viewpoint of them and know that others can get information from their point of view as well.						
5–9 years Learn what they think is not necessarily what others think. Realize others may feel differently about same situation. Understand behavior can be caused by different motives in different people.						
3–6 years Confuse what they think with what others think. Use physical remedies to handle personal problems. Easily frustrated which leads to hitting, etc.						
Semantic Interventions	Allness	Intensional Orientation		Dead-Level Reckoning		

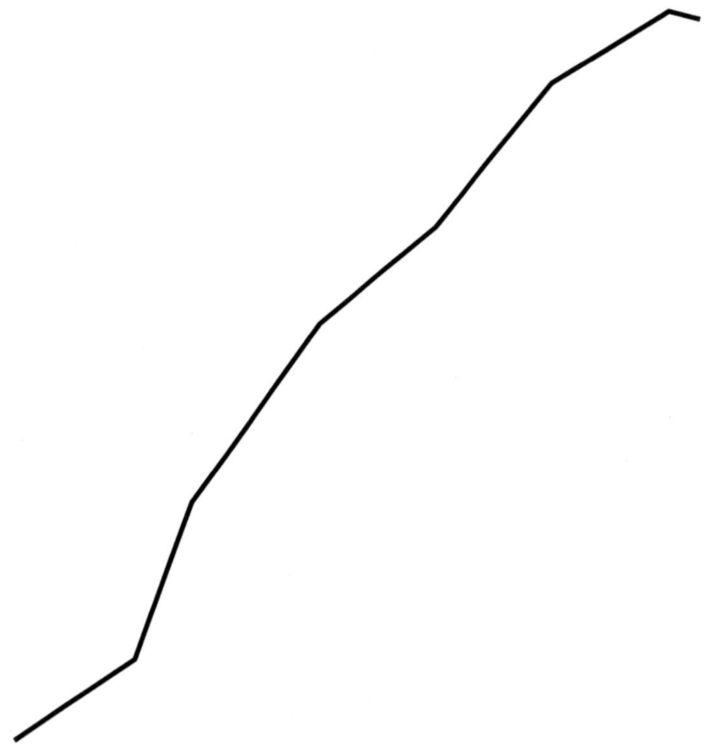

*The period of inpatient treatment for this patient was 6 weeks.

Psychosocial Analysis

Amy's psychosocial development progressed from an initial 6-12 years of age to 12-18 years of age. Clarifying her own identity of herself, she made the decision to establish a new identity and was becoming an individualized personality. She was moving away from being withdrawn and was now relating to others, an important psychosocial advance. Moving past the schizoid traits, Amy's attention was focused more on others, rather than being tied to her strong protective boundaries and egocentricity. She became more interpersonally motivated and moved away from the exclusivity of her own private world. Amy learned to trust herself to speak up for herself. She learned how to build boundaries for herself gracefully and took pride in her new skills. She eventually refused to let her family take advantage of her and was able to rely on her own judgment, which had been tested in treatment. She later resisted the shame base in her family and left home for a foster placement. As Amy began to set personal goals, explore, and understand the world, she began to break the ties of dependency and become an individual in her own right. She was beginning to refuse to accept the role of scapegoat, which was a familiar role in her family generational pattern. (See Amy's psychosocial development advancement in Table 12.3.)

Table 12.3——Case Study Research #1—Amy

Analysis of Psychosocial Development

Stages of Development	**Period of Treatment***					
	Beginning					**End**
	Weeks 1	*2*	*3*	*4*	*5*	*6*
12+ years Identity vs. Role Confusion. Adolescence is a time of transition between childhood and adulthood. They test limits, break dependent ties, establish new identities. The are becoming individuals in their own right. Work hard to clarify own definition of self, to find life goals, discover meaning to life.	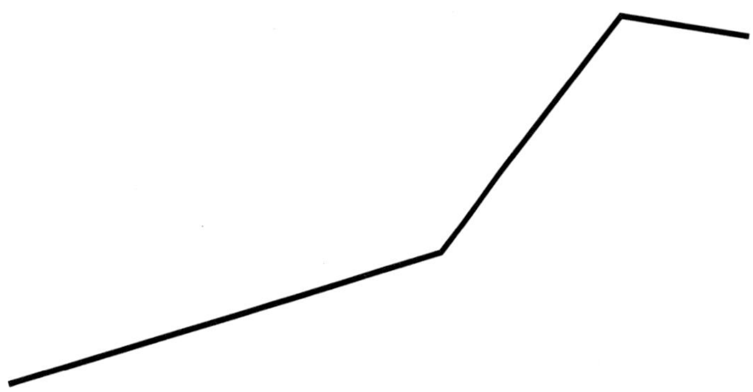					
6–12 years Industry vs. Inferiority. Need to expand understanding of world, continue to learn about sex role identity. Learn skills needed to succeed in school. Need to learn to set and achieve personal goals.						
4–6 years Initiative vs. Guilt. Children learn competence and initiative. Need to select activities they like so they can develop positive view of selves and learn to follow through on projects. If not allowed to make decisions they will feel guilt when they take initiative; will learn to let others lead and choose for them.						
1–3 years Autonomy vs. Shame and Doubt. Main struggle is leaning to rely on own judgment, finding out if "too much" independence will result in being shamed, or, if permission to explore and experiment is given.						
0–1 year Trust vs. Mistrust. If basic needs are met, individual develops basic trust level. If physical, nurturance needs are not me, individual becomes mistrustful.						
Semantic Interventions	**Allness**		**Intensional Orientation**		**Dead-Level Reckoning**	

*The period of inpatient treatment for this patient was 6 weeks.

Moral Stage Analysis

Amy was exceptionally morally developed, torn between preserving relationships and standing up for the truth. Standing up for the truth was part of her code of ethics. Although under great pressure to change her story, the patient did not waver in her assertion of the truth.

She was in Stage 6 of Kohlberg's Moral Development Scale Ratings. Even though the law in her family said to lie to protect the reputation of the family, telling the truth was the law of Amy. Perhaps she had never learned to be untruthful. She still had the trusting innocence of an 8-10-month-old child. This area of stage development is where the schizoid character traits began. Along with the developmental arrest, some individuation problems probably also began.

Interestingly, away from a dysfunctional moral set of family rules, the schizoid personality traits again allowed Amy to develop. Possibly, she never underwent the turmoil of a four-year-old child who has to give up his or her self-determined idea of what is truly right or wrong for the adult family ideas, which, in this case, were skewed. In her own private world, she was separate from the trauma organization of her family, where—no matter what the circumstances—the members had to conform to dysfunctional ideas. This separation from her family's moral code was interrupted by the rape. Out of the family structure, she eventually individuated in a more normal way, continuing past the developmental arrest and having the same moral development, but without some of the need for rigidity. Amy did not remain loyal to her family's ideals; but, instead, she moved purposely against injustice, even injustice against herself. She had developed a personhood that she understood and began to learn how to relate intimately with people that she could trust. Most of all, she had learned to trust her own judgment considering moral issues. Her moral development appeared to remain on firm footing. (See Amy's moral development advancement in Table 12.4.)

Table 12.4——Case Study Research #1—Amy

Analysis of Moral Development						
	Period of Treatment*					
Stages of Development	**Beginning**					**End**
	Weeks 1	2	3	4	5	6
Stage 6 People think civil disobedience is acceptable in order to protest unjust laws that violate universal ethics. The principle of right and wrong becomes more important than the unjust law.						
Stage 5 Individuals have a commitment to the democratic process for making and changing laws, as well as to social behavior contract and individual rights.						
Stage 4 Individuals obey because of duty and responsibility. They obey to keep social order of national system together.						
Stage 3 Individuals obey out of loyalty to families and other groups such as church, teams, etc. They obey to preserve relationships. Behavior norms are important part of how people personally think individuals should be.						
Stage 2 Individuals obey to get rewards. Rules for how to behave remain on the outside. Rules are not internalized by the individual.						
Stage 1 Individuals obey to avoid punishment. rules for how to behave remain on the outside and are not internalized by the individual.						
Semantic Interventions	**Allness**	**Intensional Orientation**		**Dead-Level Reckoning**		

*The period of inpatient treatment for this patient was 6 weeks.

Case Study Research #2—Kay

Kay was seen over a period of six years. The most interesting aspect of Kay's case was the severity of the early developmental arrest. Kay was originally diagnosed as borderline personality with psychotic features and dissociative personality disorder. She was in the 0-2 years of age in cognitive development, 3-6 years of age in social development, 0-1 year in psychosocial development, and in Stage 1 of moral development. Kay was seen over a six-year period, consisting of both inpatient and outpatient treatment.

Interventions for Case Study Research #2—Kay

Kay's difficult personality made treatment challenging. The most important conceptual information Kay needed to learn was to separate her behavior from her personhood by using an "I message." Before she could say "When you do ________, I feel ________ and that results in _________," she had to identify what her feelings were. She could only recognize angry feelings, but only after sorting through a jumble of feelings she did not understand. She needed to express her feelings verbally and not act them out. She was given a "feeling list," from which she could formally compose some verbal responses to some common insult interactions in her life. She began to talk to her children in the way she had learned, teaching them to identify and verbalize their own feelings. With five communication errors in the family semantic pattern, it was safe to predict that this family would have serious problems. Kay's polarization, "intensional" orientation, indiscrimination, static evaluation, and fact-inference confusion were all very severe. With the confusing aspects of the family communication pattern being quite evident, so was the fact that Kay was very intelligent. The high frustration generated by this combination of confusion and intelligence led to anger, which, in turn, led to violence. The degree of frustration appeared to be in direct proportion to the degree of intelligence. Deep down, Kay felt that she should be able to function better than she was.

Family Semantic Evaluation

Polarization

Polarization, a kind of communication that causes conflict because the communication implies that only two choices are available, not only caused frustration in the family, it also had prevented much early development needed in the family. Polarization robbed the individuals from forming their own inferences, opinions, and judgments. Polarization contributed to an "us versus them" mentality creating barriers to interaction with the world at large. Because the speech pattern was emotionally loaded, it contributed to feelings of inferiority in the individual. People being addressed with this type of speech would distance themselves from the emotionally-loaded speech pattern, and the person using this speech pattern would feel rejected.

Kay was given assignments to listen for the polarization speech pattern in others and to feel her feelings, naming from the feeling list. She learned to attend to the negative emotional charge when she heard this speech pattern. She found it highly frustrating to hear polarization patterns of speech that seemingly gave her only two choices, neither choice agreeing with her own opinion of situations. In therapy sessions, polarization language was named and the accompanying feeling level was verbalized. Kay found she controlled and was controlled by polarization. She learned other ways of talking and enjoyed the feelings of peaceful interaction. As she formed her own opinions and let others have their feelings, she became a skilled debater.

Kay's husband was a leader in Christian circles and spoke with total authority. Their Christian environment supported the almost infallible image of himself he had created. Kay eventually understood the confusion and frustration inside; after they divorced, she learned to form verbal defenses to deal with her former husband, choosing not to act out her feelings. As she improved her skill at not acting out physically but instead giving a verbal "I message," she gained the self-respect that often comes with self-control. She noticed the good feelings she had, and sometimes she enjoyed the power of not responding at all. Little by little, her former husband seemed to grow in his respect toward her. As her behavior improved and stopped being the focus of attention, her pastor began to speak up about the situation. Her former husband was removed from his pastoral position.

Static Evaluation

The static evaluation speaking error was addressed by asking Kay to remove the words "always" and "never" from her speech pattern. She learned that these words threw her back into her former despair. Because she had introduced change into her environment by taking responsibility for her behavior and changing her behavior, a static lifestyle was ultimately a thing of the past. She began to think in terms of possibilities. Kay was gaining control. The chaos was still going on outside; but inwardly, Kay was aware of a boundary developing between herself and the chaos.

"Intensional" Orientation

Kay's use of the "to be" verbs—am, are, and is—indicated that intensional orientation was part of her communication problems. Her speech pattern contained words that pointed inward toward her views rather than outward toward the reality being discussed. She tended to make statements of judgment rather than statements of fact. The "intensional" orientation revealed the severity of the reality error that dysfunctional speech can inflict upon its victims. For example, she would state, "He is right. Everybody knows that I am wrong." This was a statement of her reality, stated as a fact, which she projected onto others, not realizing that the idea had begun with her judgment of the situation. She began to question the absolute statements found in her speech and in her thinking. She tried to observe how others described situations and how others expressed their statements of judgment.

As Kay began to understand her process of judging, she then could determine the process of judging by others. To bring her opinions and judgment statements into more agreement with reality, she began to include sentence starters into her speech. She began to say "It seems to me," "I think," or "I feel." When hearing others use "to be" verbs, she integrated the skill to say to herself, "It seems to them," or "They think," or "They feel." The ability to integrate this skill had a calming effect and advanced her cognitive thinking.

Indiscrimination

As Kay listened to her own speech, she could see how the indiscrimination speech pattern was restraining the natural energy of her loving personality. Using language in this way led to stereotyping, causing her to have a fixed mental picture of some group that she applied to each individual of the group without regard to his or her unique qualities. Indiscrimination stopped her positive flow of good feelings toward others. For, example, she generalized individuals into categories of people, which she saw herself unable to penetrate. These were categories of people who were different from her or who would "naturally" not like her. She realized some of her perceptions of others were skewed by her fear of others. Her own language errors, which she heard herself say, reinforced this fear.

When she did not have any skills, Kay had reason to fear with no hope for recovering her good feelings; but now, when she was fearful, she used the fear to discover the truth for herself and test it out by asking questions. She stopped generalizing people into categories and was able to keep the positive flow of good feelings toward others intact, gradually extinguishing much of her fear of others.

Fact-Inference Confusion

Kay began to recognize the addictive cycle (inherited from her family of origin) revealed in the Fact-Inference-Confusion speaking pattern. Her inferences, opinions, and judgments were types of communication that needed to be used responsibly. She intervened into the cycle of despair, rage, unrealistic optimism, and skepticism by going through the steps of fact, inference, opinion, and judgment. She learned to stop, back up, and evaluate the process of her speech pattern:

1. What are the facts?
2. What inference did I make regarding the facts?
3. What was my opinion?
4. What was my judgment?

She learned she could select her inferences and avoid painful emotions. For example, she watched for her distorted belief that she was the cause of everyone's problems. She was now able to understand that sometimes people were just having a bad day. During individual and group therapy sessions, she was repeatedly asked to check out her inferences, which increased her awareness of the dysfunctional speaking pattern.

Analysis of Developmental Progress

Cognitive Development Analysis

Kay began in the 0-2 stage but at the end of treatment evaluated herself to the 12-and-over category of Piaget's Cognitive Development. She learned to make inferences beyond the information given. She put information into categories and into order. She reasoned outside of just what was familiar to her. She thought in terms of possibilities. She came to know there is more to life than meets the eye. Kay commented on her cognitive development: "I have reached the 12-year-old developmental stage. I have my own ideas and try them out." (See Kay's cognitive development advancement in Table 12.5.)

Table 12.5—Case Study Research #2—Kay

Analysis of Cognitive Development						
	Period of Treatment					
Stages of Development	**Beginning**					**End**
	Years 1	*2*	*3*	*4*	*5*	*6*
12+ years Adolescents begin to think in terms of possibilities. They see reality but know there may be more to life than meets the eye. They have ideas and try to prove them out.						
7–12 years Learn to make inferences that go beyond information given. Can put two pieces of information together and draw inferences from information given. Can put information into categories and into order. Reasoning is limited to what is familiar and known to the child.						
2–7 years Think and speak according to what they pick up with senses. Do not understand systems yet. Center on own point of view; use large amount of egocentric speech. Cannot coordinate two points of view or take into account more than one dimension at a time.						
0–2 years Learn to tell difference between physical bodies and world. Begin to understand when object goes out of sight it still exists.						
Semantic Interventions	**Polarization**	**Static Evaluation**	**Intensional Orientation**	**Indiscrimination**	**Fact-Inference Confusion**	

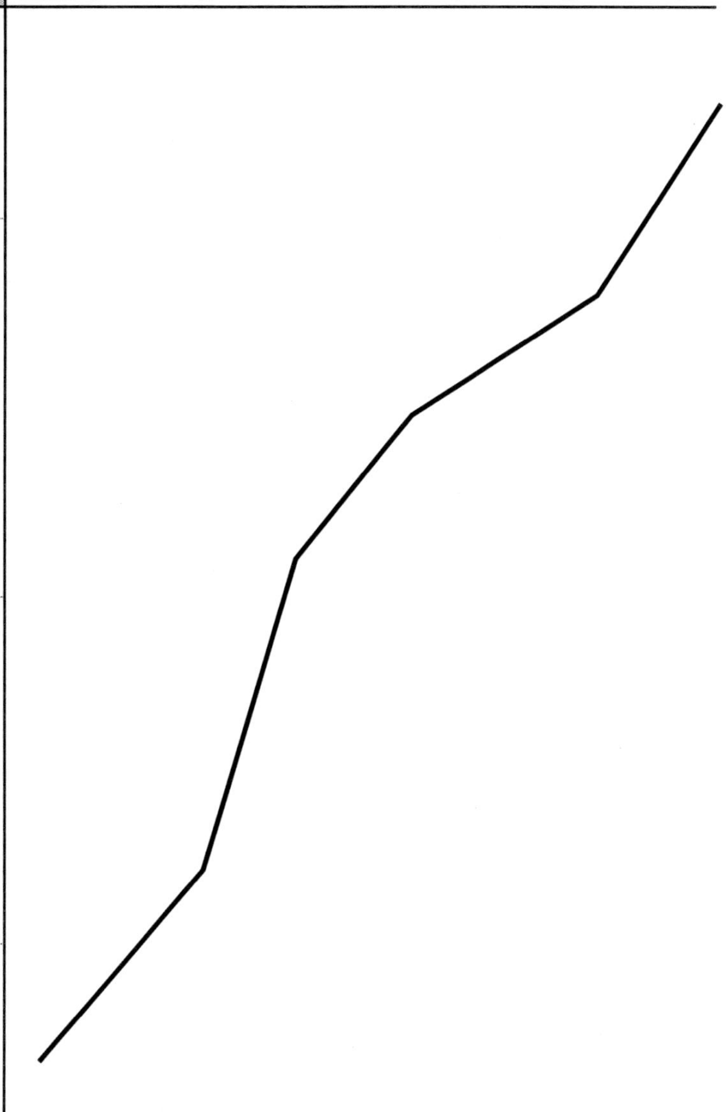

*The period of outpatient treatment for this patient was 6 years.

Social Development Analysis

The individual began treatment in the 3-6-year-old stage of Selman's Social Development rating. She rated herself in both the 7-12-year-old stage and the 10-15-year-old stage, because she could stand apart and understand what was going on between people and knew that others could do the same. She understood the viewpoints of others regarding her and knew that others get information from their viewpoints. She learned how to get information from the viewpoints of others, making it possible for her to understand their intentions. Kay commented on her advancement: "Even though I recognize my advancement, my feeling level still drops down to more immature stages."

The dynamic of recycling through lower developmental stages is considered normal for almost everyone. When advancement through missed stages comes in adulthood, because the old feelings are so overwhelming, the person is often aware of the cycle; however, with a well-established cognitive structure, the individual can find a reality base and cycle back to the appropriate developmental stage. When cycling through lower developmental stages, in order to avoid continuing rejection from others, Kay had to depend on her growing cognitive development and her practice of general semantics, while also learning to control her strong personality characteristics. (See Kay's social development advancement in Table 12.6.)

Table 12.6—Case Study Research #2—Kay

Analysis of Social Development	
Stages of Development	**Period of Treatment***
	Beginning — *Year 1*, 2, 3, 4, 5, 6 — **End**
12+ years Adolescents have the ability to see things from a national point of view, understand legal systems, moral ethics, and what is considered the traditional thing to do.	
10–15 years Know others can do the same. Individual can stand apart and understand what is going on between people.	
7–12 years Understand intentions of others. Individual can understand others' viewpoint of them and know that others can get information from their point of view as well.	
5–9 years Learn what they think is not necessarily what others think. Realize others may feel differently about same situation. Individual understands behavior can be caused by different motives in different people.	
3–6 years Confuse what they think with what others think. Use physical remedies to handle personal problems. Individual is easily frustrated which leads to hitting, etc.	
Semantic Interventions	**Polarization Static Evaluation Intensional Orientation Indiscrimination Fact-Inference Confusion**

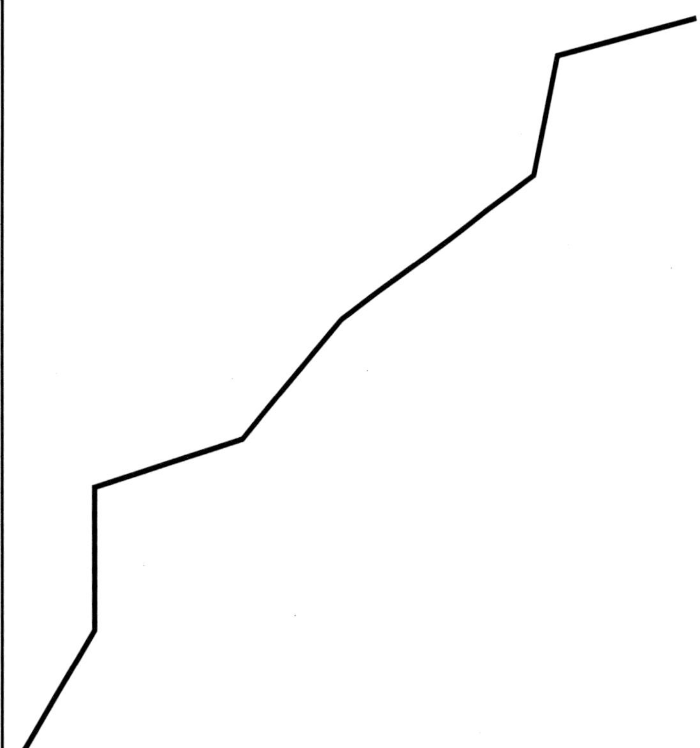

*The period of outpatient treatment for this patient was 6 years.

Psychosocial Development Analysis

Although she began in the 0-1-year-old stage of Erikson's Psychosocial Development Scale, Kay evaluated herself at the end of six years at the 12-18-year-old stage of identity versus role confusion. She saw herself as still trying to break dependent ties and establish a new identity. She worked hard to clarify her own definition of self, to find life goals, and to discover the meaning of life. She was employed in a small dental office where no one knew her past. Kay saw that she might be the healthiest employee in the office. Her employer was impressed at her ability to look at a situation, separate herself from the situation, and give her viewpoint about what needed to be done. Kay commented on her psychosocial development: "I see myself in the 12-18-year-old psychosocial development stage. I am still breaking dependent ties and establishing a personal identity. The people at work think I am all grown up." (See Kay's psychosocial development advancement in Table 12.7.)

Table 12.7—Case Study Research #2—Kay

Analysis of Psychosocial Development						
Stages of Development	**Period of Treatment***					
	Beginning					**End**
	Years 1	*2*	*3*	*4*	*5*	*6*
12+ years Identity vs. Role Confusion. Adolescence is a time of transition between childhood and adulthood. They test limits, break dependent ties, establish new identities. becoming individuals in their own right. Work hard to clarify own definition of self, to find life goals, discover meaning to life.						
6–12 years Industry vs. Inferiority. Need to expand understanding of world, continue to learn about sex role identity. Learn skills needed to succeed in school. Need to learn to set and achieve personal goals.						
4–6 years Initiative vs. Guilt. Children learn competence and initiative. Need to select activities they like so they can develop positive view of selves and learn to follow through on projects. If not allowed to make decisions they will feel guilt when they take initiative; will learn to let others lead and choose for them.						
1–3 years Autonomy vs. Shame and Doubt. Main struggle is learning to rely on own judgment, finding out if "too much" independence will result in being shamed, or, if permission to explore and experiment is given.						
0–1 year Trust vs. Mistrust. If basic needs are met, individual develops basic trust level. If physical, nurturance needs are not met, individual becomes mistrustful.						
Semantic Interventions	**Polarization Static Evaluation Intensional Orientation Indiscrimination Fact-Inference Confusion**					

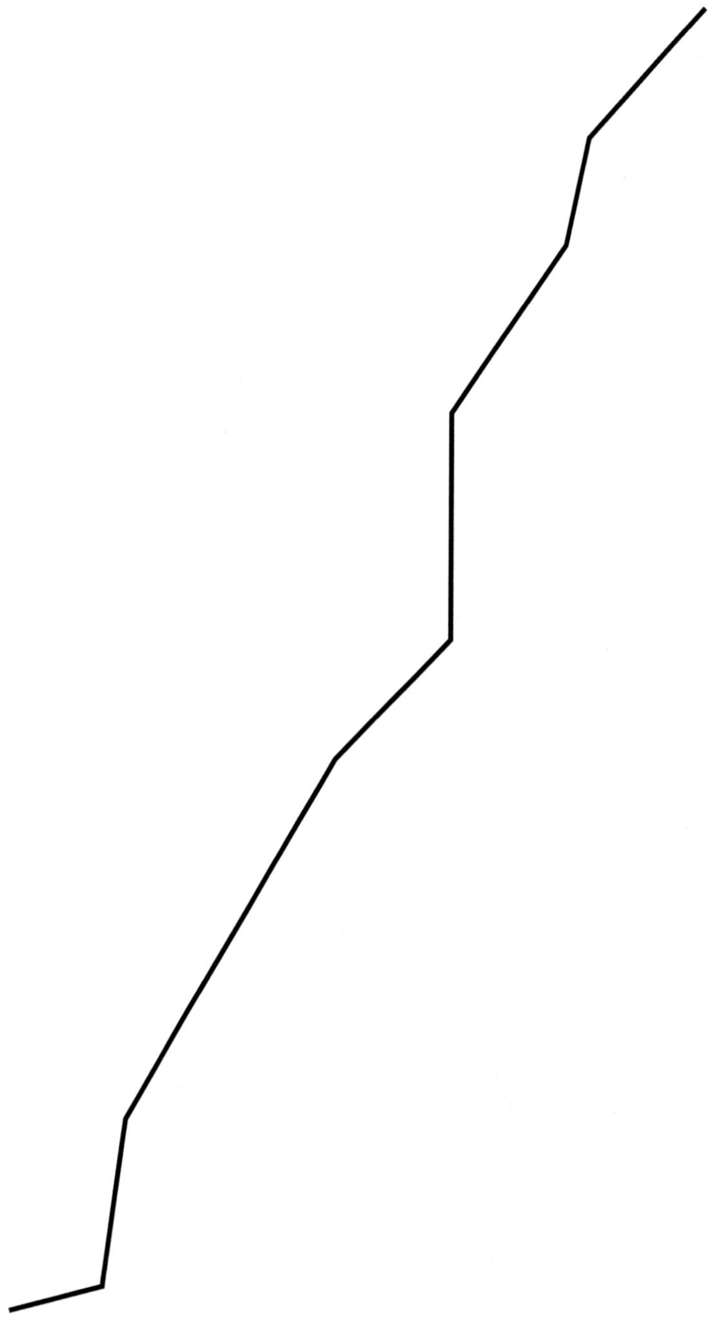

*The period of outpatient treatment for this patient was 6 years.

Moral Development Analysis

Kay began treatment at Stage 1 of Kohlberg's Moral Development Scale, only obeying rules to avoid punishment. She evaluated herself as being in Stage 3, having established a moral code and working toward internalizing the rules. Kay admitted: "I like to steal. There are perks. But I don't."

The important point about this admission was she understood this part of her make-up and could choose to keep it under control. Integration had taken place. In this case, her stealing had been a primal way of acting out loss. Progress in her moral development and cognitive development allowed her to gain control of primitive instincts, giving her more control of her behavior. She came to understand moral standards and decided to follow them with her actions. Few people will work to look deep enough to recognize their primal urges. The fact that Kay was not very developed in any area when she began therapy is important to remember. Time was spent building the personhood of Kay; however, it did not take much time before a conscience with a code of ethics came into being.

Part of the lingering attraction for stealing was the adrenaline rush, which accompanied the act. Due to the newness of Stage 3 development, the addictive nature of adrenaline rushes, and weak areas in boundary issues that were not reconciled, Kay's development remained unstable. (See Kay's moral development advancement in Table 12.8.)

Table 12.8—Case Study Research #2—Kay

Analysis of Moral Development						
Stages of Development	**Period of Treatment**					
	Beginning					**End**
	Years 1	*2*	*3*	*4*	*5*	*6*
Stage 6 People think civil disobedience is acceptable in order to protest unjust laws that violate universal ethics. The principle of right and wrong becomes more important than the unjust law.						
Stage 5 Individuals have a commitment to the democratic process for making and changing laws, as well as to social behavior contract and individual rights.						
Stage 4 Individuals obey because of duty and responsibility. They obey to keep social order of national system together.						
Stage 3 Individuals obey out of loyalty to families and other groups such as church, teams, etc. They obey to preserve relationships. Behavior norms are important part of how people personally think individuals should be.						
Stage 2 Individuals obey to get rewards. Rules for how to behave remain on the outside. The individual does not internalize rules.						
Stage 1 Individuals obey to avoid punishment. Rules for how to behave remain on the outside and are not internalized by the individual.						
Semantic Interventions	**Polarization Static Evaluation Intensional Orientation Indiscrimination Fact-Inference Confusion**					

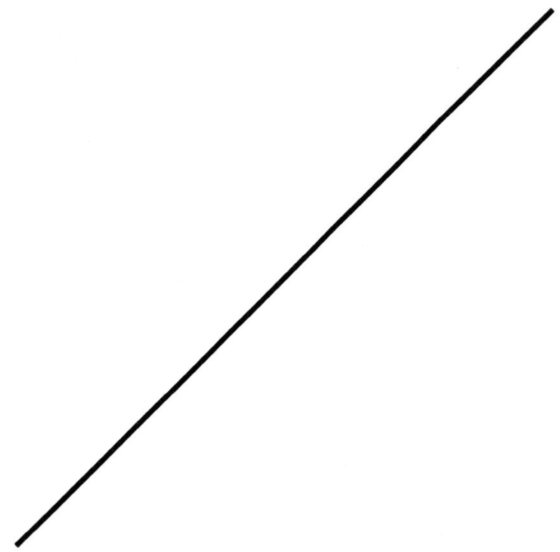

*The period of outpatient treatment for this patient was 6 years.

Case Study Research #3—Charles

Charles was adept at power and control in his relationship with others. Due to his antisocial personality disorder traits, he had problems with relationships in his home and work environments. He had been married three times and had participated in therapy for his seven children or stepchildren before he himself entered treatment for a four-month period. Charles was very intelligent but lacked the social and emotional intelligence necessary to achieve his goals.

Interventions for Case Study Research #3—Charles

The advanced cognitive ability of Charles was an asset in therapeutic interventions. Away from threat of shame or blame, he could reason toward other forms of development. For instance, he was extremely frustrated and impatient with the symptoms of the attention deficit, hyperactivity disorder (ADHD) of his stepson, Lane. Charles concentrated on what he called "the stupidity of Lane's actions." The judgment symbol, "stupid," illustrated lack of empathy in his social development and the fact-inference confusion semantic error. The frustration around Lane's behavioral differences was an excellent place to begin a therapeutic intervention. Charles already had information concerning ADHD, and his wife had explained to him that Lane's behavior was typical of children with this disorder. Although Charles was showing some sympathy due to the fact Lane could not help his behavior, he was noticeably frustrated over a particular incident. Charles had acted out his frustration with punitive behavior toward the child. Lane had taken out the garbage, forgotten his goal on the way, and had left the garbage out of the cans. Dogs had found the bags and had scattered the contents. Charles was asked to explain his thinking process regarding how he would sequentially perform the chore. He said that he would visualize the direct route, complete the task, and reenter the house. He was then asked to explain Lane's thinking process, which he could not do or even imagine. Charles showed no signs of empathetic processing.

The therapist suggested there were probably distractions along the way which stopped the progress toward Lane's original goal. The therapist wondered aloud if the child knew how to complete the thinking process based on his level of development. Charles was asked if punishment had decreased Lane's distractibility. The answer was negative, because the child had repeated the same behavior the next day.

Charles' strong demonstrations of his pseudo masculinity covered a soft heart that wanted the children in his family to succeed. His strong style of speaking also covered up his vulnerability. Polarization, fact-inference confusion, and dead-level reckoning were used to keep him safe, but also kept him separate from satisfying relationships.

Family Semantic Evaluation

Polarization

As Charles realized that he was following a family pattern of control that had harmed him severely, he lost his desire to control others. Others in the family had also learned to address the control issues and since everyone knew what the dynamics were, the polarization lost its power. The problem was that he hardly knew what else to do.

The polarization used in his language pattern covered the emptiness inside of him. To fill the void, he decided to enter law school and be purposeful about sublimating his former aggressive tendencies into a more socially acceptable use. He learned to use his powerfulness as a tool, but the drive behind the need to control others was gone. Power and control were no longer the ultimate goal, but rather, a means to an end to help others, which he discovered, was very rewarding.

Fact-Inference Confusion

Since Charles began treatment with a 3-6-year-old social developmental arrest, judgment was strongly connected to punishment. Before entering treatment, he had no other options in correcting his stepson. The fact-inference semantic dynamic of going directly to judgment instead of processing through fact, inference, opinion, and only then judgment was a factor in his arrest at a low level of moral development. By not developing further, Charles was actually training others in the family to remain at the first stage of moral development. He was denying the permission needed for Lane to think his own thoughts and feel his own feelings needed to develop further. Charles practiced processing through his fact-inference rationale. The therapist encouraged him to process as Lane probably processed, taking into account the child's fear that he would make a mistake and receive punishment.

The therapist suggested that when interacting with Lane, Charles could process for the child aloud, dividing the chore into smaller components for him and rewarding him with praise at the end of each small task. He was instructed to praise only the behavior, not any personhood trait. Later he could ask Lane what he thought the next step would be and, at that time, Lane's correct thinking could be reinforced. Eventually, the power to praise was transferred to the child, with Charles asking how Lane thought he was doing, affirming any positive comments.

Charles was urged to view the process as an opportunity to monitor his own emotions and to keep them under control. The interactions with his stepson enabled both of them to advance to a higher stage of social and moral development, observing interactions from a moral point of view and taking advantage of opportunities to try out more conventional behavior.

For Charles, learning to verbally process information through all of the steps necessary to arrive at judgment or opinion yielded rich information and encouraged others to communicate with him. He learned to listen to the views of others as they processed their facts, inferences, opinions, and judgments. Learning to process in this manner gradually moved him away from the isolation brought about by his antisocial characteristics.

Dead-Level Reckoning

The strong dead-level reckoning speech pattern was another part of the voice of the power and control issues present in Charles. His current wife had been alarmed over the growing verbal abuse Lane was receiving before the intervention. Lane was nearing the age of 11, the same age Charles' severe abuse of his other stepson, Matt, now 16, had accelerated. The continuing verbal and physical abuse of Matt after age 11 had ended the marriage of Charles and Nita.

Charles was asked if anything in his life had changed around the age of 11. He was surprised, but shortly thereafter disclosed an account of a sudden sexual attack and continuing sexual exploitation by his older guardian, beginning at age 11 and ending at age 15. Although he had not sexually acted out with any children, Charles realized that he was continuing the pattern of verbal and psychological abuse that his guardian had directed toward him. He learned that his repressed and conflicted emotions were stirred up when his stepsons reached the same age as when the abuse began in his life. Charles was projecting his feelings of self-loathing onto male children around him when they reached that age range, responding to them in abusive ways.

As he dealt with his abuse issues in therapy, he learned the dead-level reckoning patterns were symptomatic of his fear which was the cause of his controlling behavior. The controlling behavior caused others to distance from him, leaving him with feelings of abandonment, which, in turn, reinforced his feelings of fear. By identifying and verbalizing the control and recognizing the underlying issues for his fear, he learned to handle the fear of not being in absolute control.

Charles was able to change his dead-level reckoning speech patterns. He noticed people were responding to him differently, and he handled his frustration better. Charles began to be able to stop the self-destructive cycle. He apologized to his stepsons and stopped the abusive tendencies toward the two boys, improving his relationships with them.

As his defense mechanisms and interpersonal style were refined by the knowledge of developmental conceptual information, his personality began to expand, and he grew as a person. The healthy changes in Charles influenced the family system. For instance, Matthew came to work with Charles. After Matt married a high-functioning young woman, he soon reentered therapy to heal the hurts and finish the therapeutic work he had begun at age sixteen.

Charles stopped the dead-level reckoning in all areas of his life, deciding not to manipulate but to take responsibility whenever possible. He found the decision to take responsibility for his words and actions increased his self-respect and gave him legitimate power in the workplace and at home.

Analysis of Developmental Progress

Cognitive Development Analysis

The advanced cognitive development of Charles aided the conceptual intake of information necessary to begin advancement in other psychosocial, social, and moral areas of development. A cognitive adult part of his personality provided protection for the tender feelings ready to surface. Raised like a little soldier, he now used verbal firmness as a tool to draw safe boundaries between himself and others, but he did not keep the rigidity as a permanent part of his personality. As he integrated the developmental conceptual information, he better understood cause and effect, which affected his intrapersonal and interpersonal relationships. (See Charles's cognitive social development advancement in Table 12.9.)

Table 12.9—Case Study Research #3—Charles

Analysis of Cognitive Development				
Stages of Development	**Period of Treatment***			
	Beginning			**End**
	Months 1	*2*	*3*	*4*
12+ years Adolescents begin to think in terms of possibilities. They see reality but know there may be more to life than meets the eye. They have ideas and try to prove them out.				
7–12 years Learn to make inferences that go beyond information given. Can put two pieces of information together and draw inferences from information given. Can put information into categories and into order. Reasoning limited to what is familiar and known to child.				
2–7 years Think and speak according to what they pick up with senses. Do not understand systems yet. Center on own point of view; use large amount of egocentric speech. Cannot coordinate two points of view or take into account more than one dimension at a time.				
0–2 years Learn to tell difference between physical bodies and world. Begin to understand when object goes out of sight it still exists.				
Semantic Intervention	**Polarization**	**Dead-Level Reckoning**	**Fact-Inference Confusion**	

*The period of outpatient treatment for this patient was 4 months.

Social Development Analysis

At the beginning of treatment, Charles' social development was in the 3-6-year-old range. He moved away from a high-control profile and punitive mindset and continued to a 10-15-year-old plateau. He learned that others did not necessarily think as he thought or feel as he felt about a situation. He realized others could feel differently about the same situation. He understood behavior could be caused by different motives in different people. He understood others' viewpoints of him and knew others also could get information from their viewpoints. He came to understand the intention of others. He could stand apart from others and understand what was going on between people. He came to understand that others also were able to stand apart and view what was going on between people. He learned that the conversation between others did not necessarily have to be about him.

He did not reach the 12-and-older stage of social development. His sexual abuse and a first marriage to an older woman who initiated him into activities that had left him encumbered with a sexual addiction. Unless he entered treatment for his addictions and learned to handle the shame-and-blame dynamics, he would not progress further in social development or be free to see life from a more conventional point of view. (See Charles's social development in Table 12.10.)

Table 12.10—Case Study Research #3—Charles

Analysis of Social Development

Stages of Development	Period of Treatment*			
	Beginning			End
	Months 1	*2*	*3*	*4*
12+ years Adolescents have the ability to see things from a national point of view, understand legal systems, moral ethics, and what is considered the traditional thing to do.				
10–15 years Knows others can do the same. Can stand apart and understand what is going on between people.				
7–12 years Understands intentions of others. Can understand others' viewpoint of them and know that others can get information from their point of view as well.				
5–9 years Learn what they think is not necessarily what others think. Realize others may feel differently about same situation. Understand behavior can be caused by different motives in different people.				
3–6 years Confuse what they think with what others think. Use physical remedies to handle personal problems. Easily frustrated which leads to hitting, etc.				
Semantic Intervention	**Polarization**	**Dead-Level Reckoning**		**Fact-Inference Confusion**

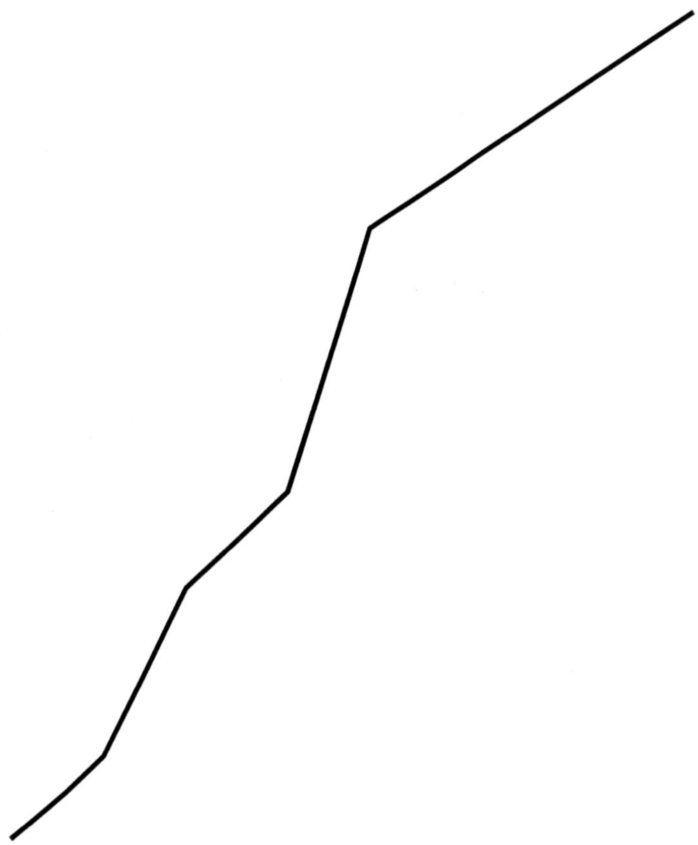

*The period of outpatient treatment for this patient was 4 months.

Psychosocial Development Analysis

Charles began treatment at the 0-1 age of psychosocial development and ended with only slight improvement. He kept a tight rein on himself to ward off strong feelings of shame. Although conceptually he was aware he could move past the perfectionist outlook and allow himself to take responsibility for any mistakes he made, the feeling of shame overwhelmed him when he made a mistake. Again, without the support of a 12-step program, he could not overcome the sexual addiction and continued to defend against shame. One night in a therapeutic group setting, he had ended an altercation with a female (with strong borderline personality traits) with a direct insult. The female involved was cautioned by the therapist about her dynamic of drawing out behavior from others using a particular verbal dynamic to extract the insult; however, Charles could not forgive himself for his less-than-perfect behavior. His loss of control in a group setting embarrassed him and the ensuing internal shame was too overwhelming for him. He left treatment immediately. (See Charles's psychosocial development achievement in Table 12.11.)

Table 12.11—Case Study Research #3—Charles

Analysis of Psychosocial Development				
Stages of Development	**Period of Treatment*** **Beginning**			**End**
	Months 1	*2*	*3*	*4*
12+ years Identity vs. Role Confusion. Adolescence is a time of transition between childhood and adulthood. They test limits, break dependent ties, establish new identities. becoming individuals in their own right. Work hard to clarify own definition of self, to find life goals, discover meaning to life.				
6–12 years Industry vs. Inferiority. Need to expand understanding of world, continue to learn about sex role identity. Learn skills needed to succeed in school. Need to learn to set and achieve personal goals.				
4–6 years Initiative vs. Guilt. Children learn competence and initiative. Need to select activities they like so they can develop positive view of selves and learn to follow through on projects. If not allowed to make decisions they will feel guilt when they take initiative; will learn to let others lead and choose for them.				
1–3 years Autonomy vs. Shame and Doubt. Main struggle is leaning to rely on own judgment, finding out if "too much" independence will result in being shamed, or, if permission to explore and experiment is given.				
0–1 year Trust vs. Mistrust. If basic needs are met, individual develops basic trust level. If physical, nurturance needs are not met, individual becomes mistrustful.				
Semantic Intervention	**Polarization**	**Dead-Level Reckoning**		**Fact-Inference Confusion**

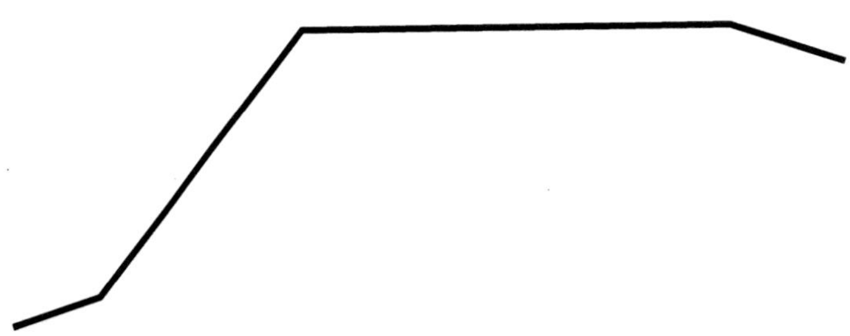

*The period of outpatient treatment for this patient was 4 months.

Moral Development Analysis

Charles advanced conceptually from a Stage 1 level to a nearly completed Stage 3 level of moral development. He passed the need for outside praise and sincerely desired to form relationships. The overwhelming feelings of shame he experienced in the group situation demonstrated he still punished himself unmercifully when he had perceived he made mistakes. The episode in the group brought up an old dynamic. He mistakenly perceived others disliked him intently because of the revelation of "who he really was," less than perfect. He felt loyal to the unspoken group norms of politeness and had violated the rule.

Charles chose not to avail himself of a 12-step group, which could have given him a chance to mature with support of others seeking similar goals. A 12-step group could have provided a focus to guide his progress and to empower him to move away from his addictive behavior. (See Charles' moral development advancement in Table 12.12.)

Table 12.12—Case Study Research #3—Charles

Analysis of Moral Development				
Stages of Development	**Period of Treatment***			
	Beginning			**End**
	Months 1	*2*	*3*	*4*
Stage 6 People think civil disobedience is acceptable in order to protest unjust laws that violate universal ethics. The principle of right and wrong becomes more important than the unjust law.				
Stage 5 Individuals have a commitment to the democratic process for making and changing laws, as well as to social behavior contract and individual rights.				
Stage 4 Individuals obey because of duty and responsibility. They obey to keep social order of national system together.				
Stage 3 Individuals obey out of loyalty to families and other groups such as church, teams, etc. They obey to preserve relationships. Behavior norms are important part of how people personally think individuals should be.				
Stage 2 Individuals obey to get rewards. Rules for how to behave remain on the outside. The individual does not internalize rules.				
Stage 1 Individuals obey to avoid punishment. Rules for how to behave remain on the outside and are not internalized by the individual.				
Semantic Intervention	**Polarization**	**Dead-Level Reckoning**	**Fact-Inference Confusion**	

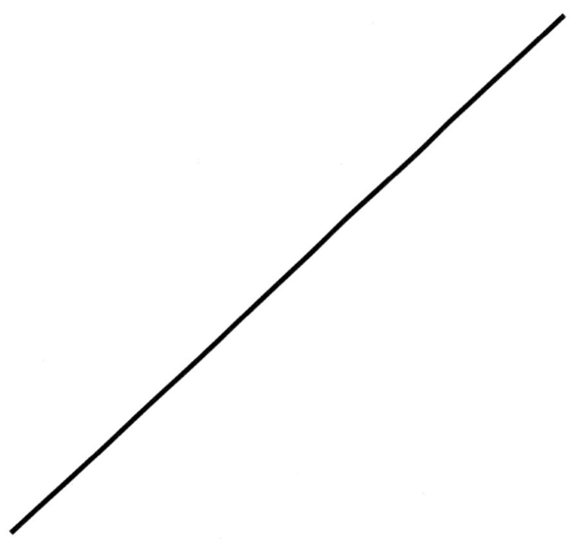

*The period of outpatient treatment for this patient was 4 months.

Case Study Research #4—Paul

Paul was seen over a four-month period. He had been court ordered into counseling after his daughter disclosed that she had been sexually abused by her father.

The cooperation of the family system was important for two reasons:

1. Paul had strong anti-social tendencies that were outside his awareness.
2. Much of the material for intervention contained information unknown to Paul.

Interventions for Case Study Research #4—Paul

Paul's low levels of development had to be addressed along with the speech tendencies that gave them power. He did care for his immediate family and extended family but offended them because proper knowledge of proper boundaries was not present. Also, he did not understand cause and effect, so many people were needed to verify the effect that his behavior had on them, or he might surmise that it was only one person's opinion.

His family cared for Paul also and for his immediate family. As some of his sisters had already been in treatment for the effects of Paul's behavior, they were very helpful in expression of feelings. Paul could see that his family was united in their determination to normalize their family system. Paul and his wife completed the semantic family evaluation.

Family Semantic Evaluation

The number and the strength of the semantic error in Paul's family, pointed to serious intrapersonal and interpersonal problems in the family system. These types of profound communication errors are often found in incarceration and recidivism.

Polarization

Paul came from a family where incest and molestation were a trans-generational pattern. The adult male figure was the abuser and determined the values of the home. The children were the victims, a pattern that began several generations ago.

In the family semantics, polarization, a communication that implies that only two choices are available to the speakers, was used to such a degree, it was almost the standard communication. The polarization communication was a signal to victims not to have their own thoughts or feelings, but to monitor the language of the perpetrator and, regardless of how one felt, agree with the language of the perpetrator. The lack of permissions to have individual thoughts and feelings had been passed down through the polarization in the language and had provided a path for generational verbal and sexual abuse.

Paul had been molested by an adolescent babysitter. He had molested two of his sisters and his own daughter. Eventually, the whole family system came into counseling, wanting to end the systemic dysfunction in their generation. Changing the semantics of polarization was a good place to begin, so the polarization language was carefully explained and cued each time it was used by the family in therapy. The family continued to monitor the tendency toward polarization at home.

Fact-Inference Confusion

The family did exercises in curbing fact-inference confusion. Paul had antisocial traits and entitlement issues, but mostly exhibited symptoms of sexual addiction, with the accompanying compulsiveness. He was surprised when he was asked what he was thinking about during the molestations of his daughter. He was visualizing what had happened to him during his molestation. He came to realize that thoughts of his own abuse were prompting his behavior. He learned that he would have to stay away from fantasy and increase his cognitive controls. Fact-inference processing helped. Paul learned through fact-inference processing to sharply divide out opinion and judgment from fact. Like most systemic problems, unless the system changed, individual treatment would probably fail. His family and his extended family were invited to attend therapeutic sessions. As his extended family joined therapy, Paul, by having to listen to his daughter and his sisters process through fact, inferences, opinion, and judgment, was confronted for the first time with the thoughts and feelings of others. He became aware of the feelings of others when he expressed his strong opinions. He understood how having these strong opinions was part of a cycle of abuse beginning with ideas of entitlement for him. He could see that these ideas of entitlement had hurt his family and gotten him in trouble with the law. He also had adopted a Christian belief system, and some cognitive dissonance set in as he considered moral standards for the first time.

Allness

A pattern of allness in communication affected the entire family. The family members had barely tasted life, afraid to think or feel, or to enter into any new situation because the family shame might be activated. They gained self-respect and confidence from doing something about their problems. In the *Uncapping Family Wisdom* program, the Communication Unit and the Developmental Stage Unit expanded their conceptual vocabulary and allowed them to look at different worldviews and grow in their strength as individuated persons.

Indiscrimination

Paul's indiscrimination speech pattern revealed a mix of positive and negative qualities chosen as reactions to lumping people or things into categories. He was a hard worker, managed his finances well, and took good physical care of his daughter—categories in which he had placed himself. Excelling in these categories allowed him to minimize other categories. He did not see himself as a sexual deviant, but minimized his sexual behavior. He saw life through a sexual screen—almost everything had to do with sexual innuendo. When he projected his own sexual curiosity onto the therapist, he was not rewarded by shock or embarrassment. Instead he was asked to accept responsibility for inappropriate behavior and was aided in engaging in normal conversation. He was surprised at being to relate to the therapist in a normal fashion. He gradually became convinced the therapist was mentally stable, and he could see merit in the other therapists whom he had placed in the "all therapists are crazy" category. He looked for indiscrimination errors in other areas of his life, which made the world a safer place for him.

Dead-Level Reckoning

The family system learned to challenge Paul's use of this communication pattern. His ability to recycle to the same conclusion in response to all reasoning was well ingrained. In his dead-level reckoning, there was an unwillingness to switch categories and he was so verbally powerful the other members of his family collaborated on a common system of speaking in order to break the speech pattern. Predictably, he had married women who themselves had been victims of sexual abuse as children, as were his sisters; but when all the women united, determined to give up a victim stance, they were a powerful wedge. While Paul was in treatment, his current wife, Carly, was a powerful advocate for his daughter. He could not deny Carly's strength. Also, two of his sisters had received therapy and had come back to face the family system problems. After everyone learned to identify the well-entrenched language error, the family no longer used the pattern themselves and pointed out Paul's use of it. The dead-level reckoning pattern lost its power. As a result, the family system stopped keeping secrets from Paul, and he left a life of emotional isolation.

Forming a Moral Code

Paul had not been exposed to the language or conceptual information of Christianity. Paul accompanied Carly to her church, where Paul had a conversion experience. Collectively, the church agreed to support and teach Paul moral conceptual information and to support the family. For the first time in his life, Paul was exposed to adult behavior, stability, discipline, and unconditional love. His problems were not hidden from the church members. His habits, once concealed by the darkness of secrecy and isolation, now were revealed in the light of new paradigms of belief and practice.

Therapy worked to bring a moral code into his personality from which all behavior was to spring regardless of support from outside. He learned to separate himself from his behavior and take charge of his behavior. He and his extended family learned about different boundaries, physical, emotional, and moral. These boundaries provided dignity for the family. His daughter became very assertive with him. Her stepmother and aunt supported and guarded her, forcing the dynamics of abuse to change.

Setting Boundaries

Although perpetration outside the family had not been a part of the pattern, Paul was cautious about children anywhere and firmly set physical and emotional boundaries. An extended family meeting was called, and Paul took the lead about revealing family facts. Sexual abuse was part of the family line, and he wanted to stop the practice in this generation. He told the children that they were never to be alone in a room with him again. He would take the responsibility of calling another adult, but they were to leave immediately. He was so serious that when he found himself alone in a fast food restaurant with a child, he found the manager and reported the potential for danger. Unknown to Paul, his behavior was observed by his sister, who chanced to enter the restaurant and saw the behavior.

This sister, who left the family system long ago and observed the system from outside, lived a normal life. She had strong feelings of anger toward her brother, who had abused her. Viewing her brother's appropriate behavior in the restaurant, she felt that there was a potential for personal trust of her brother. By learning and practicing proper boundaries, Paul eventually gained the respect of this sister who had been skeptical about his ability to change. Her opinion, that change was occurring, was considered an important marker for the probable success of treatment. At last, she too was able to state she had witnessed the growth and changes in Paul. Although treatment was considered successful, Paul still faced charges of child abuse in the courts. Paul's daughter dearly loved her father and now wished she had never told her teacher about the abuse. She felt punished. Her life had changed in positive ways and now, if her father were imprisoned, she felt she would lose everything. The therapist informed the court that if the father were sentenced, the daughter, who was now out of danger, would lose her livelihood. The church advised the court of their involvement with the family. Regardless, the police abuse investigator was determined to get a conviction, and Paul was sent to prison for child sexual abuse. His daughter was distraught with his absence and ran away to California, where her mother lived. Paul and his wife lost everything materially speaking—his home, airplane, and job, but Paul gained a new inner life and respect for himself.

He had much time to study in prison and took advantage of many educational opportunities. He continued his Bible studies, participated in groups, and acquired more self-knowledge. During his prison stay, he and his wife worked in an organization that reached out to families with relatives in prison.

Analysis of Developmental Progress

Cognitive Development Analysis

When Paul began treatment he was in the 7-12-year-old period of Piaget's Scale of Cognitive Development. Even though he had the skills found in this level, he also had some characteristics of younger years, such as, not having a full understanding of systems, becoming centered on his own point of view, and using a great deal of egocentric speech.

He advanced to the 12-year-and-above level. He began to think in terms of possibilities and knew there was more to life than the reality he could see. He looked back and evaluated his life according to the information he had acquired during treatment and the ways his thinking and behavior had changed. He stated, "I now know that what people did to me was wrong and it is not right to think that way. I know that it was wrong for me to repeat the things that were done to me. I must act as an adult and not as a teenager." (See Paul's cognitive developmental advancement in Table 12.13.)

Table 12.13—Case Study Research #4—Paul

Analysis of Cognitive Development

Stages of Development	Period of Treatment*			
	Beginning			End
	Months 1	*2*	*3*	*4*
12+ years Adolescents begin to think in terms of possibilities. They see reality but know there may be more to life than meets the eye. They have ideas and try to prove them out.	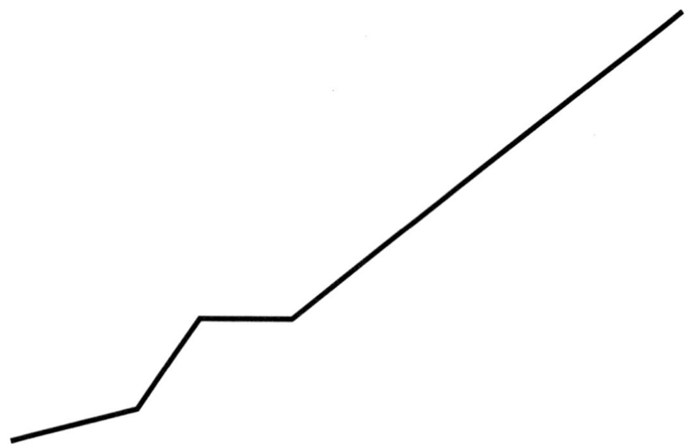			
7–12 years Learn to make inferences that go beyond information given. Can put two pieces of information together and draw inferences from information given. Can put information into categories and into order. Reasoning is limited to what is familiar and known to child.				
2–7 years Think and speak according to what they pick up with senses. Do not understand systems yet. Center on own point of view; use large amount of egocentric speech. Cannot coordinate two points of view or take into account more than one dimension at a time.				
0–2 years Learn to tell difference between physical bodies and world. Begin to understand when object goes out of sight it still exists.				
Semantic Interventions	**Polarization**	**Fact-Inference Confusion**	**Allness**	
	Indiscrimination	**Dead-Level Reckoning**		

*The period of outpatient treatment for this patient was 4 months.

Social Development Analysis

Almost beginning in the 10-15-year-old category of Selman's Social Development Scale, Paul progressed to the 12-and-above category. He explains in his own words: "I have the ability to see and understand that my new viewpoints have changed the error of my thinking. I now think out the things I do before I do them and make sure they are right." Paul meant that he could stand apart and see that he had new ways of thinking. His new viewpoints changed the error that was formerly in his style of thinking. Thinking before doing was a new skill for Paul, who formerly did what he wanted and was controlled by his compulsions. He could now stand apart and know what was going on between people. With the newfound freedom of expression in the family, the family opened up to him and shared information about their personal lives. The information about how others thought and felt helped him develop cognitively, and the sharing from others made him feel wanted. He broadened his moral code and could understand how his behavior affected an entire system. He saw things from a more conventional point of view. (See Paul's social development advancement in Table 12.14.)

Table 12.14—Case Study Research #4—Paul

Analysis of Social Development				
	Period of Treatment*			
Stages of Development	**Beginning**			**End**
	Months 1	*2*	*3*	*4*
12+ years Adolescents have the ability to see things from a national point of view, understand legal systems, moral ethics, and what is considered the traditional thing to do.	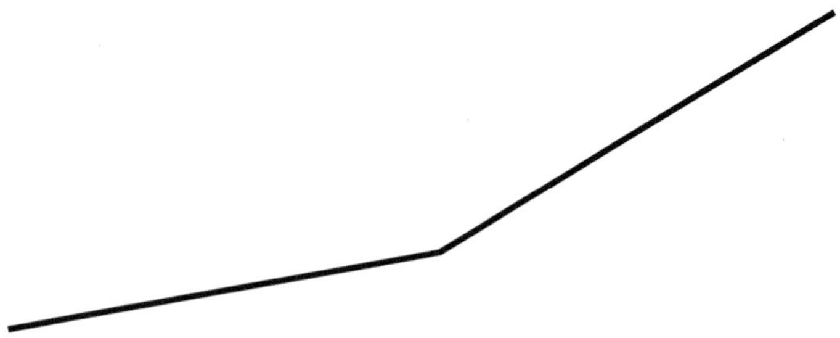			
10–15 years Knows others can do the same. Can stand apart and understand what is going on between people.				
7–12 years Understands intentions of others. Can understand others' viewpoint of them and know that others can get information from their point of view as well.				
5–9 years Learn what they think is not necessarily what others think. Realize others may feel differently about same situation. Understand behavior can be caused by different motives in different people.				
3–6 years Confuse what they think with what others think. Use physical remedies to handle personal problems. Easily frustrated which leads to hitting, etc.				
Semantic Interventions	**Polarization Fact-Inference Confusion Allness Indiscrimination Dead-Level Reckoning**			

*The period of outpatient treatment for this patient was 4 months.

Psychosocial Development Analysis

Paul entered treatment in the 6-12-year-old level of Erikson's Psychosocial Development. He progressed to the 12+-year-old level. As he learned what boundaries were needed to keep him safe and to keep others safe, he could display more adult behavior. A new world opened for him as he left the one-dimensional sexual screen and thought about the things he had never known. He left the controlling behavior to discover a freedom to establish a new identity. He began to express himself to others. As he gained conceptual knowledge and feeling vocabulary, he was able to have satisfactory intrapersonal relationships. Formerly, he had to use his hand and head movements to attempt to get his point across. Now his vocabulary increased and his body did not show tension in conversing with others. Paul explained the process in the following way: "I now find ways to express myself without showing it with my hands or body. I'm learning to connect better as an adult." (See Paul's psychosocial development advancement in Table 12.15.)

Table 12.15—Case Study Research #4—Paul

Analysis of Psychosocial Development	
Stages of Development	**Period of Treatment*** **Beginning** … **End** *Months 1* 2 3 4
12+ years Identity vs. Role Confusion. Adolescence is a time of transition between childhood and adulthood. They test limits, break dependent ties, establish new identities. becoming individuals in their own right. They work hard to clarify own definition of self, to find life goals, discover meaning to life.	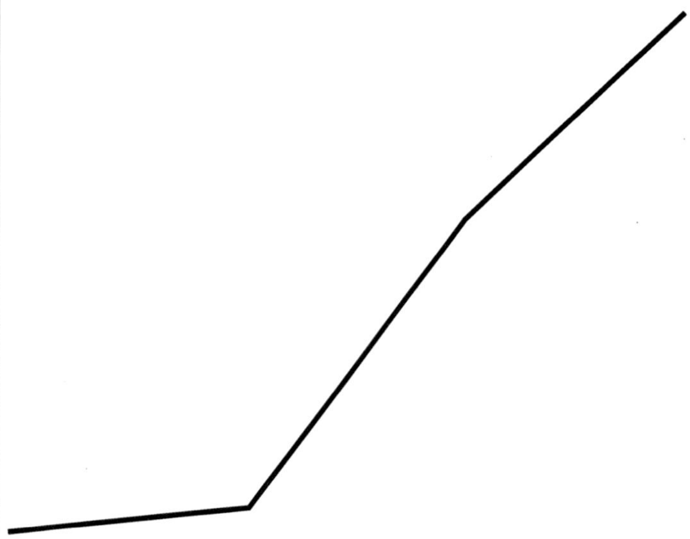
6–12 years Industry vs. Inferiority. They need to expand understanding of the world and continue to learn about sex role identity. Learn skills needed to succeed in school. Need to learn to set and achieve personal goals.	
4–6 years Initiative vs. Guilt. Children learn competence and initiative. Need to select activities they like so they can develop positive view of selves and learn to follow through on projects. If not allowed to make decisions they will feel guilt when they take initiative; will learn to let others lead and choose for them.	
1–3 years Autonomy vs. Shame and Doubt. Main struggle is leaning to rely on own judgment, finding out if "too much" independence will result in being shamed, or, if permission to explore and experiment is given.	
0–1 year Trust vs. Mistrust. If basic needs are met, individual develops basic trust level. If physical, nurturance needs are not met, individual becomes mistrustful.	
Semantic Interventions	**Polarization Fact-Inference Confusion Allness Indiscrimination Dead-Level Reckoning**

*The period of outpatient treatment for this patient was 4 months.

Moral Development Analysis

Paul started treatment in Stage 1 and developed to Stage 4 of Kohlberg's Moral Development Scale. He was able to form a moral code and the rules were internalized. Now rules made sense to him; and out of loyalty to his family and his church group, he decided to voluntarily cooperate. Because of duty and responsibility, he formed values and learned to obey. He understood rules were needed to keep the social order of the systems together. He realized his cooperation mattered and understood how he fit into the world. He explains: "Now my morals are different. I take responsibility for my actions. I have learned that morals are about myself and others. I have placed a high standard of goals for myself." (See Paul's moral development growth in Table 12.16.)

Table 12.16—Case Study Research #4—Paul

Analysis of Moral Development				
Stages of Development	**Period of Treatment***			
	Beginning			**End**
	Months 1	*2*	*3*	*4*
Stage 6 People think civil disobedience is acceptable in order to protest unjust laws that violate universal ethics. The principle of right and wrong becomes more important than the unjust law.	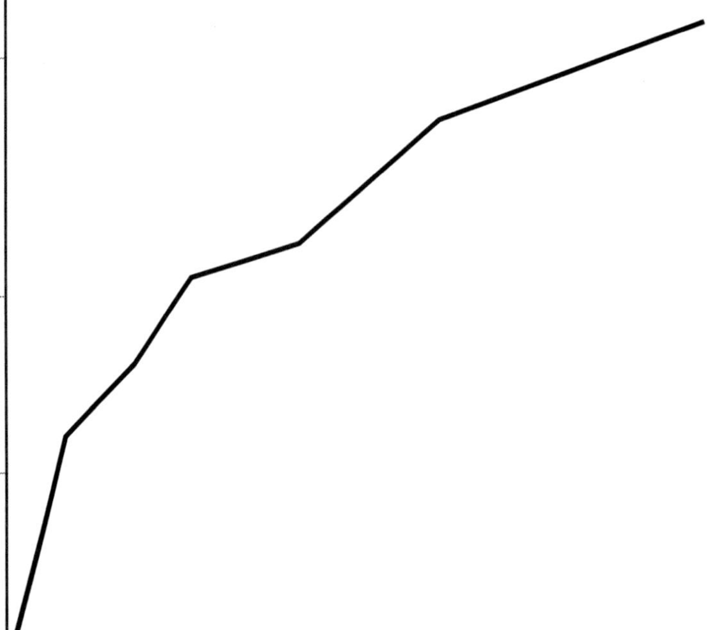			
Stage 5 Individuals have a commitment to the democratic process for making and changing laws, as well as to a social behavior contract and individual rights.				
Stage 4 Individuals obey because of duty and responsibility. They obey to keep social order of national system together.				
Stage 3 Individuals obey out of loyalty to families and other groups such as church, teams, etc. They obey to preserve relationships. Behavior norms are important part of how people personally think individuals should be.				
Stage 2 Individuals obey to get rewards. Rules for how to behave remain on the outside. The individual does not internalize rules.				
Stage 1 Individuals obey to avoid punishment. Rules for how to behave remain on the outside and are not internalized by the individual.				
Semantic Interventions	**Polarization**	**Indiscrimination**	**Fact-Inference Confusion**	**Dead-Level Reckoning** **Allness**

*The period of outpatient treatment for this patient was 4 months.

SUMMARY

To begin our search for a way to uncap family wisdom, we asked these questions:

- How do we begin to restore communities?
- How can we provide an environment where families can heal?
- How can we supply the information the families need to overcome transgenerational dysfunction?
- How can we empower the families to move into leadership positions where they can impact their communities with rich conceptual information and healthy norms?

Restoring communities ideally begins with the family unit. Then, a community is formed where everyone can learn the same thing at the same time. Then a structured environment serves to bypass shame and to keep the members of the community safe. The general semantics of the family system and the developmental evaluation of the individuals allow the families to self-evaluate to determine their own needs. Then, rich conceptual information is introduced to the family. Finally, week by week, the families integrate the information into their family unit.

In a search for the cause of the cause of the cause of the cause of the cause, abstraction levels show how to truly evaluate each case and to ultimately intervene in multi-level causes. With such intervention and the self-knowledge of the family, the families are capable of moving into leadership positions where they can impact their communities with healthy norms. With these "bottom-up" initiatives, whole communities can change; and with the change of groups of communities, society itself will feel the influence.

Table 12.17 shows the combined information of the four individual case study researches, which were reviewed in detail. It is interesting to note that the progress was dependent on the correct diagnosis of the semantic errors, the current levels of development, and the environmental atmosphere provided by those who interacted with the outpatients and the inpatients. Where the entire family system could be trained, the interventions were particularly dynamic. In an inpatient setting, the willingness of the staff to be trained provided an environment for impressive short-term advancement in development, enhancing the interventions already in place.

Multi-Case Study Research

Table 12.17—Combined Information for Case Studies 1–4

Name	Case #1 Amy	Case #2 Kay	Case #3 Charles	Case #4 Paul
Diagnosis	Schizoid Personality Disorder; Dissociative Identity Disorder	Borderline Personality Disorder	Narcissistic Personality Disorder	Antisocial Personality Disorder Narcissistic Personality Disorder Sexual Addiction
Age	14	32	45	42
Gender	Female	Female	Male	Male
Inpatient	X	X		
Outpatient		X	X	X
Length of Treatment	6 Weeks	6 Years	4 Months	4 Months
Semantic Intervention	Intensional Orientation Allness Dead-Level Reckoning	Polarization Intensional Orientation Static Evaluation Indiscrimination Fact-Inference Confusion	Polarization Fact-Inference Confusion Allness Dead-Level Reckoning	Polarization Fact-Inference Confusion Allness Indiscrimination Dead-Level Reckoning
Beginning Levels of Development				
Social	3-6 years	3-6 years	3-6 years	10-15 years
Cognitive	0-2 years	0-2 years	12+ years	7-12 years
Psychosocial	6-12 years	0-1 year	0-1 year	6-12 years
Moral	Stage 6	Stage 1	Stage 1	Stage 1
Ending Levels of Development				
Social	10-15 years	7-12 years, 10-15 years	10-15 years	12+ years
Cognitive	12+ years	12+ years	12+ years	12+ years
Psychosocial	12+ years	12+ years	0-1 year	12+ years
Moral	Stage 6	Stage 3	Stage 3	Stage 4

Case Study #2—Kay and **Case Study #4—Paul** qualify as long-term studies since they have been followed for over 20 years. Kay was called in to self-evaluate her developmental progress. She could see that she had developed as much as could be measured by the categories of development measurable for her age. Kay is a trained caretaker, and her two boys serve in the military.

Paul has moved to two states and has followed all the restrictions for a sex offender in each state. He is now living in the state where he was convicted. He has been married to the same woman for over 24 years. Paul is close to his sisters, who live locally, and interacts with them on a regular basis. Since treatment for Paul, there has been no reported sexual abuse in this family system or sexual abuse in the family that constitutes the next generation after Paul. Because his record has been clear for 20 years, Paul has plans to petition a judge to remove the level-one sex offender label.

Table 12.18—Multi-Case Study Research

Analysis of Cognitive Development	
Stages of Development	**Period of Treatment*** — Beginning … End
12+ years Adolescents begin to think in terms of possibilities. They see reality but know there may be more to life than meets the eye. They have ideas and try to prove them out.	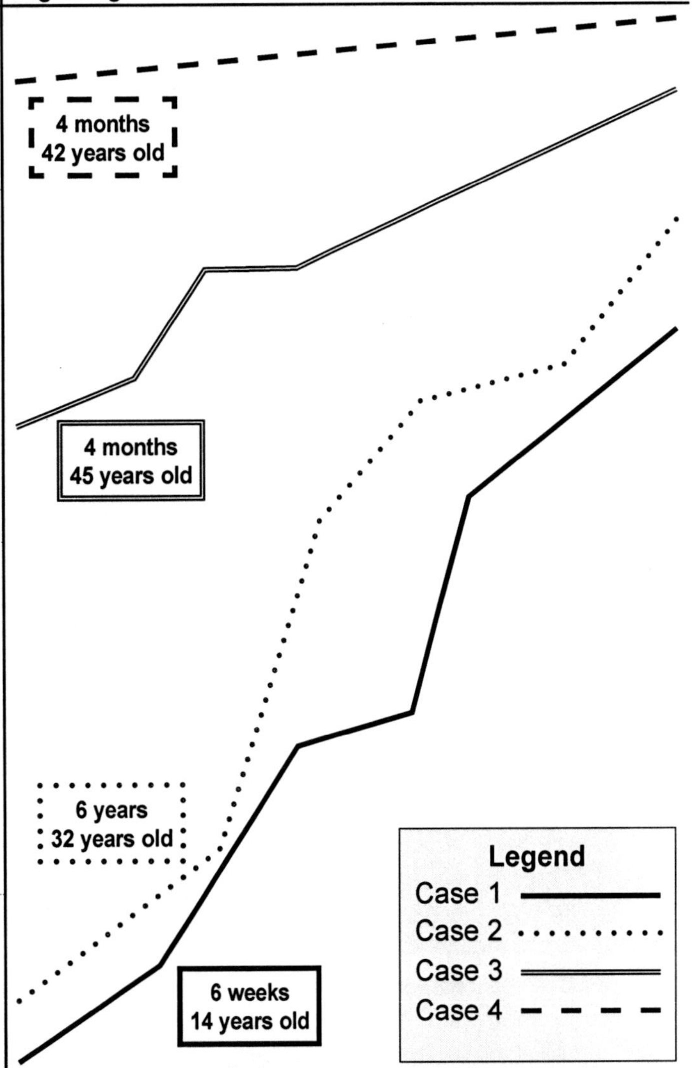
7-12 years Learn to make inferences that go beyond information given. Can put two pieces of information together and draw inferences from information given. Can put information into categories and into order. Reasoning is limited to what is familiar and known to child.	
2-7 years Think and speak according to what they pick up with senses. Do not understand systems yet. Center on own point of view; use large amount of egocentric speech. Cannot coordinate two points of view or take into account more than one dimension at a time.	
0-2 years Learn to tell difference between physical bodies and world. Begin to understand when an object goes out of sight it still exists.	
Semantic Interventions	Polarization Static Evaluation Indiscrimination Allness Sign-Symbol Confusion Fact-Inference Confusion Dead-Level Reckoning

*The period of treatment varied for each subject.

Table 12.19—Multi-Case Study Research

Analysis of Social Development

Stages of Development	Period of Treatment* (Beginning → End)
12+ years Adolescents have the ability to see things from a national point of view, understand legal systems, moral ethics, and what is considered the traditional thing to do.	
10–15 years Know others can do the same. Can stand apart and understand what is going on between people.	
7–12 years Understand intentions of others. Can understand others' viewpoint of them and know that others can get information from their point of view as well.	
5–9 years Learn what they think is not necessarily what others think. Realize others may feel differently about same situation. Understand behavior can be caused by different motives in different people.	
3–6 years Confuse what they think with what others think. Use physical remedies to handle personal problems. Easily frustrated which leads to hitting, etc.	

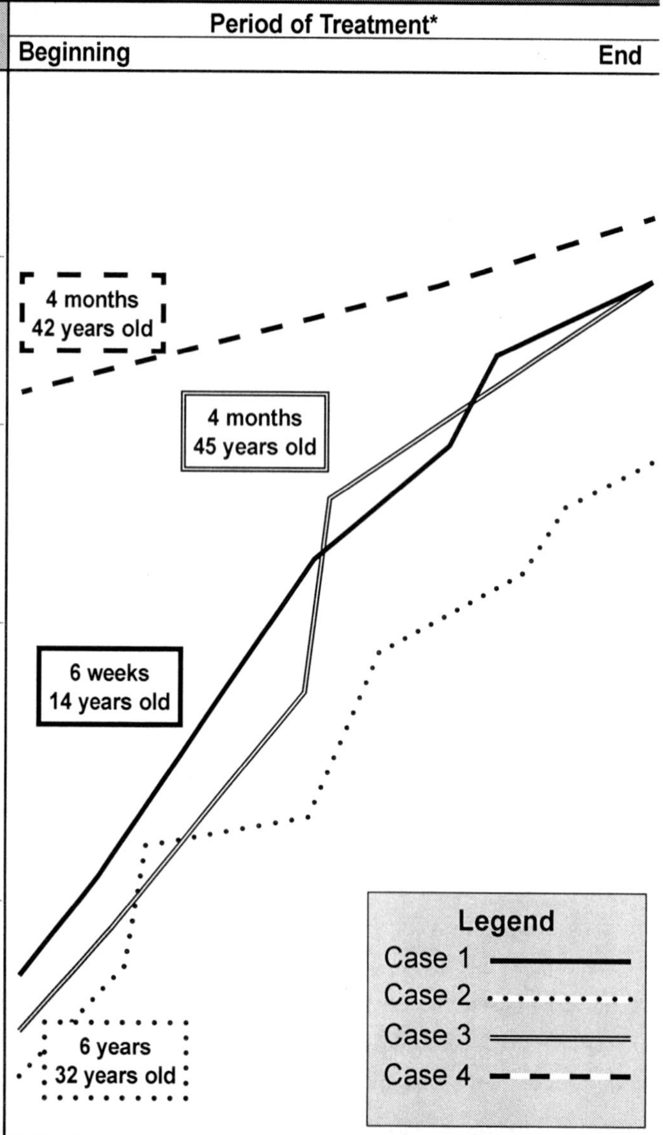

Semantic Interventions	Polarization, Static Evaluation, Indiscrimination, Allness, Sign-Symbol Confusion, Fact-Inference Confusion, Dead-Level Reckoning

*The period of treatment varied for each subject.

Table 12.20—Multi-Case Study Research

Analysis of Psychosocial Development

Stages of Development	Period of Treatment* (Beginning – End)
12 years and above *Identity vs. Role Confusion.* Adolescence is a time of transition between childhood and adulthood. They test limits, break dependent ties, establish new identities, becoming individuals in their own right. They work hard to clarify own definition of self, to find life goals, discover meaning to life.	
6-12 years *Industry vs. Inferiority.* They need to expand understanding of the world and continue to learn about sex role identity. Learn skills needed to succeed in school. Need to learn to set and achieve personal goals.	
4-6 years *Initiative vs. Guilt.* Children learn competence and initiative. Need to select activities they like so they can develop positive view of selves and learn to follow through on projects. If not allowed to make decisions they will feel guilt when they take initiative; will learn to let others lead and choose for them.	
1-3 years *Autonomy vs. Shame and Doubt.* Main struggle is leaning to rely on own judgment, finding out if "too much" independence will result in being shamed, or, if permission to explore and experiment is given.	
0-1 years *Trust vs. Mistrust.* If basic needs are met, individual develops basic trust level. If physical, nurturance needs are not met, individual becomes mistrustful.	
Semantic Interventions	**Polarization Static Evaluation Indiscrimination Allness Sign-Symbol Confusion Fact-Inference Confusion Dead-Level Reckoning**

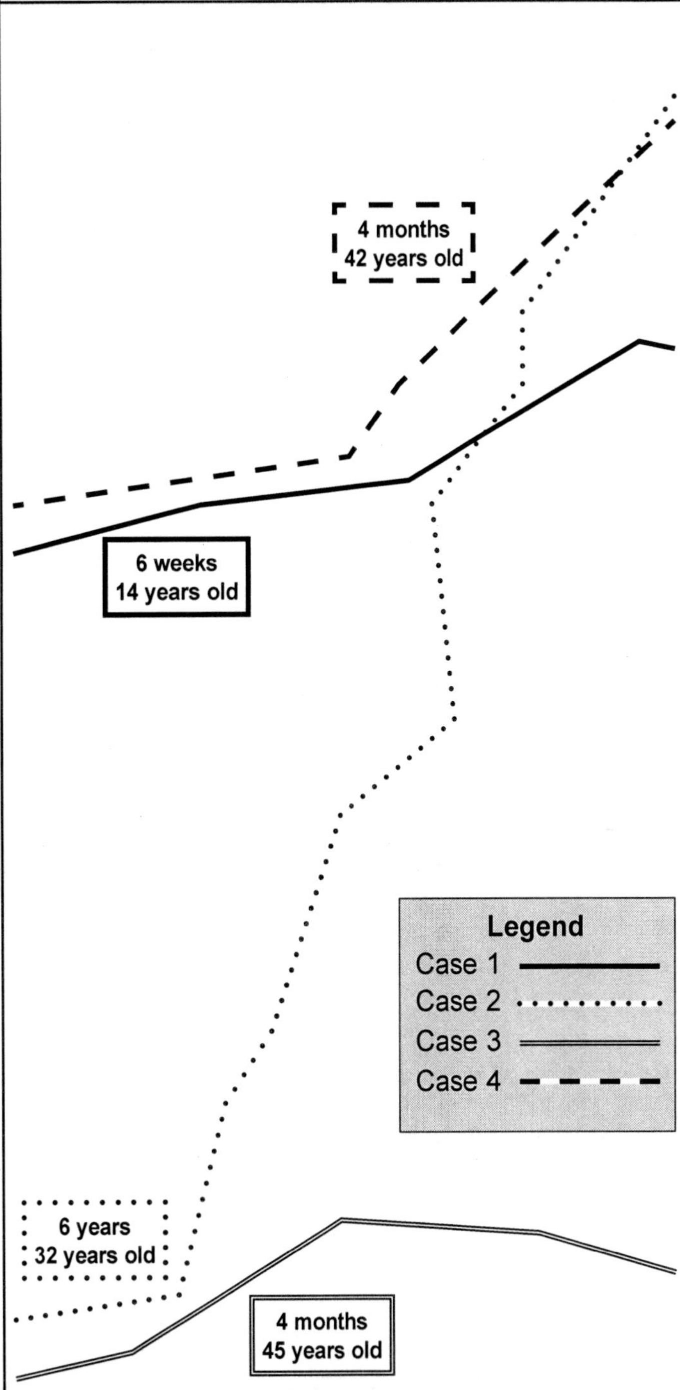

*The period of treatment varied for each subject.

Table 12.21—Multi-Case Study Research

Analysis of Moral Development

Stages of Development	Period of Treatment* — Beginning / End
Stage 6 People think civil disobedience is acceptable in order to protest unjust laws that violate universal ethics. The principle of right and wrong becomes more important than the unjust law.	
Stage 5 Individuals have a commitment to the democratic process for making and changing laws, as well as to a social behavior contract and individual rights.	
Stage 4 Individuals obey because of duty and responsibility. They obey to keep social order of national system together.	
Stage 3 Individuals obey out of loyalty to families and other groups such as church, teams, etc. They obey to preserve relationships. Behavior norms are important part of how people personally think individuals should be.	
Stage 2 Individuals obey to get rewards. Rules for how to behave remain on the outside. The individual does not internalize rules.	
Stage 1 Individuals obey rules for how to behave remain on the outside and are not internalized by the individual.	
Semantic Interventions	Polarization Static Evaluation Indiscrimination Allness Sign-Symbol Confusion Fact-Inference Confusion Dead-Level Reckoning

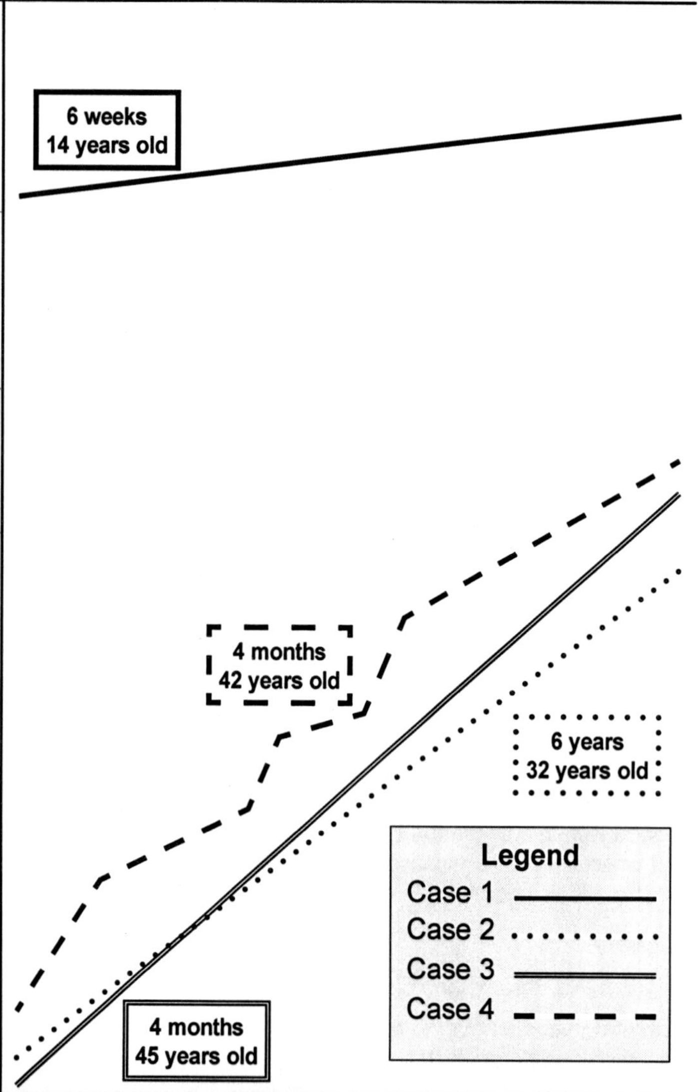

*The period of treatment varied for each subject.

Concluding Comments

Uncapping Family Wisdom: Recognizing, Treating, and Reconciling Transgenerational Dysfunction is not an introductory survey course. The program is designed for experienced staff to make operational. There will be time and place for experienced therapists to use their particular therapy or therapies of choice; but the course will be easier and less lengthy because of the conceptual information now ingrained into the clients at some level.

Twenty years ago, I came to consult and administer a program at a treatment center for women and children affected by domestic violence. One woman who was there at that time recently found me working in another city. She told me she was now teaching this material at her church and how the information had expanded her thinking. She related how the cultural information had allowed her to change her life and move into a level of employment she never thought possible.

At this point, you may have begun putting the theories together in some meaningful way yourself. One person stated that before she finished reading the book, she had already used the information when interacting with someone. I hope the information has strengthened your knowledge of professional and ethical issues that you will eventually encounter and that the information has stimulated you to consider your position regarding them. I hope you are conscious of the impact that you can have upon your world.

A Living Instrument

The program was meant to be a living instrument. Several case studies have been presented, as have the teaching of the terms and applications. The case study research benefited from the prior development of theoretical propositions to guide data collection and analysis. The investigator's job was to expand and generalize theories (analytic generalization) but not to enumerate frequencies (statistical generalization). Now is the time for investigators to enumerate frequencies (statistical generation) on the program. The program needs to be tested in other locals and in outpatient treatment locals to compare the efficacy of the program in different populations.

I would like to know your experience with the book. I would be very glad to hear how you use this information, what research you do, and your findings, along with the joys and problems you encounter along your path. Also, your suggestions for improving the program and making this book more useful in future revisions will be welcomed. You can write to me at Phillip–Monroe Publishing Company, P. O. Box 2585, Rogers, AR 72757-2585.

Sandra S. Pate,
MSW, D. Phil

References

Ward, A. (1987). Introduction to general semantics. In J. Butler (Ed.), *Insights into communication: Course syllabus for speech communication* (4th ed.) Scottsdale, AZ: Gorsuch Scarisbrick, Publishers.

INDEX

A

B

C

M

N

O

P

Q

R

S

T

U

V

W

Y

CPSIA information can be obtained at www.ICGtesting.com
Printed in the USA
BVOW05*0449310713

327270BV00003B/5/P

9 780615 455440